OUR GOD-GIVEN FUNDAMENTAL RIGHTS

Dedication

I am dedicating this work in loving memory of my younger brother, mother, and father and to those medical professionals at St. Anthony's Hospital in Denver who saved my life and provided me the opportunity to write this treatise. And, of course, to my loving wife Molly, who nursed me back to health.

I would also like to thank the many friends, theologists, and health professionals who have challenged and inspired me to be a better person.

OUR GOD-GIVEN FUNDAMENTAL RIGHTS

And the Unconstitutional Effort to Mitigate, Infringe, and Violate them

Patrick Bohan

Our God-Given Fundamental Rights by Patrick Bohan
Copyright © 2023 by Patrick Bohan
All Rights Reserved.
ISBN: 978-1-59755-747-4

Published by: ADVANTAGE BOOKS™, Longwood, FL, www.advbookstore.com

All Rights Reserved. This book and parts thereof may not be reproduced in any form, stored in a retrieval system or transmitted in any form by any means (electronic, mechanical, photocopy, recording or otherwise) without prior written permission of the author, except as provided by United States of America copyright law.

Unless otherwise indicated, Bible quotations are taken from the New American Standard Bible version, Copyright (c) 2021 by Zondervan or the New American Standard Bible version available on www.biblegateway.com.

There are a few verses taken from the Book of Mormon published by The Church of Jesus Christ Latter Day Saints.

Library of Congress Catalog Number: 2023947911

Name:	Bohan, Patrick, Author
Title:	***Our God-Given Fundamental Rights***
	Patrick Bohan
	Advantage Books, 2023
Identifiers:	ISBN Paperback: 978159757474; Hardcover: 9781597557719; eBook: 9781597557580
Subjects:	Politics & Social Sciences > Politics & Government > Ideologies & Doctrines > Conservatism & Liberalism
	Politics & Social Sciences > Politics & Government > United States > National
	Politics & Social Sciences > Politics & Government > Elections & Political Process > Political Parties

First Printing: November 2023
23 24 25 26 27 28 10 9 8 7 6 5 4 3 2 1

Table of Contents

Preface

Chapter 1, titled, "Introduction" opens by providing the thesis for this treatise. In the section titled, "Spiritual and Intellectual Growth" I discuss:

- How I stumbled into writing this book.
- My growth from a biblical skeptic into a God-fearing Christian.
- Why I support controversial political issues that fail to meet my personal values.
- Why my philosophy for drawing conclusions from the original meaning of the Constitution or construction of the law differs from published law scholars on the subject of fundamental rights.

The chapter concludes with a brief synopsis of the book and a list of solutions to the many grievances I highlight in the text concerning the abuse of government power. After all, it is futile to write a book about how the United States has strayed from its founding principles without offering solutions for the country to get back on track. The solutions will reinstate the constitutional republic as the Founders envisioned, while maximizing the liberty for each citizen to pursue their God-given fundamental rights to achieve the American dream.

The reader should keep in mind that the subjects addressed in Chapter 1 will be discussed throughout the text to provide more clarity.

Chapter 2, titled, "Can Science Rationalize the Existence of God?" focuses on a faith-based model that merges science and theology. In the faith-based model, God's language of life includes subatomic particles (quantum mechanics), DNA (genetics), and free will catalyzed by environmental factors. The result is that everyone has a unique reality or personality to satisfy God's want for diversity. Human personalities or realities are limited because they only encompass what a person can sense (see, touch, smell, taste, and feel). Therefore, quantum mechanics teaches us that reality is not what it seems. Much more exists beyond what we can sense, or beyond the ordinary world of yes and no, right and wrong, and conservative and liberal, or beyond our four-dimensional world of height, length, width, and time (spacetime). Ephesians 4:4–6 teaches us that only God holds the correct reality. Thus, those claiming to have experienced supernatural events might be sane individuals owning realities closer to God's perfect reality.

Chapter 2 also examines probability, quantum mechanics, and evolution (genetics), which suggest a God exists hypothesis is more logical than other theories posed by scientists to explain the creation of the universe and life. For example, statistical analysis highlights how improbable it was for life as we know it to evolve spontaneously into its current state without Godly interventions. For instance, the probability for one protein found in the human body to grow spontaneously into existence was about 1 chance in 10^{500}! That number is greater than all the atoms in the entire universe! And that is only the probability of creating one protein. The human body has hundreds of proteins equally improbable to form by evolution alone. Evolution is part of God's overall plan, but evolution alone cannot explain our existence. The chapter concludes by explaining the shortcomings of other scientific theories including the limitations of theories derived from the universal wave function.

In Chapter 3, "Is the Bible God's Word?", the focus shifts toward answering difficult questions about the Bible, such as the creation timeline, gigantic humans, long life expectancies, wars, violence towards women, polygamy, prayer, miracles, free will, and many more complex questions. The purpose of this chapter uncovers how I was able to resolve many difficult questions about the Bible. Being able to rationalize the many stories and miracles in the Bible is what ultimately turned a lifelong biblical skeptic into a God-fearing Christian.

In Chapter 4, "Defining and Distinguishing between Moral Principles, Virtues, and Fundamental Rights," I define and distinguish the differences between moral principles, virtues, and fundamental rights. If people follow God's moral principles, their personalities are transformed to attain the cardinal virtues God desires in His servants. God wants righteous servants because they do not infringe on the fundamental rights of other citizens. While moral principles and virtues pertain to policing the moral compass of the individual, fundamental rights refer to policing society's moral compass. More specifically, fundamental rights are lawful actions that citizens can pursue.

In order to identify fundamental rights, the properties of God-given fundamental rights are outlined in this chapter. For instance, fundamental rights are equivalent or symmetrical (like the beauty of symmetry found in math and science), non-controversial, non-political, deep-rooted in American history and culture, discerned from the Bible, and unanimously accepted. Furthermore, fundamental rights are independent of the demographic makeup, education, ideological preference, or socio-economic status of citizens. Additionally, since fundamental rights come from God and are perfect, they cannot be improved or altered. Thus, governments cannot create or enhance rights; they can only protect them. The chapter also demonstrates how the Bible influenced both the Constitution and our God-given fundamental rights. Without the Bible's influence on fundamental rights, they would not be God-given.

Some of the fundamental rights recognized in this text can be found in the Bill of Rights and the Constitution, such as the right to religious liberty, to free speech, to justice or due process, to vote, to own property, to contract, and to self-defense. That said, most of the fundamental rights recognized in this writing are unenumerated or not found in the Constitution or Bill of Rights. Historical documents, prior legislation, or landmark Supreme Court cases such as the Northwest Ordinance, the Civil Rights Act of 1866, *Pierce v. Society of Sisters*, and *Meyer v. Nebraska* can identify unenumerated fundamental rights. The comprehensive list of unenumerated fundamental rights includes the right to travel, to work a lawful profession, to pursue legal recreational activities, to obtain knowledge, to marriage, to raise a family, to friendships, to make choices that do not harm other citizens, to private activity that does not harm others, to life, to pursue happiness, to pursue health, to liberty, to safety, to antiwelfare protection, to profit from one's labor, to government protection, and to be represented in government.

Chapter 5, "Protecting Fundamental Rights and the Role of the Statutory and Natural Law in United States History," focuses on the proper constitutional methodology to protect fundamental rights by the Supreme Court. The Ninth Amendment and the Privileges and Immunities Clause of the Fourteenth Amendment should be the methodology used by the courts to defend fundamental rights, but unfortunately, they are ignored or improperly enforced. Instead, courts use a doctrine called Substantive Due Process to protect fundamental rights, which is, at best, confusing and controversial. Erroneous constitutional doctrines such as Substantive Due Process are addressed in Chapter 7.

The chapter discusses how to resolve controversial issues such as when rights conflict, enforcing inaction, accommodation laws, and determining when legislators can lawfully abridge fundamental rights. Since all people sin and fail to follow God's maximum standard of moral principles and laws, governments are formed to create statutory law. The statutory law is nothing more than the written laws of society enacted by legislators bounded by the Constitution. Natural law is a universal code of ethics bestowed on humanity from God and His word written in the Bible. Specifically, natural law is how humans interpret God's laws and incorporate His principles into the statutory law.

In Chapter 6, "The Regression of Constitutional Principles and Protections," I explain how many constitutional protections have been mitigated over the years. For example, most Americans believe the following statements are factual: Sovereignty in the United States resides with the federal government, the United States is a democracy, and the objective of the military is to fight for freedom. If history were taught correctly, Americans would learn that sovereignty in the United States resides with "We the people" (politically speaking, but Christians know God is the true sovereign), the United States is a constitutional republic, and the Founders fostered liberty above freedom. These differences may sound like minor semantics, but these differences are, in fact, major and a big deal. What the Founders created as a national government vastly differs from how we are governed today.

Next, in Chapter 7, "Government Techniques that Eliminate Natural Law and Alter Fundamental Rights", I outline the techniques individuals, groups, organizations, and the government use to violate the fundamental rights of citizens. Common strategies used to mitigate or eliminate natural law and fundamental rights include:

- Fear-mongering tactics to pass, for example, climate change legislation.
- Creating new rights that are not fundamental such as abortion rights.
- Changing the meaning of words, such as replacing equality with equity.
- Changing the meaning of constitutional clauses and amendments, which was done to the Takings Clause, for example. [1]
- Inventing fictitious constitutional doctrines such as the Separation of Church and State doctrine.

- Erroneously attempting to improve fundamental rights, which can be found in various labor laws.
- Incorrectly expanding federal grants of power beyond constitutional limits, such as by creating various departments including the Department of Education.
- Using demographic guidelines to obtain better privileges for one group of people, which is accomplished in various antidiscrimination laws.
- Writing vague and ambiguous statutes to invent and enforce crimes.

Chapter 8 is titled, "Examples of Mitigating Fundamental Rights in United States History." Here, I offer numerous present-day examples that detail the removal or mitigation of fundamental rights. These examples illustrate how the liberty to free speech, family rights, self-defense rights, religious rights, voting rights, profit rights, labor rights, educational rights, and health rights have been marginalized. For instance, the Supreme Court has a history of mitigating the right to religious liberty. The government has used the Establishment Clause of the First Amendment to enforce the Separation of Church and State doctrine to ban public parking if a vehicle has a religious sticker, prayer at a graduation ceremony, grammar school students praying before lunch, senior citizens praying at community centers, a librarian wearing a cross, college students conducting Bible study in their dorm rooms, a third grader wearing a shirt referring to Jesus, students praying at a football game, students doing research papers on religious topics, a choir singing religious songs, and having a Bible in a classroom. Courts believe the Separation of Church and State doctrine provides them the power to remove God from any public setting. That said, the Separation of Church and State doctrine has nothing to do with the exclusion of God. The Establishment Clause of the First Amendment pertains to prohibitions against the government, not a restriction against the Church or the individual to pursue religious avenues. The government's actions over the last century support liberty from religion, not liberty of religion.

Chapter 9, titled "The Revolutionary War Background Information" provides the necessary background and context for the Revolutionary War and focuses on the critical events leading up to the outbreak of the Revolutionary War. The topics include the significance of the Revolutionary and Civil Wars, an analysis of the war's timeline, and the founding of a Christian nation. Other critical events covered are taxes, The French and Indian War, the quartering of troops, a standing army, the sovereignty debate, the tea monopoly, Navigation Acts, and the Declaratory Act.

In Chapter 10, "The Revolutionary War Causation Theories and Consequences," I describe how historians have incorrectly rewritten history without God. Thus, it should come as no surprise that historical theories explaining the cause of the Revolutionary War outbreak do not include fundamental rights or God. Instead, they include the imperialism theory, the conservative theory, the progressive theory, the neo-Whig theory, the Founders impact theory, and the propaganda theory. In this chapter, theories mentioned above are refuted in favor of a hypothesis that the war was fought primarily to secure maximum liberty for citizens to pursue their God-given fundamental rights. The significant consequences of the Revolutionary War (the Constitution and Bill of Rights) support this hypothesis.

Chapter 11, titled "The Civil War Background Information" provides significant background information on the Civil War and focuses on the critical events leading up to the outbreak of the Civil War. The topics include the election of 1860, the Native American crisis, the national bank crisis, and slavery. Within the topic of slavery, there are several important issues, including expansionism, the Kansas dispute, attempts by the North and South to compromise on slavery, secession, and the infamous Supreme Court case *Dred Scott v. Sanford.*

In Chapter 12, "The Civil War Causation Theories and Consequences," I describe the objective of some historians to incorrectly rewrite history without God. Thus, it should come as no surprise that historical theories explaining the cause for the outbreak of the Civil War do not include fundamental rights or God. Instead, they include the states' powers theory, the economic theory, the cultural theory, the needless war theory, and the moral theory. In this chapter, the above-mentioned theories are refuted in favor of a hypothesis that the war was fought primarily to secure maximum liberty for citizens to pursue their God-given fundamental rights. The significant consequences of the war (Thirteenth, Fourteenth, and Fifteenth Amendments) support this hypothesis.

Chapter 13, titled, "Conclusion" includes:

- The key points from the preceding twelve chapters.
- A final example illustrating why our God-given fundamental rights, natural law, and God struggle to survive the test of time in United States history.
- Next steps, detailing my future work on the subject of fundamental rights as well as suggestions that political independents may consider to restore the Founders' vision for the United States.

Chapter 1: Introduction

The Thesis

No one has yet to definitively define humanity's essential and necessary God-given fundamental rights. The wait is over because this book unearths them from historical documents, prior legislation, scripture, and landmark Supreme Court cases. Again, the reader should keep in mind that the subjects addressed in Chapter 1 will be discussed throughout the text to provide more clarity. The premise for this book has several points:

1. A God exists hypothesis is more logical than the scientific theories that attempt to explain the creation of the universe and life without a creator.
2. Fundamental rights are God-given because they can be discerned from the Bible, which is God's word.
3. The criteria for identifying God-given fundamental rights are more diverse than the unalienable natural rights acknowledged by the Founders, including life, liberty, and property. God-given fundamental rights also comprise social, civil, political, and economic rights.
4. If the government's objective is to rewrite or erase history to portray the United States as a secular nation, then it must be their mission to mitigate, infringe, and violate the God-given fundamental rights of its citizens.
5. If historians' objective is to rewrite or erase history to portray the United States as a secular nation, then they must fabricate theories for the causation of the Revolutionary and Civil Wars that do not include fighting for the God-given fundamental rights of American citizens.
6. God-given fundamental rights are the basis for the United States' founding because they strongly influenced the Declaration of Independence and the Constitution and were the sole cause to trigger the Revolutionary and Civil Wars.
7. If the first six points are true, then United States history must include God.

Please refer to Table A1 in the Appendix for a timeline of events discussed in this text.

It is imperative to answer the following crucial questions in this text to prove all the points in the above thesis:

1. Does God exist?
2. Is the Bible God's word, and is it accurate?
3. What are our fundamental rights and what makes them God-given?
4. How are fundamental rights identified and protected?
5. How and why are constitutional principles denigrated?
6. How and why does the United States government mitigate, infringe, and violate the God-given fundamental rights of its citizens?

7. How and why do historians rewrite history to portray the United States history as a secular nation?
8. How do we know the Declaration of Independence and Constitution were divinely inspired by God?
9. How do we know that God-given fundamental rights were the basis for the United States founding?
10. How do we know that God-given fundamental rights were the cause for both the Revolutionary and Civil Wars?

Spiritual and Intellectual Growth

During his confirmation hearing to the Supreme Court, Justice Neil Gorsuch said something profound. Gorsuch said, "A judge who likes every outcome he reaches is very likely a bad judge." [2] What Gorsuch meant was his decisions must follow the law, not his heart. Gorsuch understands that it is okay to have empathy and compassion for people that come before him, but those feelings should not influence his rulings to uphold the law – even if he disagrees with the law.

Devising a cohesive theory to explain how science, history, constitutional law, and theology are related is impossible to accomplish especially if the theory must satisfy one's limited personal experiences and principles. Therefore, just as with Justice Gorsuch, not every conclusion in this book meets my personal values. How can I write a book that does not meet all my values? A decade and half of dealing with a debilitating neurological disorder and a near death trauma humbled me to seek more knowledge and venture past many of my biases and narrow philosophies. When I was most vulnerable, I began to read the Bible. The Bible is littered with verses about renewing our minds to gain new knowledge and wisdom. My four favorite Bible verses about gaining knowledge and wisdom are as follows:

1. 1 Corinthians 3:18, "Take care that no one deceives himself. If anyone among you thinks that he is wise in this age, he must become foolish, so that he may become wise."
2. Romans 12:2, "And do not be conformed to this world, but be transformed by the renewing of your mind, so that you may prove what the will of God is, that which is good and acceptable and perfect."
3. 2 Corinthians 4:16, "Therefore we do not lose heart, but though our outer person is decaying, yet our inner person is being renewed day by day."
4. Proverbs 3:13, "Blessed is a person who finds wisdom, and one who obtains understanding."

The Bible opened my mind to learning new perspectives and to venture past the biases, opinions, and prejudices holding me back from gaining wisdom. Wisdom turned me from a life-long biblical skeptic into a God-fearing Christian who routinely studies scripture. It is, indeed, possible to teach an old dog new tricks with newfound wisdom!

I have never been a strong believer in gun ownership or religion due to disturbing experiences as a youth. Having faith in God and having faith in religion are two separate issues. That said, I fully support the First and Second Amendment right for any person to practice religious liberty or to own a gun for self-defense purposes respectively. Gun ownership and religion may not meet my personal values, but our Founders must have had a good reason to enshrine those ideals in the Constitution. I was able to rationalize that (1) religious liberty is the same as the right to conscious thought and that (2) gun rights are the same as the right to self-defense.

To be sure, Christians may object to a few of my conclusions in this text. For instance, some may object to my conclusion that the creation timeline told in Genesis is merely a model for mankind to celebrate the larger creation or that I conclude civil unions should be supported by a civil society. Although gay marriage does not meet my personal values, I came to rationalize a pro-civil union conclusion for several reasons:

- For any government to operate fairly, it must treat all citizens the same. The Constitution provides that the federal government is to protect "We the people" equally. The government cannot offer privileges tied to any fundamental right such as marriage, which includes reduced tax rates, to only a select few of its citizens. That said, I am very clear that churches and organizations cannot be compelled to believe or do anything that goes against their values. Churches should be free to believe the creation happened in seven days and to marry only those couples who hold the same ideals as the church. Organizations and churches do not have to follow the same guidelines as the government because they are protected by the First Amendment's freedom of association and religious liberty provisions. Therefore, churches and any organization are free to cater to like-minded people. Even if some in society believe religious practices discriminate against homosexuals, churches are in their right to bar homosexual marriage so long as they do not physically harm or prevent homosexuals from seeking other avenues for gay marriage.
- The Bible is clear, homosexuality is a sin. But we all sin and in our judgement of homosexuality we, in turn, sin. Christians try to deny contract and marriage rights to homosexuals and homosexuals applaud the use the Separation of Church and State doctrine to erroneously erase Christianity from the history books and even attempt to deny Christians the right to display their faith on public grounds. Moreover, state and federal governments use accommodation laws to compel businesses to serve customers whose values do not meet the values of the store owners. It is an unfortunate vicious cycle of events.
- A civil society must tolerate the diverse values held by everyone. In order to gain tolerance, one must practice many moral principles found in the Bible to treat everyone the same and to show love, compassion, and kindness towards our neighbors.

The United States is a Christian nation and the Declaration of Independence and Constitution were divinely influenced. However, I suggest people must accept and tolerate unholy behavior because the message of tolerance is important in both the Constitution and Bible. For instance, the First Amendment's free speech and religious liberty clauses allow people to violate two of the Ten Commandments. God's Ten Commandments, written in Exodus 20, instructs His servants to worship only Him and furthermore, His servants should never use His name in vain. Free speech enables people to use offensive speech, including taking God's name in vain. Religious liberty allows people to worship whatever god or gods they wish. In fact, freedom of conscious thought protects atheists who do not wish to worship any god. Similarly, Romans 14:1 proclaims the same principle, "Now accept the one who is weak in faith, but not to have quarrels over opinions." The principle of tolerance is what makes both the United States Constitution and the Bible powerful documents. The bottom line, however, is that the key to any civil society is tolerance.

If people follow 1 Corinthians 3:18, Romans 2:12, 2 Corinthians 4:16, and Proverbs 3:13 and gain more wisdom, then they will automatically become more tolerant by gaining knowledge and understanding of different viewpoints. My only hope is that this book helps foster wisdom and tolerance to open our minds and heart to a healthy dialogue. With any newfound wisdom, people will unearth the principle that everything in society is not going to follow the limited and flawed values of any one person or organization. Only God holds the correct value system and humans not only have limited values, but flawed values. Until society accepts the principle that ALL humans are highly flawed, society will continue to devolve into hate, anger, and polarization instead of tolerance for our neighbors as we tolerate ourselves.

The solution is simple. No one needs to change their value system but merely tolerate the value system of other people in society. Society needs to leave the judgment of sins that do not violate the rights of others where it belongs – with God. Of course, the judicial system is required to serve judgment or due process on those persons in society who violate the rights of their fellow citizens. In the grand scheme of promoting national tranquility and equal fundamental rights, individual or personal values are important. Especially the personal value or virtue of tolerance to accept the diverse standards of everyone in society collectively. As we shall learn, natural law philosopher John Locke suggests citizens must make sacrifices when they enter into a civil society for the greater good of everyone. Sacrifices would include tolerating the diverse standards of everyone in society.

Although law scholars such as Randy Barnett, Tim Sandefur, and Richard Epstein strongly influenced me to pursue wisdom in both constitutional law and natural law, I doubt they would also agree with my findings in this text. For instance, Barnett suggests that the Fourteenth Amendment is the gem of the Constitution and was necessary because the original Constitution legitimized slavery. I agree that the Fourteenth Amendment became the gem of the Constitution, but only because Chief Justice Marshall's ruling in *Barron v. Baltimore* incorrectly held that the Bill of Rights did not apply to the states. *Barron v. Baltimore* and the ignorance of jurists and politicians led to the redaction of the Ninth Amendment or the true gem of the Constitution. If the Bill or Rights (including the Ninth Amendment) were applied to the states, the Constitution could not protect slavery. Furthermore, I will likely be criticized for using the Bible to formulate a non-originalist constitutional theory to obtain a desired result in my fundamental rights theory. But even Barnett admits that "higher positive law" is part of constitutional law construction. What Barnett refers to as higher positive law is how natural law influences the constitutional, civil, and the statutory laws of society. If the preceding sentence is true, and if it is true that the Bible influenced the founding of America and the Constitution, then shouldn't the Bible be part of constitutional originalism construction? [3]

Like Barnett and his findings in his book *The Original Meaning of the Fourteenth Amendment*, the results that transpired in this text differed from what I anticipated. I certainly did not think that when I was reading the Bible, it would convert me. Nor did I think that when I was studying law it would lead me to the Bible. Nor did I think that when studying natural law philosopher John Locke, I would learn that the natural law rights of life, liberty, and property have such an expansive umbrella to include economic, social, civil, and political rights. For example, I do not agree with Barnett's finding that liberty had a narrow meaning at the time of the founding. Just as property had a broad natural law meaning, so did liberty. I believe Barnett's error is he believes liberty and freedom are synonymous. The Founding Fathers believed liberty was the power for humanity to pursue all fundamental rights, whereas freedom only encompassed the liberty to pursue fundamental rights allowed by the government or a majority. All that I uncovered while writing this book changed my opinion about how I view the world. [4]

I respect law scholars' theories and admire the extensive research they have done to reach their conclusions. However, I am left scratching my head trying to understand how their list of fundamental rights includes some enumerated rights, civil rights, or political rights – but excludes other obvious rights. Moreover, how is it possible that their list may include some rights that are controversial, divisive, or conflict with other obvious rights. Since Barnett and coauthor Evan Bernick are silent on a full list of rights protected by their theory, their criterion for establishing rights certainly seems to protect controversial rights and does not follow a simple natural law principle that fundamental rights should be agreed upon in unanimity.

For any scientific hypothesis or law theory to have any legitimacy, it must have consistency. I believe the confusion or lack of consistency regarding other fundamental right theories stems from the fact that there is no way for law scholars to know what transpired behind closed doors during the debates about the framing of any law. It appears as if many fundamental right theories follow the irregularities of legislation. Legislation is loaded with inconsistencies due to "pork" and carves out exceptions to garner votes for its approval. Although law scholars can uncover the truth, congressional truths are inconsistent and unreliable because the nature of politics is to bargain and buy votes to pass legislation. For example, many of the framers of the Fourteenth Amendment said publicly that the privileges and immunities protected by the amendment did not support political rights such as the right to vote for newly freed slaves. However, less than two years later, the same men passed the Fifteenth Amendment granting black men the right to vote. It seems intuitively obvious the framers of the Fourteenth Amendment believed it protected political privileges and immunities such as the right to vote, but to garner votes for its passage they denied that fact. The framers of the Thirteenth, Fourteenth, and Fifteenth Amendments took baby steps to grant rights to newly freed slaves. It is not that they felt political rights were not fundamental rights, they did not want to bring about too much change at one time that may alarm Southern politicians. [5]

A few years back Barnett and coauthor Josh Blackman of their book, *An Introduction to Constitutional Law: 100 Supreme Court Cases Everyone Should Know*, challenged users on a podcast to give them a list of cases they should include in their top 100 cases that they may have overlooked. I could think of many such as *Reynolds v. Simms, Everson v. Board of Education,* or *Calder v. Bull.* Instead, I emailed Josh about an obscure Eleventh Amendment case, *Prout v. Starr*, which I felt best illustrated the true meaning of the Eleventh Amendment than cases they selected such as *Hans. v. Louisiana* or *Seminole Tribe v. Florida.* Blackman responded, "I had not heard of it." That was the end of it, the case closed! After all, if they had not heard of it, then how could it be important. It never occurred to Blackman that the jurisprudence in Prout may be worth considering. Although I am inexperienced, if scholars are willing to go out of their inner circle and embrace new ideas, they may learn something from even a novice.

It would be prudent for law scholars to consider the Bible, *Prout v. Starr*, and the Ninth Amendment to resolve an accurate list of fundamental rights. Following the jurisprudence set in *Prout v. Starr* would make it impossible to exclude enumerated rights from any list of fundamental rights. For instance, both the Free Exercise and Establishment clauses would be fundamental rights to secure religious liberty. Some law scholars erroneously exclude the Establishment Clause as being a part of the fundamental right to religious liberty. The sound logic behind the Ninth Amendment would make it impossible to exclude natural, social, economic, political, or civil unenumerated rights from any list of fundamental rights. For instance, the political right to sit on a jury would not be excluded as being fundamental regardless of what the framers of the Fourteenth Amendment intended. Publicly the framers of the Fourteenth Amendment did not intend for the amendment include political rights as fundamental rights. After all, Prout specifically enforces that the Fourteenth Amendment does not trump the Ninth Amendment unless specifically designed for that purpose. It was not! *Prout v. Starr*, the Ninth Amendment, and the Bible make formulating a consistent list of fundamental rights possible.

Although Barnett and Bernick are right that many scholars develop theories solely to meet their belief system. They also need to understand that scholars overanalyze everything and make matters much more complicated than they need to. I was an average engineer when it came to intellect. What made me an above average engineer was not getting bogged down in theory and instead finding and using the most simplistic solution to solve a problem. That is what made Einstein brilliant – the simplistic solutions he found to problems. I would never argue that I am smarter than doctors, law professors, theologists, and scientists. I would, however, argue that I am more practical than most. My strength is not getting side-tracked by all the doctrines, acronyms, theories, and terms but instead trying to rationalize the simplest or least convoluted answer to the problem.

Synopsis

A God exists hypothesis makes more sense than the plethora of scientific explanations for the creation of the universe and life. A God exists hypothesis is more logical because scientific theories fail to address the information conundrum, violations to the second law of thermodynamics, or the challenges posed by infinite solutions to equations. God's ingenious language of life includes subatomic particles, DNA, and free will, which are catalyzed by evolution and environmental factors. Evolution and free will made God happy because every creature has a unique phenotype. Evolution and free will satisfied God's want for diversity. On the flip side, free will made God angry because man fell into sin. The only way to control and civilize such a diverse society of fallen people was for God to create His laws or moral principles. Thus, God created His moral principles and commandments, or God's Law, to guide humans to live righteous lives. By following God's law or the moral principles, revealed in the Bible, people can attain virtuous traits. People who have virtuous traits do not violate the fundamental rights of other citizens. Unfortunately, all citizens sin, and society is full of crime, corruption, and evil.

While moral principles and virtues pertain to policing the individual's moral compass, God-given fundamental rights aim to police society's moral compass. Fundamental rights are God-given because they are defined in the Bible as well as historical documents and Supreme Court cases. Governments are created to produce civil or statutory laws for society to ensure the God-given fundamental rights of citizens are protected from sinners, crime, corruption, and evil. Civil or statutory law must be administered equally regardless of citizens' demographic makeup, economic status, or ideological beliefs. The statutory law's objective is, therefore, to protect, deter, and seek punishment and retribution from those in society who are unrighteous and violate the fundamental rights of their neighbors. In the United States, citizens tacitly consent to be governed through the social contract found in the Declaration of Independence and the statutory law dictated by the Constitution, both of which were divinely influenced. As we will learn, these documents are divinely influenced because the Founders incorporated scripture into the Declaration of Independence and Constitution via a process called natural law. The true meaning of the Constitution uncovers the importance of our God-given fundamental rights and the correct cause for the outbreak of both the Revolutionary and Civil Wars.

Unfortunately, in our present societal and governmental system, the process described in the preceding paragraph is reversed. Instead of God being the most sovereign entity for defining moral principles and fundamental rights, the government has confiscated this power. In modern society, governments create civil or statutory laws to protect fictitious fundamental and moral principles such as protecting abortion, creating climate legislation, or by defining human beings by their skin tone, economic standing, or gender instead of by their true rights. Fictitious moral principles and fundamental rights desecrate and make a mockery of the Bible and God's law. Moral principles and God's law have been compromised by partisan politics, biases, and opinions, instead of resolving disputes and conflicts with truths, knowledge, wisdom, and the rule of right. [6]

On one hand, it is easy to propose a thesis on fundamental rights and show that abortion, illegal immigration, welfare, diversity, and health insurance do not qualify as rights. On the other hand, it is difficult to outline potential solutions to these very real complex problems. First, God teaches us we should seek wisdom to understand both sides of the issue and have compassion, kindness, understanding, and wisdom to move forward. Second, this book is about the Constitution and grants of power that the federal government possesses to protect the fundamental rights of citizens. A solution may be as simple as allowing each individual state to decide what is right for them and their constituents. Americans can vote with their feet and move to a state of their liking. The evidence in this text supports federalism and placing more power back to the states to resolve issues beyond the grants of power provided to the federal government. That is the beauty of the American federalism system, it is fifty nations within one united nation. State solutions to issues, however, are limited because they cannot involve experimentation with the fundamental rights of citizens. Of course, we will learn, that state and federal governments do, indeed, incorrectly experiment with fundamental rights.

By following the fundamental rights proposed in this text, it is possible to achieve some level of compromise, efficiency, understanding, and benefit for both sides of controversial issues. For instance, although abortion is not a fundamental right, the fundamental right to pursue health would protect any woman who needs an abortion to save her life. Charity controlled by the private sector would be more efficient than government welfare. Smart guns would be more beneficial to both parties involved in the Second Amendment debate. A private sector solution using carbon capture would be advantageous to both sides of the climate debate. Understanding that the First Amendment not only protects the liberty to free speech and religion but all conscious thought may provide pause to those that want to limit free speech and religious rights. Understanding that voting disenfranchisement affects rural America more than urban America may change some perceptions about voting laws. Understanding education is the great American equalizer and not diversity may help bridge the racial divide. Understanding judgment of others sexuality is just as much a sin as homosexuality may foster more acceptance for gay marriage. There are solutions, but to attain solutions we must venture past all our biases and opinions to achieve what God wants in his servants: Wisdom for the greater good of society.

List of Solutions to the many Grievances Highlighted in the Book

Below is a list of solutions to the many grievances I highlight with the federal government in this text. The below solutions would increase perceptions, trust, and legitimize public consent of the federal government: [7] [8]

1. States should follow Article V of the Constitution and hold an annual constitutional amendment conference. At the conference, each state receives one vote, and those proposals that receive a two-

thirds majority legally become amendment proposals to the Constitution. Once amendment proposals garner three-fourths of the states' approval, they become amendments to the Constitution. The beauty of this method of amending the Constitution is it bypasses Congress.

2. Pass an amendment that allows states the right to veto or nullify federal legislation with three-fifths majority.
3. Pass an amendment that places 12-year term limits on the House of Representatives, Senate, and Supreme Court.
4. Repeal the Eleventh, Sixteenth, and Seventeenth Amendments.
5. States that opt out of federal legislation shall receive a tax rebate, so they are not coerced by the federal government to sign on to legislation they oppose.
6. Pass an amendment that protects citizenship by requiring a national identification card for privileges to work, vote, education, receive benefits, etc.
7. Pass a balanced budget amendment to control the 31 trillion-dollar national debt.
8. Reinstate Republican principles such as those checks and balances to secure bipartisanship. For example, requiring two-thirds Senate majority to pass appropriations bills and to confirm nominations to important federal posts.
9. Pass an amendment allowing the executive branch the power to a line-item veto. A line-item veto will prevent unnecessary and wasteful spending practices in omnibus spending bills. Since the President can only pass spending bills in their entirety, there is no mechanism to weed out the wasteful pet projects politicians try to win for their state or districts.
10. Pass an amendment to define United States citizens fundamental natural rights (like Table I) that should be the focus of all legislative regulations and laws. Laws and regulations outside the scope of protecting the rights of all United States citizens and federal grants of powers should be voided by the courts. Documenting a comprehensive list of fundamental rights will reinforce that sovereignty resides with "We the people," and the government should face the burden of proving legislation that infringes on fundamental rights is a reasonable necessity to achieve a constitutional objective. The purpose of this amendment should also be to restore free speech, property, contract, work, religion, and gun rights to their original constitutional meaning.
11. Restore federalism and states' powers. In other words, uphold the Tenth Amendment.

12. Restore the original constitutional definition of the Interstate Commerce Clause, which means trade between the states and nothing more.

13. Restore the original constitutional definition of the Necessary and Proper Clause, which means the government may act if, and only if, there is both a compelling reason and they use the least evasive method to achieve their constitutional objective (common sense and the rule of right).

14. Abolish the departments of education, agriculture, energy, environmental protection agency, labor, health and human services, federal reserve, internal revenue service, and housing and urban development. Most of these powers should fall to state and local governments. The internal revenue service may be abolished after repealing the Sixteenth Amendment and implementing a fair tax or national sales tax.

15. Restrict the authority of federal law enforcement to only those crimes enumerated in the Constitution: Counterfeiting, treason, slavery, and high crimes. Federal enforcement can also protect federal institutions such as those for national intelligence, national security, immigration services, the Post Office, military, and other legal federal departments and agencies.

16. Draft an amendment: In the name of national unity each citizen of the United States has equal fundamental rights. The United States is a country defined by equal rights, not diversity. There shall be no laws that regulate race, gender, ethnicity, socio-economic status or any other demographic that is used to create polarity, division, and displacement of rights. The objective of political parties and the government is to protect the rights of everyone equally and not to impose their beliefs on the minority party.

17. Pass a school choice amendment: Parents have the right to choose the school for their child's education and tax money should follow the child to the school they attend.

18. Pass an amendment that climate change legislation cannot violate fundamental rights by restricting carbon emissions. Instead, the focus should be on carbon capture. After NASA was cut by Obama, the private sector took charge and has been successfully putting men in space. Similarly, if we challenge the private sector with the carbon capture job, it too can be solved.

19. Pass an amendment stating emergency powers and laws are temporary and must be renewed on a yearly basis. These laws must be applied equally and must be the least evasive method of achieving its objective.

20. "None of the above" needs to be a choice on voting ballots. If "none of the above" wins, then parties must nominate alternates for the office in question. "None of the above" on ballots may force candidates to show they can reach out and connect with disgruntled voters. It could be eye opening to see how disconnected parties and their candidates are with the American people.

Notice, all the above grievances are about returning to the original meaning of the Constitution by correcting past indiscretions. I am not proposing any radical changes to the original meaning or purpose of the Constitution, which is to protect the fundamental rights of all citizens equally.

Solution to Rogue Federal Enforcement Agencies [9]

Several actions could reverse the alarming trend of prosecutorial liberty to conjure up crimes and victims discussed in Chapter 7:

- Place the onus on government enforcement agencies to pay the criminal costs and restitution for exonerated defendants. Overzealous prosecutors should be held legally accountable when they knowingly change the meaning and purpose of statutes to prosecute innocent persons or companies.
- The justice system should end the practice of incentivizing whistleblowers and making deals with defendants to testify against persons higher in the corporate or political pecking order. Whistleblowers and defendants with deals are incentivized to lie. Moreover, it is a federal crime to bribe or coach witnesses to make false statements, but the prosecution is not held to the same standard as the defense when it comes to witness tampering. For the justice system to be fair and consistent, the prosecution needs to be held to the same standard as the defense.
- Judges need to enforce ex post facto law protection and dismiss cases where prosecutors invent or create new ways to enforce ambiguous statutes. Ex post facto law protection is in the Constitution and prevents people from being prosecuted for doing what were legal activities before a new law turned the activities into a crime.
- Eliminate crimes without victims. The objective of the government is to protect the fundamental rights of citizens equally. The government can only mitigate fundamental rights to protect the health and wellbeing of citizens. Any constitutional law that infringes on rights must be deemed reasonable, necessary, and its ends must justify the means. It is not the duty of prosecutors and judges to determine when immorality without victims becomes a crime. God is the judge of immoral actions (without victims), not prosecutors wishing to play God. Certainly, immoral behavior in private should not be a crime nor should perjury, conspiracy, and obstruction without a victim. Immoral behavior done in the public sphere is open to much debate. Nudity and lewd behavior in public is certainly offensive but are the people who witness this behavior victims of physical harm? More importantly, where is the line drawn between acceptable and unacceptable

behavior? These laws are open to much interpretation by the judge, and it is beyond the scope of this text. I would only inject that any violation of public immorality without physical harm should only result in a fine and community service, not imprisonment. Mental anguish without physical harm is real. Nevertheless, these cases should probably be resolved in civil, not criminal court. [10]

- We need a strict enforcement of separation of powers between the judicial and executive branches. Eliminate the political weaponization of both the state and federal judicial systems, which can only be accomplished by either dissolving a politically charged justice department or by making the justice department neutral and not an extension of gubernatorial and presidential administrations.
- Gag orders preventing defense attorneys from discussing cases need to be scrutinized. The only way for defendants to receive a fair trial is when they have the opportunity to discuss the nature of their case with the press prior to a trial. The media has regularly been an extension of government prosecutions because they are oblivious to the questionable tactics used by enforcement agencies. The defense should have the same opportunity as prosecutors when accessing the press. [11]

Part I: Rationalizing the Existence of God [12]

Chapter 2: Can Science Rationalize the Existence of God?

God's Language of Life Creates the Flesh and Soul

Subatomic Particles [13 14]

Subatomic particles comprise all matter and forces in the universe. The standard model equation is a quantum physics equation that explains many happenings in the universe. The standard model equation includes a plethora of subatomic particles, such as 36 different quarks and 12 different leptons. Also in the standard model equation are gluons, W, and Z force particles that bind the quark and lepton subatomic particles to form protons, neutrons, and electrons. The standard model equation also includes the God Particle or the Higgs boson particle. The Higgs boson particle is often referred to as the God Particle because human life would not exist without it. That said, human life could not exist without any of the particles that have been discovered. Subatomic particles are characterized by two groups: Matter and forces. Matter particles (fermions) include protons, neutrons, electrons, quarks, and neutrinos, whereas force particles (bosons) include gluons, W, Z, gravitons, and photons (light). [15]

Quantum entanglement is an example of one bizarre quantum mechanics theory with some credence. Quantum entanglement suggests that any two subatomic particles in the universe may be entangled, or their probabilistic state is dependent on each other. Entanglement not only defies our current reality; it also defies our current laws of physics (Einstein's theory of relativity) because $E=mc^2$ no longer applies. That is because entanglement suggests that subatomic particle interactions can travel much faster than the speed of light constant, c, in the above equation. Up to this point, science reveals that nothing in the universe travels faster than light, but entanglement suggests communication, interaction, or dependency between subatomic particles can occur instantaneously among particles at opposite ends of the universe (millions of light years apart).

Thus, it may certainly be plausible that the subatomic particles within one person can interact with those subatomic particles that make up other people. If that is true, then it is possible that when people feel connected or fall in love, the fate or destiny of their subatomic particles is dependent. Additionally, entanglement may also suggest that an observer's subatomic particles may influence or change the outcome of experiments. Entanglement may mean that data and facts uncovered from scientific experiments may not be true. Everything in the universe is connected and much more mysterious than we ever imagined. In other words, the state of human subatomic particles can be influenced by environmental conditions and perhaps God.

DNA and Environmental Factors

Our environment is everything and is the basic principle behind God's master plan. More specifically, our environment is what crafts everyone's personality, identity, or reality. No person is perfect; each person has a flawed DNA genome with a certain number of unique mutations. That said, about 99% of the human genome is the same regardless of race or gender. Thus, diversity has nothing to do with our race and gender but everything to do with our specific environmental experiences. What defines us is how our genes are expressed. Gene expression is the result of epigenetic changes (evolution) from our exposure to environmental factors. Since no two people experience the same environment, this is what defines our phenotype, diversity, or uniqueness. A person may have a mutation indicating a high prevalence of certain cancer or Alzheimer's Disease. Nevertheless, gene mutations may never be expressed if the body never faces certain environmental conditions. God provides us with a unique environment, DNA, gut bacteria, and subatomic particle probabilities. Then our free will choices and other environmental factors shape our reality and subconscious into our identity. The environment defines everything about us, such as how we will sin and how we will love. God's evolutionary plan also means the adversity each person faces is also unique since free will and environmental conditions are exclusive to each person. We all face distinct challenges in finding our way to God and faith. When Jesus was asked if the man born blind was because he or his parents sinned, Jesus responded in John 9:3, "It was neither that this man sinned, nor his parents; but it was so that the works of God may be displayed in him." Jesus is referring to God's want for variety. [16]

Human reality is restricted, in part, by the evolutionary limits of our senses. [17] For example, our eyes can detect wavelengths of color, but the eyes cannot detect large wavelengths that encompass radio or TV electromagnetic fields or small wavelengths that comprise gamma and x-ray electromagnetic fields. We may be aware of these electromagnetic fields, but are they really part of our reality, or do we just take them for granted? [18] We all believe the space we inhabit is continuous, but on the contrary, it is finite. The resolution of a computer or TV screen is determined by the number of pixels (the precision of an analog-to-digital converter – A2D). The pixel size cannot be subdivided any further to improve resolution (without getting a new TV or computer). Today, the resolution is so good we do not even notice the pixels. Similarly, space is made up of very small volumes that cannot be subdivided any further. These volumes of space are so small (Planck length) we do not know they exist because our reality cannot sense them. There is much more to our reality if we can venture past our senses and those factors that inhibit or place boundaries on our reality.

Free Will

Life is primarily controlled and dictated by free will choices. There are three arguments that support free will over fate or life that is predetermined by God. First, if life is predetermined, then why does the Bible teach people to pray? If the fate of humans is predetermined, prayer would be a meaningless exercise. Second, if life is predetermined, then that also means that God orchestrates evil and chaos. It tends to make more sense that God is a stabilizing factor in the universe who is opposed to evil. Evil is the result of the fall of man and, therefore, evil is carried out by the free will choices of man. What about Satan and the Devil? Are they real? Perhaps, but in my opinion, the Devil provides religious followers a reason to explain the evil behavior of Godly creations such as Adolph Hitler or Joseph Stalin. Whether or not the Devil exists, one thing is for certain, evil exists. Finally, God provides everyone with choices. For instance, in *Revelation 3:20,* God provides everyone with a choice to pick Him or rebuke Him. God may provide guidance and advice, but He does not make decisions for human beings. Nonetheless, each person must live with the consequences of their decisions. Besides, since free will is not very complicated and our everyday choices are not very complex, it seems unlikely that God is involved in these mundane decisions. Everyone seems to have a routine that requires little thought. [19]

Many of our choices are so basic that society is primarily binary: True or false, yes or no, Republican or Democrat, and so forth. Saint Paul in 2 Corinthians 1:18 suggests, "But as God is faithful, our word to you is not yes and no." In other words, only God can act in the certainty of "yes." There is more to the universe than what our simplistic binary reality perceives. If our free will choices guide us beyond our everyday choices and we seek more wisdom for the greater good of society, then perhaps God is guiding us and showing us the way. More importantly, if we act on that guidance, we are listening to Him.

The Flesh, Soul, Spirit, and Sin

The body and soul discussed in the Bible make up human reality. The body is referred to as the flesh in the Bible and is comprised of, among other things, DNA, subatomic particles, and the senses. Everyone has the same body or vessel to house the soul and spirit. The body, in turn, uses free will to interact with environmental conditions to create the soul or a unique and diverse identity or reality for each person. The human spirit discussed in the Bible is a sixth sense that allows people to enter a relationship with God and live more righteous lives. The sixth sense allows humans to venture into the unknown (beyond our senses) and view the universe through God's lens. [20] In much the same way, the sixth sense may explain the concept of neural plasticity. Neural plasticity describes how exercise can condition the muscles and brain to find new and alternate communication pathways to avoid diseased nerves and muscles. Neural plasticity can help a person who should be requiring assistance to walk to live a normal lifestyle. In the same way, the brain can be rewired so functional senses are heightened to help the blind or deaf to compensate for their handicap. Similarly, the spirit or the sixth sense retrains the body and soul to develop new neurological pathways and to heighten the senses to learn what exists beyond the very limited human reality.

How is eternal life referred to in John 3:16 possible? Dr. Chuck Missler defines the soul as the internal software of the human being. Missler's internal software is equivalent to my definition of diversity and human identity or reality, which includes perceptions, attitudes, memory, and personality. Human reality or internal software is physically much different than the body and flesh because it has no mass. Missler concludes that anything without mass is eternal and can live forever because it will never decay. [21]

All sins must be created equal. One sin is no more relevant or worse in the eyes of God. Sure, some sins have more retribution or punishment assigned to them in the criminal justice system, but a sin is a sin. People who boast about not committing any of the bad sins fail to understand this point. People who think that sins are unequal may justify, for example, saying hurtful things because, in their estimation, it is not a bad sin. All sins are equal for four reasons. First, sins should not be marginalized. Second, all sins defile the flesh, soul, and spirit. Third, sins that are merely bad manners can have a profound negative effect on nations. Sam Adams said, "Neither the wisest nor the wisest laws will secure liberty and happiness if a people whose manners are universally corrupt." Founding Father John Witherspoon said, "A corruption of manners makes a people ripe for destruction." The Founders knew that liberty could not exist in the face of bad manners. Bad manners foster the inability to listen, debate, and tolerate opposing views. Present-day society has moved into an unprecedented age of anger, hate, polarity, and intolerance that could be a sign the United States is in its infancy or its downfall and demise. Finally, sins are equal because they are guided by the principles that explain the simplicity and beauty of the universe and human nature – symmetry. [22] [23]

What is Normal?

Reality refers to the world or state of things as they exist. In the quantum world, reality is the interaction or relationship between things that result in events. My definition of reality explains how things are perceived by each individual relative to their vantage point and environment. C.S. Lewis states that reality is incorrigibly plural in that all things come from God and are related, but all things are not the same. Lewis and I agree that our realities come from God and are similar, but we each have a different reality. Most states of nature or realities of human beings are similar (overlap or interlocked), yet they are not identical. If you asked every person in the world to provide a detailed description of the same basic chair, there would be many similarities, but every description would be different. We are all connected (the same senses); at the same time, we are all unique or differentiated by our environmental factors. [24]

Quantum physicist David Bohm was the first to suggest there may be two realities: A higher order implicate reality that may encompass spirituality, and a lower order explicate reality. Genesis 1:31 implies in the beginning, there was one order, but after the fall of man, a lower-order reality may have been initiated with new laws of physics that do not explain the higher-order reality of the universe. The fall of man may explain why we are struggling with understanding the physics behind subatomic particles since they are part of another reality, a distinct set of laws of science. Dr. Missler points out in his book *Cosmic Codes* that Nobel Prize-winning physicist Brian Josephson believes Bohm's concepts may introduce God into scientific theories. [25]

John 8:31–32 suggests that only God holds the truth. If that is accurate, then that means only God holds the correct reality. If that is correct, then each human may not only have a unique reality but a flawed reality. Human reality is unique and flawed because it is dependent on limited environmental factors catalyzed by God's language of life (subatomic particles, DNA, and free will). Since the environment, subatomic particles, DNA, and free will choices are unique to each person; everyone has a diverse and unique reality, but at the same time, a flawed reality. Therefore, the only way for humans to know the truth is to reform their reality by living sin free and having a relationship with God. Then, and only then, may humans gain precise knowledge, understanding, and wisdom to uncover the mysteries of the universe. Therein lies the problem, not only is our present-day population moving further from God but so too is our scientific brain trust. How did Einstein understand our universe so well? Thinking like God and having a relationship with God is what made Albert Einstein and Georges Lemaitre centuries ahead of their time. By thinking like God, they were able to produce accurate theories by visualizing a universe that God may create. Einstein theorized the cosmological constant (dark energy), and Lemaitre hypothesized the universe began when an infinitely old singularity exploded (big bang) decades before they would be proven. Until modern scientists start believing in and thinking like God, progress in understanding the universe will be stagnant, even in the face of vast technological advances.[26]

If God owns the perfect reality and each person not only has different realities but imperfect realities, then do we really know what normal is? Normal is different for each person! For example, in my reality, I have never experienced a supernatural event. However, that does not mean others that claim to have had supernatural experiences are lying. Supernatural experiences may be part of their reality and the result of how their subatomic particles behave or align with God. Until we can view the universe through the same lens as God, our realities or identities (personalities, ideas, theories, conclusions, etc.) will remain flawed. I truly believe those with a theistic belief system have a more perfected reality, whereas those with an atheistic point of view have realities that are defective and devolving. [27]

The Probability for Human Life to Form on Earth

Consider the human body for a moment. According to Dr. Chuck Missler, in his book *Cosmic Codes*, he states the probability of creating hemoglobin (only one of the thousands of proteins in the human body) is about one in 10^{500}. [28] Stephen Meyer, author of *Return of the God Hypothesis*, estimates the probability that one simple protein spontaneously came to exist and created the first living organism is about one chance in 10^{164}. Those numbers are not even fathomable in our reality because they are vastly larger than the number of atoms that exist in the entire universe which is estimated to be 10^{80}. [29] Keep in mind that this is the probability of creating one protein. The creation of other proteins has similar odds. Now, consider the odds that thousands of proteins will combine to form a human being. Those odds are beyond astronomical! The human body is indeed a scientific marvel. Furthermore, the number of neural connections and the vast amount of information stored in the brain make the human body the best and most efficient communication system. Creating a protein and intelligent life only scratch the surface of the miraculous and sophisticated nature of the human body, and they explain why the odds of creating human life are trillions upon trillions of times greater than all the atoms in the universe.

The probability of creating life from a biological and chemical standpoint was addressed in the prior paragraph. However, the probability of having an environment conducive for human life from a physics standpoint was not considered. For life to exist on Earth, about one million things with little chance of happening had to come to fruition. For example, consider the force of gravity or the strong nuclear force. If these forces are a tad higher or lower, everything fails; the universe falls apart. If the Milky Way did not have an unusually low entropy compared to other galaxies, then we would not be here. If stars did not have supernova explosions, then heavy elements for living organisms to survive would not be available on Earth. If the weight of subatomic particles was not exact, then life could not exist. If the rate at which the universe expands was not precisely what it is, then life could not exist. If the Earth did not develop an atmosphere or a magnetic field, no life as we know it would survive the sun's deadly radiation. Even in more recent evolutionary times, if a giant asteroid did not strike the Earth and kill off the dinosaurs, then it is improbable that life as we know it would exist today. Even the creation of our moon is critical to our existence—illustrating that human life is a miracle. Stephen Meyer places the probability for Earth to develop a low entropy level at one chance in 10^{123}. Just as unsurprising, Meyer claims the probability of creating a universe suitable for life over a sterile universe is also improbable with only one chance out of every 10^{98} universes created! [30] Thousands, if not millions, of unlikely events led to the creation of human life on Earth. Some scientists support a concept known as the anthropic principle or the theory that the Earth was designed specifically for human life. The anthropic principle suggests that life on Earth was just a stroke of luck and occurred without any help from God. However, even most scientists cannot accept that life on Earth was pure luck because that would rule out any chance of finding any solutions as to why we or our universe exists in the first place. [31] [32] [33] That God exists seems to be a much more logical explanation for the creation of the universe than scientific theories that suggest our existence is pure luck, which is especially true considering that the stroke of luck was an astronomically improbable event.

The Second Law of Thermodynamics: Information and Missing Information [34]

Science and math like to define what the Bible refers to as wisdom, understanding, facts, truth, and knowledge as information. More specifically, information can be defined in terms of bits. When I worked in the field of semiconductors, my specialty was testing analog to digital converters (A2Ds). A2Ds are used to convert analog information to digital information and are found embedded in all our digital products. If a product had an 8-bit A2D, that means 8 bits of analog information are transferred to the digital realm and may be represented by 2^8, or 256 states. The states define the precision or accuracy of the A2D. A 16-bit A2D has 2^{16}, or 65,536 states. The more bits of information an A2D can covert, the more precise the information that is converted from the analog world. More resolution or information means better-quality pictures are taken from a digital camera, and better-quality images are displayed on a digital TV or computer screen.

Of importance to science and math is missing information, or information we do not know. Missing information is represented in science by the second law of thermodynamics, which states that the missing information or entropy of the universe is always increasing. Said differently, everything wears out. More specifically, our universe and stars are finite and cannot exist forever. Missing information and entropy represent the chaos and randomness of the universe. As we uncover more information, it reveals much more that we do not know or understand. Furthermore, our ignorance prevents us from learning new information. We may think we know the truth and facts about the world, but instead, our brains are filled with misinformation from non-credible sources, biases, opinions, and prejudices. Moreover, even if we own the truths and facts about certain information, it does not mean we have the wisdom to draw the correct conclusions. [35]

Chaos results from missing information such as when there is a lack of communication. If someone could miraculously uncover missing information, it could be used to restore order in the universe. Moreover, if someone could miraculously add information to offset what information is lost to entropy, then that would also constitute a stabilizing event in the universe. Evidence suggests that organization found within the universe is just as influential as the chaos or disorder that results from continually increasing entropy (second law of thermodynamics). There seems to be an organizing principle of universal order that has avoided scientific detection, and it may explain our existence. If true, it is not out of the realm of possibility that this stabilizing force may produce irregularities in what our reality may consider normal or uniform – a miracle. If this organizing or stabilizing principle is the work of God restoring missing or adding new information, scientists will never unravel this mystery. [36] As I will discuss later in this chapter, scientific theories to explain the creation of the universe and life are highly flawed. Since scientific theories are flawed, it is more reasonable to assume the correct hypothesis is that an intelligent designer has periodically injected genetic information into the ecosystem which has resulted in the creation of life and the introduction of thousands of new species.

Quantum physics has ignored thermodynamics in its standard model equation. A unified quantum equation that includes the four major forces of the universe will be incomplete unless new fields are added to the equation to comprehend thermodynamics. Thermodynamics is the study of heat that all forms of energy produce. Heat describes everything in the universe. In fact, satellite pictures of the universe reveal electromagnetic radiation emitted at the time of the big bang 14 billion years ago. In other words, not only is heat a map or a picture of the past, but the transfer of heat may help scientists predict what the future of the universe holds (similarly, telescopes enable us to see into the past). The universe is filled with both the very hot (stars and black holes) and very cold reaches of space. For these reasons, quantum physics has potentially made a huge error by omitting thermodynamics – heat and entropy – in its equations to describe the universe.

Symmetry [37] [38]

Aristotle wrote, "The mathematical sciences particularly exhibit order, symmetry, and limitation; and these are the greatest form of beauty." [39] The laws of mathematics and science are based on symmetry. Symmetry is important for several reasons. First, it creates order out of chaos. Second, it makes it possible to predict future outcomes. For instance, elements and subatomic particles can be predicted before they are discovered. Elements fit in a predictable pattern in the periodic table of elements, and symmetry also predicts that opposing particles, such as antimatter particles, exist. Third, symmetry unifies unrelated things, such as linking gravity, electromagnetic forces, and matter. Fourth, symmetry reveals the unexpected such as subatomic particles having spin. Finally, symmetry eliminates diverging equations that result in unwanted infinities; symmetry makes for finite solutions to equations.

Isaac Newton taught us that planets, asteroids, and moons move in symmetrical patterns determined by the force of gravity acting on them. James Maxwell taught us that the equations for the electromagnetic force were the same for either the magnetic or electrical fields; thus, they are symmetrical. Albert Einstein's theories of relativity proved that spacetime or gravitational fields, as well as energy and mass ($E=mc^2$), are symmetrical. Einstein demonstrated that there was no such thing as the conservation of energy (E) or mass (m), but instead conservation of energy and mass collectively. Both the weak and strong nuclear forces are symmetrical. The strong nuclear force is what holds the nucleus of atoms together since positively charged protons should repel each other. The weak nuclear force explains why unstable atoms or elements decay.

If the laws of science follow symmetry, it begs to reason that the laws of human nature should also follow symmetry. There are extremes, good and evil, and of course, there are various degrees of goodness and evilness in between. Thus, symmetry suggests that natural disasters, crime, pain, and suffering are a necessity of life. Similarly, the Book of Revelation teaches us that society must face pain, suffering, and adversity before the second coming of Christ.

Carbon Dating

The existence of God may be found in Bible prophecies. My favorite prophecy is found in Isaiah 53, which predicts the coming of Jesus several centuries before his arrival. The Bible has predicted hundreds of historical events. Isaiah was written about 700 BC, but a copy of the Book of Isaiah found in the Dead Sea Scrolls was carbon-dated to about 200 BC. The Dead Sea Scrolls version of Isaiah was a copy of the original. Thus, even the copied version of Isaiah's prophecies was written well before the birth of Christ. In fact, the 10th anniversary expanded edition of the Rose Book of Bible Charts, Maps, and Timelines details one hundred archeological finds (manuscripts, artifacts, ancient cities, etc.) that corroborate Bible verses and records. [40]

The Imperfections of the Many Scientific Theories to Explain our Existence

Biologist Richard Lewontin wrote in 1997, "We take the side of science in spite of the patent absurdity of some of its constructs. Moreover, materialism is absolute, for we cannot allow a Divine Foot in the door." Removing God as a possibility for designing the universe seems to be the chief objective of naturalists. Unfortunately, many scientists are naturalists or materialists who have one mission and that is to develop any theory that removes the possibility of God as our creator. Occam's razor is a philosophical principle that posits the simplest solution to a problem is generally the correct one. God is certainly the simplest explanation for our existence then the many imperfect, outlandish, flawed, and desperation theories discussed in this section. [41]

Evolution

Evolution explains how organisms adapt to environmental changes. However, evolution cannot explain two important issues regarding our existence. First, evolution cannot explain the spontaneous creation of the first living organism. When creating life, DNA and information are required to make proteins. The creation of proteins was identified as an improbable event in the preceding section on probability because each DNA molecule contains vast amounts of information. In other words, DNA is a complex biological computer that cannot be synthetically created by simply combining the elements that make up life. In fact, the only thing scientists have identified that can create information are intelligent beings such as man or God. Competing scientific theories to the God hypothesis only brings more relevancy to God or an intelligent designer as the source of the information to form the first living organism. For instance, scientists point to a principle called panspermia to explain how life was introduced on Earth. Panspermia proposes that life is alien and came to Earth via a comet, meteor, or spaceship. Perhaps, but again, panspermia does not answer the original question posed in this paragraph: How did the first living organism, alien or not, originate? [42]

Finally, evolution cannot explain how new species form. Genetic mutations are more likely to degrade genetic function than create and improve species. Genetic information is lost, not gained from a vast majority of mutations. Human mutations usually result in illness, disease, and deformity, but not increased functionality. Furthermore, fossil discoveries are deficient to explain the creation of many species. Evolution, by definition, happens slowly with small information gains between each generation of species. However, fossil discoveries suggest the bridge from some species to other species requires incredible gains of genetic information that are astronomically improbable. In fact, there are dozens of generations of species that need to be unearthed to prove the theory of evolution can create new species. Furthermore, Stephen Meyer suggests the odds evolution created one simple protein in a new species from a genetic mutation in another species is only one chance in 10^{37}. And that is the probability to create one new protein. Of course, each new species requires hundreds of new proteins with equally improbable odds to form via the evolutionary process. Although the odds to create a new protein from a species is much better than the odds described earlier of a protein forming spontaneously, it is still improbable. In other words, it is astronomically improbable that new species were introduced by evolution alone. [43]

Scientists have synthesized ribonucleic acid (RNA) and developmental gene regulatory networks (dGRN) from controlled experiments. These findings have many scientists suggesting that life can be spontaneously created. Nevertheless, a controlled experiment consists of scientists imputing information to obtain a desired result. Experiments do not prove the spontaneous origins of life or new species. However, they do prove information is required from scientists to create life or a new species. Unfortunately, scientists have no explanation as to what is the source of that information to create new species (other than God). [44] I am not saying evolution is fiction and does not happen. Even if evolution and epigenetic changes do not result in new species, evolution is important for species to survive by adapting to environmental changes. The human body makes epigenetic changes daily to adapt to its surroundings. For instance, our bodies evolve and acclimate to lower oxygen levels when we travel to places located at higher elevations.

The Theory of Everything [45]

Spacetime includes the four dimensions familiar to human beings – height, width, and length comprise the three dimensions of space, and time is the fourth dimension. In 1905, Einstein proved that space and time were the same, and it was called spacetime. In doing so, Einstein showed that there is an intermediate zone or extended present where there is no past or future. The intermediate zone depends on the relative location to the event that is being observed. The greater the distance in relation to the event, the greater the intermediate zone. In our reality, our senses cannot detect this intermediate zone when viewing events happening around us because it is only a few nanoseconds. If the event is on Mars, then relative to Earth, the extended present is about 15 minutes. That means there are 15 minutes on Mars where events are unaccountable. The present is an illusion, and there is no such thing as now.

By 1915, Einstein's model of the universe changed when he proved that spacetime was equivalent to gravitational fields. Einstein's brilliance would combine Newton's laws of gravity with the concept of fields introduced by James Maxwell for the electromagnetic force to devise the concept of the gravitational field. Gravitational fields explain how spacetime is curved and warped. The magnitude of spacetime curvature depends on its proximity to the gravitational force of celestial objects.

The quest for a God equation or a theory of everything that explains the birth and evolution of our universe is focused on unifying the four major forces of the universe into one equation: Gravity, electromagnetic, weak nuclear, and strong nuclear. Albert Einstein's theories of relativity explain the force of gravity, which, in turn, helps us understand the large-scale mysteries of the universe, such as uncovering the secrets behind black holes, the expanding universe, and the big bang. Quantum mechanics helps us understand the small-scale mysteries of the universe, such as how subatomic particles behave. In quantum physics, the interaction between subatomic particles is what matters. The time the interaction took place is not important. Spacetime has little importance in the quantum vision of the world. The current standard model equation explains almost everything in the universe because it unifies three of the universe's four forces: The strong nuclear force, the weak nuclear force, and the electromagnetic force, but not gravity.

Over the past 40 to 50 years, the mission has been to unite quantum mechanics' standard model equation with gravity and the theory of relativity. Currently, string theory and loop theory are trying to combine gravitational fields into the standard model equation that will unify all four forces of nature and will explain everything about the universe. [46] String theory suggests that subatomic particles are not finite points but tiny vibrating strings. The unusual phenomenon regarding string theory is that the math only works in ten or eleven dimensions. Our universe may have decayed from ten or eleven dimensions to four dimensions before it could remain stable. Or conceivably, human reality moves in four dimensions, but atoms behave as if they are in ten dimensions. Whatever the explanation, it must defy logic. [47]

Once scientists uncover the unified theory of everything, it still may not answer the million-dollar question of where did the theory of everything come from? One must not lose sight that once a unified theory of everything is formulated, it will not, as some presume, disprove God. On the contrary, the theory of everything equation may explain the formation, death, and evolution of universes, but it will not explain where the equation came from, what existed before the big bang, what gives the equation substance, and how were the initial and boundary conditions selected in the equation. Thomas Aquinas hypothesized that everything in the universe moves, and he rationalizes that God must be the source that sets everything in motion. The theory of everything will not explain what Aquinas hypothesized centuries ago – what set everything in motion. If every event, such as the big bang, has a cause, scientists cannot say definitively what caused an infinitely old singularity to explode and set the formation of the universe in motion. God is, of course, one logical hypothesis to explain this riddle. [48]

The Multiverse Theory

The multiverse theory suggests there are an infinite number of universes. Since the possible states each subatomic particle may exhibit are infinite, then an infinite number of universes would allow each subatomic particle to reside in all its possible states. Let us evaluate an example, the multiverse theory suggests there are an infinite number of universes containing a planet exactly like Earth. Every person in the world would exist on the Earth-like planet in each universe, but their experiences and behaviors will be different to account for the infinite number of states that their subatomic particles may experience. For example, in one universe, I may be typing; in another, I may be sleeping; and in another, I may be riding a horse. In each of the infinite multiverses, I am doing something different. The multiverse theory seems far-fetched, so the answer to this riddle may be as simple as our reality is what we sense (see, hear, taste, smell, or feel). Said differently, what we sense puts our subatomic particles into a definitive state, and all this multiverse talk is phooey. After all, this is the exact same thing happens to subatomic particles. Information about subatomic particles is only available when they are in a definitive state, which only occurs when they interact with other particles. When particles do not interact, they do not reveal any information. It is as if they disappeared. Similarly, once our senses interact with the world, our subatomic state is defined. Physicist Carlo Rovelli rationalizes our realities are in a deterministic state in the following manner: "The apparent determinism of the macroscopic world is due to the fact that microscopic randomness cancels out on average." [49]

The multiverse or parallel universe theory addresses the problem discussed earlier about the exceedingly low probability of creating not only a universe like the Milky Way, but also a planet that can support human life. If there are an infinite number of universes, then the multiverse theory explains why everything in our universe is precisely fine-tuned for life to exist. After all, if there are an infinite number of universes, then the probability that one universe will support life is much more realistic. Even if the multiverse theory is true, again, it does not answer three points. First, how are the boundary conditions to give the equation substance defined. Second, the multiverse theory introduces unpredictable problems that arise from an infinite number of solutions. Finally, the multiverse theory does not explain what set everything in motion to form the universe. There is absolutely no evidence that an infinite number of universes exist, and most scientists agree the theory is preposterous. Nevertheless, scientists support the theory because in their incorrect estimation, it eliminates the need for the universe to have a creator. [50]

Loop Theory or the Big Bounce Theory

In loop theory, the belief is that the universe started with a big bounce, not a big bang. The big bounce explains that our universe expands until equilibrium is reached, and then the universe collapses onto itself like an enormous crunch. The universe collapses to the size of a Planck length (10^{-35} m), and then a new big bounce creates a new universe, and the process is repeated indefinitely. The big bounce or loop theory was created to remove the God hypothesis by answering some unresolved questions surrounding the big bang theory. For instance, the big bounce suggests the universe is infinitely old, removing the notion that the big bang started from a singularity. Therefore, the big bounce theory removes the need to explain the unknown creation element (perhaps God) that set the universe in motion. A singularity is an infinitely small and infinitely dense point in space. The big bang theory suggests the creation of the universe began when a singularity exploded and set everything in motion. Loop theory has some issues because it is difficult to explain how the second law of thermodynamics is not violated – that chaos and entropy are always increasing. A crunching universe would seem to suggest that order is being reestablished in the universe, and entropy must therefore decrease until the next big bounce begins. [51] [52]

On one hand, if the big bounce theory *does not* violate the second law of thermodynamics, then each subsequent universe would result in less energy and shorter cycles until the universe dies. Thus, the universe cannot be infinitely old, so the big bounce theory is wrong. If, on the other hand, the big bounce theory *does* violate the second law of thermodynamics, it suggests an unexplained stabilizing element in the universe that could also be explained by the God hypothesis. [53]

The Universal Wave Function

Light particles, photons, behave both as a wave and particle. Experiments show photons stop behaving like a wave and turn into a particle once they are observed. Observation causes the photon wave function to collapse and it becomes a particle. The universal wave function is used by physicists to explain how our universe came to exist. Like the photon wave function, something must cause the universal wave function to collapse and create a visual universe. For the universal wave function to collapse and create an infinite number of universes, it seems as if it would require God or some cosmic onlooker to collapse the wave function. Thus, physicists have tried to introduce new theories to eliminate God by resolving the observation conundrum as a cause for the collapsing universal wave function.

The multiverse theory discussed earlier and the even more problematic mathematical universe theory are two examples of theories trying to eliminate the observation conundrum. The multiverse theory does not explain where the information to define the universal wave function equation comes from nor does it explain where the information comes from to provide the equation substance. To address the information paradox posed in the multiverse theory, cosmologist Max Tegmark introduced the mathematical universe theory. The problem with the mathematical universe theory is it implies that the uniformity of the laws of physics that guide naturalists are but a figment of their imagination. The mathematical universe theory must accommodate an infinite number of mathematical possibilities and, therefore, the laws of physics can and will change at a given time. For example, gravity will fluctuate and is not a uniform constant as scientists have presumed for centuries. [54]

Stephen Hawking and other naturalist scientists have formulated other theories from the universal wave function to hypothesize that the universe was "created from nothing." Hawking and others suggest that the laws of physics predated the universe (matter, energy, and spacetime) and subsequently created everything spontaneously. But the laws of physics require boundary and initial conditions as well as interactions to achieve a result. The laws of physics do nothing unless there are interactions (cause and effect) between matter and forces. Thus, it seems intuitively obvious, the universe cannot be created from nothing. There needs to be an intelligent designer to explain our existence or, as Hawking put it, to "breathe fire into the equations and make the universe for them to describe." Yet, Hawking's theory fails to address the preceding statement he made to explain the source of the information that formulated the laws of physics, set the boundary and initial conditions, and created the right interactions to achieve our universe. [55] [56]

Hawking's nothing into something equation requires negative or imaginary time to eliminate the singularity that set off the big bang. Removing singularities would eliminate any reason to consider the universe had a creator. As Hawking put it, "If the universe is really self-contained, having no boundary or edge, it would have neither a beginner nor end; it would simply be. What place, then, for a creator?" Of course, nothing in the real world emulates imaginary time and imaginary time is just another bizarre theory so naturalists can declare God does not exist. You be the judge. Does God exist or are we the result of pure luck and some kind of spontaneous creation from nothing? If one can believe we came from nothing, then why is so far-fetched to believe we are result of an intelligent designer's plan. [57]

Chapter 3: Is the Bible God's Word?

Rationalizing the Bible

In this chapter, I inject some personal opinions about subjects based on how I understand the facts. My interpretation will obviously be different from others, but there is one thing we can agree on: There is much we do not understand about God, the Bible, and science. Hopefully, my interpretation can open debate, discussion, and dialogue.

The purpose of this chapter is to describe how I resolved many questions I had about the Bible. Being able to rationalize the many stories, miracles, and happenings in the Bible turned a lifelong biblical sceptic into a God-fearing Christian. The task of rationalizing the Bible required gaining knowledge, understanding, and wisdom through many hours of prayer and contemplation.

Creationism

Creationists believe in a literal reading of the Bible. The story of the creation told in Genesis not only fuels atheist arguments contrary to the existence of God, but it is the reason for a large fracture between Christian denominations. Dr. Henry Morris is an expert in the field of creationism within the Christian community. Dr. Morris labels my point of view on the creation as a progressive creation fundamentalist. These creationist labels produce an unnecessary fracture among Christians. Founding-era reverend George Whitefield stated, "God help us all to forget having names and to become Christians in deed and in truth." Christians should not be branded, labeled, and divided by denominations or ideas. Christians should unite, not fight, and Christians should learn to agree to disagree. While I accept Dr. Morris' point of view, I highlight the different perspective of a progressive creationist who not only believes the creation of the universe took billions of years but how that point of view can still support a literal reading of Genesis. [58] [59]

Time

According to Dr. Morris, the creation happened in seven days using the same time frame humans are accustomed to using on Earth. Furthermore, he estimates this event happened about 6,000 years ago. 2 Peter 3:8 reminds us, "But do not let this one fact escape your notice, beloved, that with the Lord one day is like a thousand years, and a thousand years like one day." Similarly, King David wrote in Psalms 90:4, "For a thousand years in Your sight are like yesterday when it passes by, or like a watch in the night." If the Genesis reading of the creation is to be taken literally, then is Peter a liar and King David mistaken? Dr. Morris never addresses these conflicting statements in the Bible. Dr. Morris concludes, "Obviously, none of us really knows" what the "waters above the firmament" means in Genesis 1:6–8. If Dr. Morris is unsure about this, then how can he be so sure about the content in the rest of Genesis, which is equally open to the interpretation of the reader? [60]

Dr. Morris contends that scripture is clear that man is to precisely model the creation in Genesis by working six days and then taking the Sabbath or the seventh day off (Exodus 20:9–11). Exodus 20:9–11 does not disprove that a day to God is eons. God may allow Christians to celebrate the Sabbath by modeling God's creation. For instance, a map is an accurate representation of a larger area. Similarly, Exodus 20:9–11 may provide humankind with an accurate representation to model the larger creation. Humanity celebrates the creation on a weekly basis although the actual timeline for the creation lasted billions of years. [61]

As Dr. Morris claims, "Time cannot be separated or removed from any of the universe." But time is merely a practical reference used by humans. Time is dependent on the force of gravity and, therefore, varies throughout the universe and does not have any practical meaning to God. Einstein saw no need for time in the universe when he replaced spacetime with gravitational fields in his theory of relativity. Furthermore, according to Dr. Morris, the sole purpose of the stars, sun, and moon is so humans can establish a time reference on Earth for a day, year, and season. Dr. Morris seems to forget that the sun, moon, and stars were not created until day four in Genesis. Thus, there was no time reference for the first three days of Genesis. Besides, Dr. Morris neglects the primary purpose of the sun, moon, and stars: Life would not exist without them. [62]

Einstein taught us that time and space vary throughout the universe. Time varies for a person living on the ground floor compared to a person living on the second floor. It is only a billionth of a second per day, but time varies, and it is dependent on the gravitational force. No one can say for certain what time reference God uses or if He even uses time at all. Since time and space vary throughout the universe, it is impossible to say what a day to God was or is. Physicist and priest Georges Lemaitre would say "a day without yesterday" when explaining the creation of the universe from a singularity with the big bang. In other words, no time existed before the big bang. [63] We learned in the previous chapter that space and time do not matter in quantum physics. Of relevance in quantum physics is how particles interact, not the time at which they interact. Thus, to God, time may not matter and has no place in the universe. The only thing that matters is how events interact. [64]

Evolution

Dr. Morris writes, "As long as people have been looking at the stars, they have never seen a single star evolve. We do occasionally see stars disintegrate, but that's not evolution." In truth, stars do not disintegrate; they explode in a supernova. One such star was discovered before it exploded into a supernova. The discovery revealed that stars go through significant internal evolutionary changes before they explode. [65] [66] In fact, supernova explosions can evolve into a mysterious black hole. [67]

Dr. Morris believes God could not have used evolution because it is an "inefficient, cruel, and wasteful process." A few pages later, Dr. Morris describes the evolution of the Earth's climate because, as he explains, God initially made "our planet milder and more habitable than we experience today." Dr. Morris explains how human life has evolved, such as having decreased life expectancies. Dr. Morris clarifies that animals have evolved because they have become smaller. Finally, Dr. Morris makes it clear that plants evolve because they "adapt to any environmental changes." In other words, life evolves. [68] Dr. Morris also argues that animals and plants can only produce "its kind." They have no power to evolve over time into another creature. Dr. Morris concludes, "That is, within each kind is the design power to adapt quickly to environmental conditions." What is confounding, however, is when Dr. Morris suggests, "Anyone of these fossils could have been the dead ancestor of the living Leviathan that God describes to Job." What this sentence explains is the evolution of Leviathan from another kind! This is precisely what Dr. Morris suggests cannot happen. [69]

There are three points of interest in the preceding paragraph. First, even Dr. Morris reveals evolution happens and is part of God's plan. Second, Dr. Morris' point about the inability of species producing another kind certainly hold weight even if he contradicts his hypothesis by describing the evolution of Leviathan from another kind. As I point out in the last chapter, even small genetic information gains to create new species are highly improbable. Therefore, the evidence points to an intelligent designer to explain the formation of the universe, the introduction of life, and the introduction of new species. Finally, Dr. Morris' observation that human life expectancies have decreased is important. Decreased life expectancies illustrate how mutations or evolutionary changes are more likely to decrease – not increase – genetic information.

According to Dr. Morris, evolution is improbable because God does not experiment, nor would He produce inferior things. When God says everything is "good," according to Dr. Morris it means everything was and is perfect and flawless. [70] This is not true. Adam and Eve were flawed because they had the capacity to sin. Why was God tempting Adam and Eve if they were perfect? It is because God tests the loyalty of everyone. And tests are a form of experimentation. From my perspective, God is the ultimate scientist. Furthermore, there is no such thing as a perfect living creature, every form of life contains thousands of genetic flaws or mutations. What Dr. Morris fails to comprehend is that imperfections such as sin and evil are a necessity to maintain stability (symmetry) in the universe. Universal balance is explained in 2 Nephi 2, in The Book of Mormon, that Adam fell so that man could have emotions. After all, experiencing happiness, love, and joy are not possible without opposing emotions, such as anger and hate that are the result of evil and sin.

Higher Order

Dr. Morris claims there is a "higher order" on Earth and man is the top dog because God asked Adam to rule and have dominion over the Garden of Eden. Of course, Adam was the only choice for the job, but what did Adam and Eve do with their power? They sinned. Providing Adam with power led directly to the fall of man. If God maintains stability out of chaos, then societal hierarchical constructs do not work. Those on the top of the pyramid, or those with the most power, tend to become greedy and selfish. It makes more sense that everything on Earth is connected and to maintain order, there must be symmetry and no hierarchical system. God rules supreme, but on Earth, everything has equal importance. Dr. Morris' misstep is not understanding that all matter reveals wisdom about our creation. [71]

Dr. Morris argues that plants and vegetation are not living organisms when he writes they "are not alive!" Dr. Morris concludes life must have certain properties such as the ability to move, bleed, breathe, think, and have a spirit and soul. Why is it important to restrict life to a few properties and neglect other properties? All matter and forces should be considered life because they are all created from Godly subatomic particles. Light, wind, water, fire, rocks, insects, plants, gravity, the electromagnetic force, and dirt are alive because they are created and formed from Godly particles. The holy spirit is wind, water, and fire, and they move and communicate with the human spirit. [72] Quantum entanglement emphasizes the point that the universe acts, not as discrete parts of a whole. All matter and forces are connected and have a conscious to reveal wisdom. Thus, there is no higher order of life or matter, everything is equal because all matter and forces are connected. Dr. Morris contradicts his definition of life when he concludes millions of sea creatures are living things, yet, lobsters, crabs, and starfish have no blood. God explains, in Genesis, how He made a woman from a rib and dirt. Why would God use nonliving matter to create a woman? Because ribs and dirt are living substances. [73] [74]

Why Do Bad Things Happen to Good People?

Why do bad things happen to good people? The Bible is clear that nations, not just individuals, must abide by God's laws. Proverbs 14:34 declares, "Righteousness exalts a nation, but sin is a disgrace to any people." There are many biblical examples of the Israeli people being judged and punished collectively for their sins. In the United States, good people pay the price for poor government policies such as slavery, eugenics, abortion, internment, and a host of other laws that violate His laws. If the United States was truly divinely inspired, as the Founders believed, then the United States would also be judged collectively by God for its sins against humanity.

Why would a perfect God make an imperfect world full of pain, suffering, sin, and evil? Without evil and harm, then there would be no reason for moral principles and for people to do acts of altruism. For human beings to gain knowledge, understanding, and wisdom and to become better persons, there must be adversity, pain, and suffering. Human imperfections amplify acts of love, compassion, gratitude, goodness, kindness, and forgiveness! Like science and mathematics, nature is symmetrical.

Why has there been so much harm done in the name of religion? Remember, everyone has fallen into a life of sin. Since all people sin and are imperfect, they may hide behind the guise of religion and do harm. There have been many wars fought in the name of religion, but most people using religion as an excuse to fight a war are extremists or fundamentalists who are pushing their ideals, not the ideals of God.

Supernatural Events

It is not uncommon for people to claim they experienced supernatural events or had interactions with God. For people claiming they interacted with God, there are three choices: (1) They are lying, (2) they are delusional, or (3) they are telling the truth. Many stories about Godly experiences come from credible people and their stories are reasonable. Their stories are reasonable because they do not include miracles or God having to break His laws of nature and science. In fact, they describe their supernatural experience with God as being difficult in that He expects more from them to be better people for the common good of society. God is acting as a therapist, counselor, friend, and mentor to provide valuable guidance and motivation. Importantly, He leaves it up to the people in the relationship to heed His advice. God does not act on their behalf. There is a simple solution for anyone who has never experienced a supernatural event. They can either expand their reality or seek Godly advice throughout the Bible. Stories about encounters with God from credible sources that do not include God breaking his laws of science should be considered truthful unless proven otherwise. Remember, we live in a society where people are innocent until proven guilty. Likewise, people should be considered truthful unless they are not credible, or it is proven they are lying. We treat scientific theories the same way: They are credible until proven otherwise. [75]

Prayer

There are many types of prayers, including prayers for worship (Hebrews 13:15), faith (James 5:13–16), consecration (Matthew 26:26–27), thanksgiving (Psalms 100:4), and contemplation (Romans 8:26–27). People can pray for anything, but the most common type of prayer are prayers of petition (intercession Daniel 9:1–27). I believe intercession prayers are prayers for others, not oneself. I also do not believe God intervenes to answer prayers of petition other than to provide guidance. Moreover, God leaves it up to the individual to act on their own volition to heed His guidance. God does not make the tough decisions for us.

Sure, Jesus said in Luke 11:9, "So I say to you, ask, and it will be given to you; seek, and you will find; knock, and it will be opened to you." At the same time, in Hebrews 11:39–40, Paul writes that many righteous people "did not receive what was promised because God had provided something better for us." If we wish to petition God for favors in our prayers, He will hear us (1 John 5:14) and provide us the justice we deserve (Luke 18:7–8) in the form of love, compassion, and forgiveness. And if we are lucky, God may also provide us with guidance, support, counseling, motivation, and advice.

I regard the purpose of prayer as resembling the words of President John Kennedy's 1961 inaugural address that was influenced by John 6:28 "Ask not what your country can do for you. Ask what you can do for your country." [76] In the biblical story of the prophet Samuel, his mother, Hannah, prays for a son but agrees to offer him up to God. Hannah kept her word and gave Samuel to the Church (God) where he thrived as a prophet. Prayer should be about giving and sacrifice and not about wanting, like asking God how we can use our suffering and pain to help others in need. The whole concept of Christianity is based on the greatest sacrifice in world history. God gave up his son, Jesus, who died for our sins.

Einstein abandoned the concept of a personal God who hears and answers prayers. Einstein articulated a new moral philosophy in that it was more profound and productive to understand God through truths, knowledge, and wisdom. Einstein's God sought universal order and beauty through His scientific principles. As Einstein cleverly put it, "God does not play dice with the world." [77] Einstein also noted, "Subtle is the Lord, but malicious He is not." In trying to understand "God's thoughts" to uncover the mysteries of the universe, Einstein had a relationship with God. Einstein, like God, sought the most simplistic solution to unravel the mysteries of the universe. Astrologist Arthur Eddington claimed that the beauty and elegance of Einstein's theories and equations warranted no scientific proof because they were so logical. Therefore, to Einstein, it would make no sense for God to violate His scientific principles and create unnecessary chaos by answering prayers. For Einstein, it makes more sense to pray to understand God's scientific laws to uncover the technical mysteries of the universe. Unraveling medical mysteries would certainly be a scientific marvel to cure spinal injuries, cancer, Alzheimer's, and other elusive secrets. I would make one clarification to Einstein's personal God revelation. I believe God can be personal so long as He merely provides advice and guidance and leaves it up to people to act of their own volition. Then He is not circumventing His laws of universal order. [78] [79]

Most religious followers would object to the idea that God does not interfere with human life. Nevertheless, a hands-off God does not mean He is completely detached from human beings. On the contrary, God surely has empathy for good souls lost to disease, catastrophes, or war. God may still produce miracles regularly by, for instance, introducing new species into our ecosystem or keeping the Earth safe from deadly gamma ray radiation or other chaotic events in the universe. Humans may be unaware of these miracles despite the hundreds of new species discovered each year. [80] It is commonly believed God intervenes to fight demons and evil every day. Perhaps, but as previously discussed, it is also important to understand that evil exists, so that man does not forget the value of kindness, forgiveness, love, and goodness. Evil is an unfortunate result from the fall of man to maintain a balance between the laws of human nature and His moral principles and commandments. I am not suggesting that God could not intervene and answer prayers; I say He chooses to listen to our petitions in prayer and provide guidance, but He does not directly answer prayers.

Miracles

The word miracle is used in everyday language. It often describes events that may happen in our lives. We often say it is a miracle when someone survives cancer. In many cases, survival from cancer may have been highly improbable, but is it a miracle? A miracle must have a zero percent chance of happening, and a miracle must have a significant purpose. Miracles are acts of God because a miracle should accomplish the impossible. Thus, the problem with miracles is that humans use this word too often to describe fantastic events, such as winning the lottery and surviving a lethal illness. No question miracles happen and are God driven, but they are extremely rare. C.S. Lewis agrees that miracles are rare and witnesses to miracles are probably mistaken. [81]

There is no miracle as significant as the experiment we call life. The formation of life was shown in Chapter 2 to indeed be a miracle, whereas most other improbable things that may happen in our lives are not miracles but wonderful events. Wonderful events are improbable but happen every day without the direct involvement of God. The word miracle should be reserved for events such as the birth of Jesus Christ or other biblical miracles. To suggest that God regularly intervenes in our lives to perform miracles downplays true miracles and purposeful events that God partakes. Think of it this way, how many people have survived cancer compared to how many have walked on water or been a virgin's baby. Wonderful events may transpire when scientists uncover some of God's secrets. In medicine, scientists can generate wonderful events by finding cures to overcome life-threatening illnesses, but revealing a small part of God's scientific thoughts is no miracle. The miracle would be to unravel all of God's thoughts, and doctors and scientists are a long way from accomplishing that.

The Bible covers many miracles, and in fact, they are not rare. Jesus accomplished many miracles in the New Testament and by His Father in the Old Testament. However, if Jesus and God did not perform miracles, then who would have written the story of Jesus and His Father in the Bible? Would there be any Christian religion? Probably not. Miracles were needed for two reasons. First, for people to believe in God and Jesus, and second, so man (prophets) would document His being in the Bible. People needed proof of God's existence, and miracles were a convincing way to accomplish this task. Since we have access to the Bible, miracles are no longer needed to persuade us of His existence or to convince us of His message of love and forgiveness. That message has been received loud and clear in the Bible.

C.S. Lewis also notes that those who dismiss biblical miracles usually cite in their defense the uniform state of nature. In the opinion of naysayers, if nature is uniform, miracles cannot happen because uniformity cannot be violated. Nevertheless, Lewis astutely observes that if nature were truly uniform, the future would be predictable because it would resemble the past. Remember the mathematical universe theory discussed in Chapter 2? The mathematical universe theory attempts to disprove God, yet all it disproves is that nature is not uniform. Every theory to disprove God only disproves other theories that try to disprove God.[82]

There are two ways God may communicate: Miracles and guidance. Miraculous communications include the direct involvement of God. Miraculous communications are choices made by God that may violate the laws of science and human nature. Guidance communications are much more prevalent and do not break the laws of science and human nature. Guidance from God may be like the guidance one may receive from reading the Bible. [83]

The concept of a God who changes destinies does not make sense because that will create a butterfly effect. Since every cause has an effect, any change in one destiny will change the destinies of thousands of people, for better or worse, around the globe. The butterfly effect is like the principle of chaos or randomness discussed earlier. The butterfly effect suggests even small events can have an enormous chaotic impact on the universe. In the previous chapter, it was concluded that God as a stabilizing force makes more sense than God as a chaotic force. A neutral God who does not interfere is explained in Luke 22:42 "Father, if You are willing, remove this cup from Me; yet not My will, but Yours be done."

It is presumed God regularly intervenes to miraculously heal people. It makes little sense that God is picking winners and losers by, for instance, curing some good people from cancer but letting other good people succumb to the disease. Apostle Peter said in Acts 10:34, "I most certainly understand now that God is not one to show partiality." Again, in Romans 2:11, Paul wrote, "For there is no partiality with God." Instead, it is faith in God that increases healing powers. For instance, people of faith are more likely to survive traumatic events and deal with adversity better than those with negative attitudes and who have little or no faith. Matthew 9:22 explains how the power of prayer and faith in God from within is what heals. Said differently, faith and a strong mental attitude boost the immune response. For example, when the bleeding woman touched Jesus' cloak, she was healed. However, Jesus explained to her it was her faith that healed, not that it was a miracle (Luke 8:43–48). [84]

The most difficult aspect of understanding the Bible and God is which text should be taken literally and which text should be taken figuratively. Since Christianity is based on an immaculate conception miracle, the Bible must be taken literally. One cannot choose which biblical miracles to accept and which to disregard. Nevertheless, parables or metaphoric descriptions of biblical events beyond the writer's senses should be taken figuratively. Keep in mind, we all talk figuratively when describing things that are beyond the limits of our senses.

Halting the Sun

Is there any way we can rationalize miracles such as God halting the sun? Did God break His laws of science when He paused the sun so Israel could win a battle (Joshua 10:12–14)? If God truly broke his laws of stability, science, and nature by stopping the sun, it would have resulted in a cataclysmic effect on the entire solar system. There are several ways this may have happened. First, God halted time, not the sun. After all, quantum physics teaches us that time is the one thing in the universe that can be manipulated. Second, it was a perception that the sun stopped, not that God stopped the sun. Third, it may have been an illusion created from an atypical event such as an eclipse. Finally, God may temporarily suspend the laws of nature and science to perform miracles to prove His existence. [85] [86]

Multiplying Bread and Wine and Fertility Miracles

C.S. Lewis classifies miracles as old creation and new creation. The new creation is unique and would encompass events that defy logic, such as miracles that reverse events (raising the dead) or when Jesus walked on water. Old creation events include miracles of destruction, healing, and fertility. In other words, old creation miracles include events common to our state of nature. For example, acts of destruction, such as climate disasters, are common in our worldly events. Additionally, as far as healing power is concerned, it is common for people to survive deadly diseases. Fertility miracles include the virgin conception, the conception of the elder, turning water into wine, and even food expansion. While biblical fertility miracles are improbable, they are within our state of nature (birth). Older women having children or multiplying food to feed five thousand people is unusual but does not defy our state of nature or reality because birth and food growth are not uncommon. God would not have to defy the laws of science to achieve those miracle objectives. Whereas new creation miracles are unlike anything we are accustomed to seeing in our reality, they defy the laws of human nature and science. New creation miracles are futuristic, and our state of nature has not yet progressed to such a physical condition to support such events. [87]

Raising the Dead and Walking on Water

According to C.S. Lewis, new creation miracles include the resurrection and ascension of Jesus, bringing Lazarus back from the dead, and Jesus walking on water. Is it possible there was a time when processes could be reversed? Was there a way to create order out of disorder or reverse entropy or add information to bring the dead back to life. Since loop theory suggests the universe can reverse itself, is it improbable to think Jesus was raised from the dead? Is there an unidentified stabilizing factor in our universe that may create order out of chaos by adding information? I already suggest that God may be responsible for adding missing or new information to introduce new species. If so, then Lazarus rising from the dead is not impossible (reversing the chaotic process of death with the stability of life). We hear many stories of people regaining life after being declared dead, so maybe coming back from the dead is not even out of the realm of possibilities in our reality. Furthermore, is it possible that one person's reality is such that they can put their mind over matter to do superhuman feats, including lifting cars to save a life, walking on burning coals, or even walking on water? If we can believe in spirituality or in what does not exist–life with no personality, no time, no space, no history, no mass, or no environment, then why can we not believe in biblical miracles? [88]

If we truly think about the miracles posed in the Bible, most of them call for time manipulation. Halting the sun, bringing back the dead, turning water into wine, multiplying food (more time for crops to grow), giving birth at an old age and so forth. And according to science and quantum physics, time is the one thing in the universe that can be manipulated. Time can be slowed or sped up by altering the effects of gravity and the speed at which we travel. Of course, manipulating gravity would also account for the act of Jesus walking on water. Remember, quantum physics theories deal with manipulating time such as with imaginary time or reversing time to find reasonable results to the universal wave function. So, the miracles posed in the Bible are quite possible from a scientific standpoint. It merely requires manipulating time and an unidentified stabilizing factor, something that can replace missing information and turn chaotic events into stable events.

Gigantism

How is it possible to explain the giants referred to in the Bible, such as Goliath? After all, the tallest men and women on record are several feet shorter than Goliath. Gigantism is the product of excessive growth hormone (GH). Thus, it is plausible that the differences between present-day humans and humans that lived several millennium ago can be merely explained by the evolution of GH. [89]

Slavery

Contemplation was necessary to rationalize the many times Jesus referred to "slaves" in the Bible. The word slave has a broad meaning in the Bible; it is His word for an employee or even a student. Jesus refers to His Disciples and Apostles as slaves because their entire purpose in life was to serve Him. Thus, the term slave in the Bible does not reflect how we would use the term today. For instance, in Ephesians 6:9 and Colossians 4:1, Paul suggests that masters must treat enslaved people with justice and fairness. Justice and fairness are not words that would describe modern slavery. There are, of course, enslaved people in the Bible that do meet our current definition of slavery. Hagar was one of the first enslaved people mentioned in Genesis. God and Hagar have a relationship even though she is not a Jew, but an Egyptian. We learn that God understands the hardships of slavery and offers compassion to enslaved people even if they are non-Christians.

Proverbs 22:7 "the borrower becomes the lender's slave" and John 8:34 "everyone who commits sin is a slave to sin" are further proof of the broad definition of slavery in the Bible. Proverbs 22:7 and John 8:34 essentially make everyone a slave since everyone sins and borrows property, which is not how slavery is narrowly defined today. In fact, the first civil rights leader in America and formerly enslaved person Frederick Douglass said that Americans have trampled on both the Constitution and the Bible because slavery is not supported in either document. In truth, the Bible admonishes the narrow definition of slavery that Americans understand today. To argue against slavery, the Founders would often cite Exodus 21:16, "Now one who kidnaps someone, whether he sells him or he is found in his possession, shall certainly be put to death." [90] Isaiah 61:1 was also a popular verse used by early American politicians in support of ending slavery, "The Spirit of the Lord GOD is upon me, because the LORD anointed me to bring good news to the humble; he has sent me to bind up the brokenhearted, to proclaim release to captives and freedom to prisoners." Southern slaveowners would defend slavery primarily because the institution converted slaves to Christianity. The slaveowner conversion theory had two serious flaws. First, most enslaved people were prohibited from practicing religion. Second, Muslim extremists used the same conversion theory to defend enslaving, reforming, and converting Christians to Islam.

Polygamy

How can the biblical practice of polygamy be explained? Nothing in the Bible condones the practice of polygamy and nothing suggests that polygamy existed until Lamech (the son of Cain) broke the practice of monogamy. The Bible is clear that Lamech was not a good person. Polygamy was a practice that came about from the fall of man. In The Book of Mormon Jacob 2, God commands men only to have one wife and no mistresses. [91] Polygamy may also be explained because marriage during biblical times was seen more as an economic transaction between families than as an act of true love.

Mistreatment of Women

There are two women with the name Tamar in the Bible. Both of their stories are very difficult and heart-wrenching to read. The first Tamar can be found in Genesis 38. Tamar is married to Judah's evil son, Er. God kills Er, and Tamar is then wed to Judah's selfish son, Onan. God also kills off the sinful Onan. Since Judah was unwilling to let Tamar marry his third son (Shelah), as per Jewish custom, Tamar became deceitful. Tamar tricks Judah into sleeping with her, becomes impregnated, and has twin boys. One of the boys, Perez, according to biblical genealogy is in the direct lineage of Jesus Christ. In the second Book of Samuel (2 Samuel 13), we find the second Tamar, the daughter of King David. Tamar was raped by her brother, Amnon. Although King David and Tamar's other brother, Absalom, are angry at Amnon, they do nothing to punish him. Two years later, Absalom kills Amnon, but it is for political gain, not as revenge for what he had done to his sister. Both Judah and King David treat women horribly, despite being two of the most famous and distinguished men directly in the ancestry of Jesus. Why are these horrific stories in the Bible? These stories are important because they represent the "Me Too" movement over three centuries ago. God sees the struggles of both women, and He gives them a voice to tell their stories in the Bible so they can be vindicated and find justice in a society dominated by men.

Many women in the Bible are much more accomplished than their male counterparts. In Judges, one of Israel's most influential political leaders, judges, military leaders, and prophets was Deborah. Jael, Judith, and Rahab's courage changed the destiny of Israel. Women were common in Jesus' inner circle. In fact, Jesus transcends race and gender in a male-dominated time and place in world history (see the story of the Samaritan woman in John 4). Similarly, the Jewish Persian Queen Esther risked her life to save the Jewish people from total extermination at the hand of the King's chief minister, Haman. [92]

Do God and Jesus Seek to Polarize Society?

In Luke 12:51–52, Jesus says, "Do you think I came to provide peace on Earth? No, I tell you, but rather a division, for from now on, five members in one household will be divided, three against two and two against three." Without contemplating this statement, I would have thought Jesus to be a divider, not a uniter. However, Jesus was not trying to create war and chaos on Earth; instead, His objective was to foster open debate (contemplation) about Christianity. The way He sees it, if He can make a believer out of one or two family members, then they can convert others in their family to Christianity. God is seen as divider because He often refers to the "chosen people" in the Bible. On the surface, this sounds as if God is biased and entrance into His religion is exclusive. However, if we genuinely contemplate about God's intentions, He is not discriminating; instead, the chosen are selected to lead the unchosen.

Long Life Expectancies

How can the long-life expectancy of early biblical figures be explained? The history of humanity unveiled in Genesis is one of evolution. Genesis describes the fall of man that was the beginning of vast evolutionary changes to both the personality and wellbeing of humanity whose life expectancies steadily declined. [93]

The Harsh Nature of Deuteronomy

There are laws in Deuteronomy for stoning stubborn and rebellious children (that do not honor their parents), punishing mediums, prohibited tattoos, and laws to punish those who are promiscuous, gay, or crossdressers. The Deuteronomy dilemma posed by some of its outdated laws has been resolved through natural and statutory law. Thousands of years ago, criminal laws focused on punishing persons for defiling themselves and violating the rights of others. However, today, we are more accustomed to laws that focus on only punishing those actions that harm or violate the rights of others. Fewer present-day laws in the United States target persons for self-destructive behavior. After all, we all have bad and sinful habits that defile the body and soul. Drug use is an example of one self-destructive activity still punished by the law. Although criminal charges may not be associated with sinful self-destructive behavior such as watching pornography and being selfish, everyone must eventually answer to God.

Justifiable Wars [94]

Only justifiable wars are sanctioned by God. A justifiable war has seven principles:

1. To be declared by a government and not a private company or citizen.
2. There is a just cause for the war.
3. The war must be fought over the right intention, such as to end genocide.
4. The war must be against an eviler nation. The nation going to war may be evil, but it should be less evil than its opponent.
5. The war's outcome should be more beneficial than choosing not to go to war. For example, the proportionality of the loss of life should be less than what is gained from the war.
6. There must be a high probability of success.
7. War should be the last resort after all other peaceful alternatives have been exhausted.

Did the American Revolution violate Romans 13:1–2 which reads "Every person is to be subject to the governing authorities. For there is no authority except from God, and those which exist are established by God. Therefore whoever resists authority has opposed the ordinance of God; and they who have opposed will receive condemnation upon themselves."

Natural law philosopher John Locke and the Founders believed the Bible must be considered in its entirety. To that end, God has justified dozens of biblical wars considered self-defense or exhausted every possible legal and peaceful avenue. For example, 1 Chronicles 5:22 reads, "For many fell mortally wounded, because the war was of God. And they settled in their place until the exile." Founding father and Chief Justice John Jay explains why a loving God would support war: [95] [96]

> I think it follows that the right to wage just war and necessary war is admitted and not abolished by the Gospel... It is true that even just war is attended with evils, and so likewise is the administration of government and of justice, but is that a good reason for abolishing either of them? They are a means by which greater evils are averted.

Protestant reformer, John Calvin, would argue that Christians acting collectively or individually did not have the power to overthrow a government; however, officials within a corrupt government had the power to remove a tyrannical leader. In 1750, pastor Jonathon Mayhew said, "When magistrates act contrary to their office … when they rob and ruin the public, instead of being guardians of peace and welfare; they immediately cease to be the ordinance and ministers of God." Thus, according to Calvin, Mayhew, Jay, Locke, and the Bible, the Founders were right to wage war against a tyrannical King. [97]

Keeping within the boundaries of the above criteria, it is difficult to uncover any justifiable war in world history. As we shall learn, the American Revolution did not have a high probability of success, and it could be disputed if the Continental Congress were a legitimate government that had the people's consent to make such a decision. That said, for a revolution to be justifiable, it must only meet four of the seven requirements: A majority of the population must consent to a revolution, there must be a just cause, the conflict must be the last resort, and the conflict should be for the right intention. The American Revolution meets these requirements. For example, the colonies had cause and good intentions to break away from England to form a nation with a better form of government and better protections for individual rights.

On one hand, the Civil War can be argued that it failed to meet all seven requirements because the war was marred with high civilian casualties. If saving the Union was the goal of the war, attacks on civilians and non-military targets made post-war peace and reconstruction challenging to resolve. Furthermore, establishing black code laws following the war failed to free enslaved people entirely, so it took decades to meet the most critical objective of the war to end slavery and provide enslaved people with equal rights. On the other hand, the war accomplished its goal to save the Union, and the process for enslaved people to earn equal rights had begun.

The South's reason for the Civil War was "unjust" because their intention was evil and did not meet the standards set by natural law to protect the fundamental rights of all persons equally. However, the North's reason and intention for the war can be argued that it was, indeed, a just war.

The Case for Why God Exists

In Chapter 2, science was discussed to rationalize the existence of God, and in Chapter 3, science was used to justify many events in the Bible. It is essential to elaborate and expand on the findings in Chapter 2 and provide a little more clarity. Like any theory, the theory of God is true until it is unequivocally proven false. If the big bang theory is correct, then science cannot explain the beginning of time since the universe started from a singularity. Some unexplained force caused an infinitely old singularity to explode and start the formation of the universe. Since singularities have infinite gravity and density, science has no explanation for them. Science can only work within finite boundaries; once infinities are introduced, equations become unsolvable. Thus, at the beginning of time, God just may well have set the creation in motion. At this point, there is no other logical explanation.

Many theories have been developed to overcome singularities and eliminate the God creation element. Science likes to deal with finite numbers, not infinities. When solutions to equations result in infinities or when boundary conditions for equations are infinite, then scientists truly do not understand the implications of those results. However, physicists proceed to introduce infinite solutions, such as the multiverse or mathematical universe theories, as a reason to explain why God does not exist. Physicists face a conundrum because if they remove infinities by placing boundary and initial conditions on the universal wave function equation, they introduce information that is not explained at the beginning of the universe. Thus, by trying to eliminate the God hypothesis, physicists are in a vicious cycle of creating bizarre and unsubstantiated theories that never resolve both the information conundrum and those mathematical challenges related to infinities.

I do not suggest that science proves the existence of God; rather, I suggest that a God exists hypothesis is a simpler solution than the many scientific theories that fail to explain the origin of life, the formation of new species, and the creation of the universe. Scientists may say that I use God to explain gaps in scientific discoveries, but I am convinced that scientists may never resolve the mysteries of the universe using the current laws of physics and nature. Further, the more scientists try to fill the gaps with bizarre scientific theories, the more it seems to justify the God hypothesis. Besides, scientists do what they accuse theists of doing—filling the gaps with their preferred solution. [98]

Evolution allows nature to generate some level of order out of randomness when it creates new information. However, evolution alone could not create homo sapiens since the odds of that happening were beyond astronomical. Thus, other stabilizing factors or influences that can generate new information had to aid the creation of homo sapiens. Perhaps God influenced evolutionary changes to stack the odds in favor of the creation of homo sapiens, such as bypassing the evolution process by introducing all the proteins for life before He let evolution take hold. Similarly, God may have stacked the odds in favor of making the Earth compatible with life, such as by introducing water. It is highly improbable that life began just by chance without some stabilizing factors. Yes, it is dangerous to implant God as the reason for stabilizing our solar system and the evolutionary processes, but if God set the rules of human nature (natural law) and science, then He set the rules for this stabilizing factor. Any stabilizing factor would defy our current understanding of thermodynamics, that disorder and entropy are continually increasing.

For some reason, proof of God is held to a higher standard than any other concept, theory, idea, or principle. And for some reason, the concept of God is fought more vigorously by non-believers than any other idea, principle, concept, or theory. The double standard posed by some demanding proof of God but offering no proof that God does not exist has done much harm to society because it has led to individuals and governments violating the rights of people to pursue their religious liberty. Sure, I get it, religious extremists also violate citizens' rights, but extreme atheism is no different. Extremism, no matter what side of the equation, causes unnecessary polarity and divisiveness. Tolerance of both theism and atheism should be the objective in any civilized society. [99]

Most atheists adhere to the strict policy that without any scientific proof for the existence of God, then God does not exist. There is no definitive scientific proof of God, but there is no proof that God does not exist. What atheists forget is that all human beings learn more from personal experience or even from the experiences of others than from what any scientific theory may teach us. For example, jurists must sift through non-scientific testimony and circumstantial evidence to determine the fate of a human being. To be able to make such a critical decision, a jurist must weigh the credibility of the source and the reliability of the information. Non-scientific evidence is routinely used to determine scientific theories, and thus, we should not be hasty to dismiss non-scientific evidence that can support the existence of God. For instance, 99% of the populous have no scientific training, nor do they have any understanding of mathematical models. While understanding climate change may not be as fuzzy as understanding the existence of God, there are many more unknowns about climate change then what we know. Yet, the world is full of millions of experts on the subject. [100]

Georges Lemaitre was both a Catholic priest and theoretical physicist in the twentieth century. Lemaitre is credited as the first person to theorize that the universe started from a singularity with the big bang. Although Lemaitre would suggest that he provided the atheist a reason to deny God and for the believer to feel unconnected with God, I would disagree. I feel a closer connection to both science and God. It is comforting to believe that God may have put everything in motion. Science has not only helped me rationalize the existence of God; it has helped me rationalize the events that transpire in the Bible. [101]

Part II: Defining and Protecting God-Given Fundamental Rights [102]

Chapter 4: Defining and Distinguishing Between Moral Principles, Virtues, and Fundamental Rights

Moral principles and virtuous traits are the foundation or building blocks to define fundamental rights, which, in turn, are the building blocks of the statutory law. As Saint Paul writes in Galatians, "But the fruit of the Spirit is love, joy, peace, patience, kindness, goodness, faithfulness, gentleness, and self-control; against such things, there is no law." In other words, without the building blocks of moral principles, our fundamental rights and statutory law would not exist.

Moral Principles

Examples of moral principles and where they may be found in the Bible are outlined in the Appendix at the end of this book in List A1. Some examples of moral principles include that one should: Treat others like you would treat yourself, forgive others, be modest, be humble, be kind, be good, profess love, have self-control, be patient, be empathetic, be grateful, be tolerant, follow the laws of society, and do not lie, cheat, be deceitful, display hate, show anger, fall into temptation, or steal.

Many moral principles are evident in the hundreds of stories told in the Bible. The story of David and Goliath is one of the most famous. It is a story about the battle between good and evil and how bravery and courage can overcome adversity. Like many biblical stories, the story about David and Saul is also about good versus evil. Some biblical stories are about people who lack moral values. For example, the famous story about Samson and Delilah is focused on deception; thus, the moral of that story is that we should not become deceitful like Delilah. Similarly, the stories of Adam and Eve, Abel and Cain, David and Bathsheba, Jonah and the fish, and others are about the fall of man into sin. Of course, sinful people do not always adhere to moral principles.

Shannon Bream posed one great Bible study question in her book, *The Women of the Bible Speak*. In Joshua, was it acceptable for Rahab to lie because it helped the people of Israel? Similarly, was Jael's deceit and murder acceptable (Book of the Judges) to help Israel? [103] Rahab and Jael obviously break moral principles. What makes their actions acceptable is that they both take place in a war justified by God to defend Israel. As we learned in the previous chapter, justifiable wars are exceptions to upholding moral principles.

Moral principles are what separates humans from other forms of life since only humans have rational thought and the ability to honestly know the difference between right and wrong. Even atheists and most criminals believe in moral principles, whether they acknowledge it or not. When morally challenged persons are asked why they violated the rights of another person, they offer an excuse or lie. They knew the difference between right and wrong but tried to justify their actions.

C.S. Lewis wrote in Mere Christianity that moral principles "are tough as nails." [104] This statement means that moral principles cannot be subdivided or changed because they cannot be improved. They are already perfect because they are made in God's image, which is why they are also referred to as God's law. Furthermore, moral principles are equivalent and symmetrical. Like mathematics, when two things are equal, they are in balance and symmetrical. In other words, one moral principle is no more important than any other moral principle.

Virtuous Traits

People who follow God's moral principles develop virtuous traits which are also defined in the Bible. Virtues are like moral principles in that they are also equal and symmetrical. Virtuous traits help us strive to be better people even when faced with the most extreme types of adversity. In his book *Character Carved in Stone*, Pat Williams writes about the twelve leadership virtues that Army West Point tries to instill in its cadets: Compassion, courage, dedication, determination, dignity, discipline, integrity, loyalty, perseverance, responsibility, service, and trust. Williams explains virtues are not traits we are born with but earned through hard work. [105] Acquired virtues and moral principles are much different from God-given fundamental rights inherited by all persons from God. Said differently, we are all born with the same fundamental rights, but it requires citizens to follow moral principles to develop virtuous traits to ensure the fundamental rights of citizens are not infringed. All virtuous traits and where they can be found in the Bible are listed at the end of this book in List A2 in the Appendix. Other virtues include prudence, respect, generosity, temperance, and humility.

Fundamental Rights

While virtues are unique to each citizen, fundamental rights are the same for everyone, as defined in historical documents, constitutional law, and the Bible. Moral principles and virtues police the moral compass of the individual, whereas fundamental rights police the moral compass of society.

In Table A2 in the Appendix I highlight those virtues and moral principles that correspond to a particular God-given fundamental right shown in Table I below. For example, the right to pursue lawful recreational activities may be a competition. In a competition, people may demonstrate moral principles such as respect, tolerance, and honesty with their opposition. They also may exhibit the virtues of self-control, dedication, courage, perseverance, energy, and hard work to prepare for the competition.

Table I: Fundamental Rights and where they are Defined in American History and the Bible

Fundamental Right	**Historical Document or Court Case**	**Biblical Verse**
To Free Speech	The Bill of Rights	Romans 14:1, Deuteronomy 1:16–17, Matthew 12:36, 1 Corinthians 10:29, and Acts 18:9–10
To Religious Liberty or Liberty of Conscious Thought	The Bill of Rights, *Meyer v. Nebraska*, and The Northwest Ordinance of 1787	Galatians 5:1 and 3:27–29, 2 Timothy 3:12, 1 Peter 2:16, John 1:12–13, Acts 5:29, Joshua 24:15, Exodus 20:2–22:20, 1 Corinthians 1:22–23, Matthew 7:15–16, and Revelation 3:20
To Self-Defense	The Bill of Rights	Exodus 22:2 and Luke 11:21
To Justice or Due Process (Includes many of the clauses in the first eight amendments such as protections from illegal searches and seizures, the right to a trial by jury, the ability to confront witnesses, protection from self-incrimination, protection from having to quarter troops, double jeopardy protection, the right to have a speedy trial, protection from cruel and unjust punishment, and a right to an impartial trial to name a few.)	The Constitution, The Bill of Rights, *Corfield v. Coryell*, The Northwest Ordinance of 1787, and The Civil Rights Act of 1866	Numbers 35:24 – 25, Luke 7:1–10, Mark 10:35–45, 1 Corinthians 16:13–14, Galatians 6:9–10, Exodus 21:24, Acts 25, Ezekiel 18:20, Proverbs 3:21–27, 18:17, and 19:20, Deuteronomy 16:18–20, Romans 7:14, 3:28, Ecclesiastes 8:11, Matthew 26:63, and Psalms 37:23–29
To Contract	The Constitution, *Meyer v. Nebraska,* The Northwest Ordinance of 1787, The Civil	Matthew 21:33–46, Leviticus 19:35 and 25:16–34, Numbers 30:1–16, Proverbs 20:10,

	Rights Act 1866, and *Pierce v. Society of Sisters*	20:23, and 22:26–27, and Ezekiel 18:6
To Property	The Bill of Rights, *Corfield v. Coryell*, The Northwest Ordinance of 1787, and The Civil Rights Act of 1866	Genesis 1:26–28, Exodus 20:15–17 and 21:29, Leviticus 25:10, Jeremiah 29:5, and Deuteronomy 19:14
To Vote	The Constitution	Exodus 18:21 and Deuteronomy 1:13
To Sit on a Jury	Civil Rights Act of 1957, *Strauder v. West Virginia, ex Parte Virginia,* and *Virginia v. Rivas*	Numbers 35:24–25
To Work a Lawful Profession (Including the political right to hold a public office)	*Meyer v. Nebraska* and *Corfield v. Coryell*	Ecclesiastes 3:12–13 and 5:18, Colossians 3:23, Ephesians 4:28, 2 Thessalonians 3:10, Galatians 6:4–5, Proverbs 12:11 and 12:24, and 1 Timothy 5:8
To Make Choices that do not Harm other Citizens	There are many Supreme Court decisions protecting controversial choices people make. For instance, *Texas v. Johnson* defends the choice of protestors to burn the American flag. Choices can be controversial so long as they do not harm other citizens.	Revelation 3:20, Galatians 5:1 and 5:16–17, James 1:13–14, Genesis 2:17, Proverbs 22:6, 2 Corinthians 5:10, and 1 Peter 4:17
To Pursue Health	*Gonzales v. Raich* (Incorrectly decided)	1 Corinthians 6:19–20, Matthew 9:12, 1 Timothy 4:8, and Proverbs 14:30
To Pursue Lawful Recreational Activities	There are hundreds of Supreme Court decisions	Ecclesiastes 11:9, 3:12–13, and 8:15

	protecting lawful activities that people pursue. For instance, in *Herrera v. Wyoming,* the Court protected Native Americans who hunt on Indian Reservations without a license.	
To Travel	*Corfield v. Coryell* and The Civil Rights Act of 1866	Proverbs 2:7–8 and 3:21–24, Psalms 32:7–8 and 23:3–4, 2 Corinthians 8:16–19, Jonah 3:4, Numbers 10:33, and Genesis 29:1–4
To Safety and Protection	*Corfield v. Coryell*	2 Timothy 4:18, Proverbs 18:10, 2:7–10, and 14:26, Psalms 4:8, 3:4–6, and 32:7–8, Isaiah 49:25, Genesis 28:15, Leviticus 25:18, 2 Samuel 22:31, Deuteronomy 31:8, and Ephesians 6:11–13
To Marriage	*Meyer v. Nebraska, Loving v. Virginia, Obergefell v. Hodges,* and *Pierce v. Society of Sisters*	Genesis 2:18–25 and 1:28, Ephesians 5:25 and 5:33, Colossians 3:19, and Proverbs 12:4
To Obtain Knowledge	*Meyer v. Nebraska*, The Northwest Ordinance of 1787, and *Pierce v. Society of Sisters*	Proverbs 2:6, 9:10, 1:7, 18:15, 11:2, 18:2, 15:33, 17:24, 14:29, 19:20, and 24:3, Isaiah 11:2, and Job 12:12
To Family Rights	*Meyer v. Nebraska, Pierce v. Society of Sisters, Troxel v. Granville,* and *Griswold v. Connecticut*	Psalms 127:3–5 and 133:1, Exodus 20:12, Acts 16:31–34, Colossians 3:13 and 3:20, 1 Timothy 3–5, Ephesians 6:1–2 and 6:4, Genesis 18:19,

		Proverbs 22:6, 6:20, 15:20, and 1:8, and Matthew 15:4
To Equality	*Corfield v. Coryell, Prout v. Starr,* The Northwest Ordinance of 1787, and The Civil Rights Act of 1866	Numbers 12:1–15 and 16:1–35, Galatians 5:13–15 and 19–21, Acts 10:34, Romans 2–11, James 3:13–18, Leviticus 19:14, Proverbs 17:5, 22:2, 28:3, and 31:10–31, Matthew 21:33–46, James 2:9, Exodus 23:3, 23:6, and 23:9, Leviticus 19:15 and 19:33–34, 1 Samuel 16:7, Deuteronomy 1:16–17, Proverbs 24:23, 28:21, 29:7, 29:13, and 31:8, and Ezekiel 18:8
To Profit	*Corfield v. Coryell, Calder v. Bull,* and *Loan Association v. Topeka*	Proverbs 14:23, 21:5, and 13:11, Luke 19, Deuteronomy 14:22, Acts 20:35, Isaiah 48:17, and Colossians 3:23
To Representation in Government	Article I, Section 2 of the Constitution and The Northwest Ordinance of 1787	Exodus 18:21, Deuteronomy 1:13, 1 Samuel 8, and Ecclesiastes 4:9–10
To Actions done in Private that do not harm another Citizen	*Griswold v. Connecticut*	Luke 12:2–3, Hebrews 4:12–13, 1 Timothy 5:13, Proverbs 20:19 and 25:9–10, Matthew 6:6, and Psalms 64:2–3
To the Antiwelfare Right or the Right to a Non-Discriminatory Tax System	*Calder v. Bull,* Article I, Section 8, Clause 1 of the Constitution, and The Takings Clause of the Fifth Amendment	Exodus 23:3–6, Leviticus 19:15, Proverbs 29:14, Galatians 3:28, and Deuteronomy 15:11

Right to Friendship or Association	*DeJong v. Oregon, Bates v. Little Rock,* and *Americans for Prosperity v. Bonta*	Proverbs 27:6–17, 18:24, 16:29, 17:9, 17:17, 22:24–25, 13:20, and 12:26, 1 Corinthians 15:33, Ecclesiastes 4:9–10, Job 6:14, Psalms 133:1, Romans 12:10, John 15:13, and Luke 6:31
To Life	The Declaration of Independence	Genesis 1:28, John 3:16, and Psalms 139:13–16
To Liberty	The Declaration of Independence	Genesis 1:28, Galatians 5:1–2, 2 Corinthians 3:17, Psalms 119:45, and Leviticus 25:10
To Pursue Happiness	The Declaration of Independence	Ecclesiastes 11:9 and 3:12–13
To a Writ of Habeas Corpus (Part of the Right to Justice – This is a judicial term used to describe if a person's arrest and detention is warranted.)	Article 1, Section 9, Clause 2 of the Constitution	Deuteronomy 19:16–18 Jesus was a perfect example of a person falsely accused and denied a writ of habeas corpus.
From Ex Post Facto Laws (Part of the Right to Justice – A retroactive law that criminalizes behavior before it was a crime.)	Article 1, Section 9, Clause 3 of the Constitution	Jesus was a perfect example of a person who was convicted using ex post facto laws. Jesus never broke any commandments in the Bible. Instead, the Pharisees accused Him of breaking their version of the commandments.
From Bills of Attainder (Part of the Right to Justice – This clause prevents Congress from declaring an individual or group of people are guilty of a crime without a trial.)	Article 1, Section 9, Clause 3 of the Constitution	Ezekiel 18:20

Table I is by no means a comprehensive list. First, I am sure there are more essential God-given fundamental rights that I neglected to mention. After all, each person possesses hundreds of fundamental rights that they may pursue on a daily basis. Second, by scouring more historical documents, Supreme Court cases, and biblical verses, hundreds of more examples can probably be uncovered to support the above-mentioned fundamental rights.

Some of the fundamental rights recognized in Table I can be found in the Bill of Rights and the Constitution such as the right to religious liberty, to free speech, to justice or due process, to vote, to own property, to contract, and to self-defense. That said, most of the fundamental rights recognized in this writing are unenumerated or not found in the Constitution or Bill of Rights. In this text, the most obvious and necessary fundamental rights are generically identified to encompass all human rights. For example, the right to make moral choices or to pursue health would cover the right to brush your teeth and to take a shower. A generic or broad definition of fundamental rights can be dangerous because they may be used to encompass criminal activity such as choosing to do harm to another person. To overcome this conundrum, conditions must be placed on some fundamental rights. The right to work a lawful job places limits on the right to work. The right to choose or the right to privacy is predicated on the condition the choice or the action done in private does not harm another person.

If everyone followed God's moral principles and achieved virtuous traits, infringing on the fundamental rights in Table I would be impossible. The mission of all our behaviors and actions ought to be the moral choice for the common good of society. Likewise, according to John Locke, it is the main objective of the government to protect the fundamental rights of citizens for the common good. The common good requires the government to protect the sovereignty of both the United States and the individual so fundamental rights are not infringed.

Principles and Properties of Fundamental Rights [106]

Most of the debate surrounding the Fourteenth Amendment's Privileges and Immunities Clause surrounds the fact that we have no clear consensus as to what constitutes a privilege and immunity protected by the amendment. Privileges and immunities is a term synonymous with fundamental rights. The information in this section tries to define both the principles and properties that comprise privileges and immunities or fundamental rights as well as the criteria required for a right to be considered worthy of constitutional protection.

Privileges and immunities were narrowly and vaguely defined by Senators John Bingham and Jacob Howard during the ratification of the Fourteenth Amendment in 1868 as only those rights found in the circuit court decision *Corfield v. Coryell* and the Bill of Rights. Although Bingham and Howard also agree that privileges and immunities can include unenumerated rights, they fail to provide a comprehensive list aside from those identified in Corfield. [107]

Law Scholars Evan Bernick and Randy Barnett provide the best list of fundamental rights but there are some shortcomings to their theory. First, their book, *The Original Meaning of the Fourteenth Amendment*, is not for most Americans because it requires a strong knowledge of the law to comprehend. Second, the only unenumerated rights that Bernick and Barnett protect, aside from those in the Civil Rights Act of 1866 and *Corfield v. Coryell* are family rights, the right to self-defense, the right to work, and the right to equality. Other than that, they are silent and do not mention the right to obtain knowledge, to recreation, to travel, to pursue health, to profit, to choose, to privacy, and a few others. Third, they fail to recognize procedural rights as fundamental. I refer to procedural rights as justice or due process rights that can be found in the first eight amendments and within the Constitution such as a right to be free from self-incrimination or protection from ex post facto laws. The basic premise to the American law system is everyone is innocent until proven guilty. If procedural rights are not included to protect the right to justice or due process, then the basic principle of innocence until proven guilty cannot be fully protected. Finally, while Bernick and Barnett identify fewer fundamental rights, their less stringent criteria for fundamental rights to garner constitutional protection would allow for a much more extensive list. My requirement of unanimity is not a rule considered by Bernick and Barnett. [108]

The criteria used by Bernick and Barnett for fundamental rights to garner constitutional protection only requires the right to be protected in a supermajority of the states over the past 30 years. My guidelines are much more stringent since majorities and even supermajorities often need to be corrected. In Chapter 8, I outline some fictious rights that modern politicians have often erroneously referred to as fundamental rights such as healthcare, welfare, abortion, diversity, and illegal immigration. Many of the before mentioned fictious rights have been a deep-rooted tradition for over 30 years within many states and supported by the federal government. Would Bernick and Barnett grant these fictitious rights fundamental status? I believe they would! There are other differences in our theories such as allowing rights to be rescinded and not agreeing that natural rights can include economic, political, civil, and social rights. I make no distinction between economic, political, civil, and social rights because it complicates the process. [109]

The most important property and criteria a fundamental right must possess was defined by natural law philosopher John Locke as the "fewest people have dared to deny." Our fundamental rights are those rights that are unanimously supported by the citizens of the United States. [110]

Fundamental rights cannot be subdivided or made any better. They cannot be denied or taken away because we are all born with these rights. They are also not government-created entitlements. Fundamental rights should be controlled by the individual, discerned from biblical text, protected by historical documents or Supreme Court cases, pertain to legal actions, they cannot be controversial or a political issue, fundamental rights should be protected equally, and fundamental rights are "deep rooted in American society and culture" (*Glucksberg v. Washington* 1997). Fundamental rights are natural rights because they were introduced to us by

God and perfected in His image. Thus, fundamental rights cannot evolve, be altered, or change over time. Importantly, political issues are different from political rights. Political rights such as the right to vote, sit on juries, or attain public office are protected fundamental rights. Political issues are controversial and refer to subjects such as abortion, illegal immigration, diversity, welfare, and healthcare insurance which are not fundamental rights.

Fundamental rights are integral to society. If moral principles or fundamental rights are altered, then society is negatively affected. A society with altered rights and moral principles is no longer whole, but it becomes a fraction of what it was. Until the government and political parties accept this principle, expect fundamental rights and constitutional checks and balances to protect those rights to be mitigated.

Notice that fundamental rights and God's moral principles have nothing to do with a person's color, gender, sexual orientation, mental capacity, or socio-economic status. They have nothing to do with identity politics, whose purpose is to create conflict and friction by segregating groups of people into categories who are taught to despise each other. They are not about preferential groups of people wanting more rights at the expense of other groups of people. They are not about political ideologies, cancel culture, critical race theory, bullying, opinion media sources, or other types of propaganda and indoctrination. Instead, fundamental rights are about personal free will, decisions, and behavior. Life is complicated, but understanding fundamental rights and moral principles is simple. We are all different, but we all enjoy the same rights and are held to the same standard of moral principles.

Fundamental rights are symmetrical and interrelated. Philosopher Aristotle supports this concept by suggesting that there should be no hierarchy of rights. [111] Just as there is no hierarchical status between God, Jesus, and the Holy Spirit, there is also supposed to be no hierarchy ranking among moral principles, fundamental rights, or clauses of the Constitution. One may think of constitutional provisions, fundamental rights, and moral principles structured as a circle instead of as a pyramid. Pyramid hierarchy constructions are destructive and are destroying society by making people more selfish. Pyramid constructions define the power order of organizations, societies, companies, and groups. The more power one attains (the higher they are in the pyramid), the more selfish one may become using their power to achieve their personal agenda. [112] A circular construction indicates that fundamental rights, constitutional provisions, and moral principles all have the same value and importance. Just as symmetry is important in mathematics and science, it is equally important in defining human nature.

The Supreme Court protecting a right does not make it fundamental nor does the Supreme Court failing to protect a right mean it is not fundamental. *Gonzales v. Raich* is listed as an example in Table I regarding the right pursue health, but Raich, in my opinion, was incorrectly decided. Raich is addressed in more detail in Chapter 8. Many of the rights listed in Table I have been protected but not necessarily elevated to fundamental right status by the courts. Why do courts fail to advance obvious fundamental rights? Because they may be presumed to be fundamental. Nevertheless, the extensive overreach of federal and state governments never leads me to think any right is presumed fundamental unless it is truly protected.

The Bible and its Influence on the Constitution and Our God-Given Fundamental Rights [113]

This section demonstrates how closely the Bible, Constitution, and our God-given fundamental rights are related.

The Right to Conscious Thought or Our Right to Religious Liberty

In Revelation 3:20 God says, "Behold, I stand at the door and knock; if anyone hears My voice and opens the door, I will come in to him and will dine with him, and he with Me." In Revelation 3:20, God provides us with religious liberty because He provides us with a choice to pick Him (to answer the door) or to venture down another path. God may provide us with guidance but He allows each person to make their own decisions which is called free will. For example, God provided Adam and Eve with guidance; unfortunately, both Adam and Eve chose not to heed God's counseling, resulting in the fall of mankind. The fall of mankind from the sins of Adam and Eve demonstrates two important points. First, the fall of man illustrates how sins can affect society collectively. Second, man's fall also explains why sin and misery exist in our present society in the form of violence, hate, crime, illness, tragedy, and accidents. To be clear, everyone has a fundamental right to have evil thoughts so long as they do not act those thoughts. Unfortunately, the fall of man has led mankind to become more sinful because people are more likely to act on their evil thoughts causing needless misery, suffering, and pain throughout the world. Religious liberty is found in the First Amendment of the United States Constitution: "Congress shall make no law respecting an establishment of religion or prohibiting the free exercise thereof."

Liberty of Speech and Liberty to Associate with Whomever We Wish for Our Acquaintances or Friendships

Acts 18:9–10 establishes free speech when Luke wrote, "And the Lord said to Paul by a vision at night, 'Do not be afraid any longer, but go on speaking and do not be silent; for I am with you, and no one will attack you to harm you, for I have many people in this city.'" In the preceding verse, God urges Saint Paul to spread Christianity despite facing ridicule and possible punishment from Jewish elders and the Roman Empire. Similarly, our Founding Fathers provided us with freedom of speech so no person is punished for their religious or political points of view. Furthermore, liberty of speech protects like-minded people to congregate and associate. For instance, Baptists are like-minded people who regularly associate, congregate, and develop strong bonds and friendships. Liberty of speech is found in the First Amendment of the United States Constitution which states Congress shall make no law "abridging the freedom of speech, or of the press; or the right of the people peaceably to assemble, and to petition the Government for a redress of grievances." To petition the government for a redress of grievances simply implies people have the right to ask the government for justice or due process if they believe their rights have been violated.

Due process, Justice, Retribution, Protection, and Safety from Those Who may Sin and Violate the Rights of Other Citizens in Society

Justice is a complicated fundamental right because due process must focus on both the protection of the accused, since they are presumed innocent until proven guilty, as well as the victims of crime. The information in this section on due process and justice focuses on the rights of the accused. King Solomon provides his wisdom in Proverbs 18:17, "The first to plead his case seems right, until another comes and examines us." King Solomon suggests that there are two sides to every event or story. Thus, the proceeding verse depicts the due process right to allow defendants to confront witnesses against them so defendants can tell their side of the story. The Confrontation Clause is found in the Sixth Amendment of the United States Constitution which states, "In all criminal prosecutions, the accused shall enjoy the right…to be confronted with the witnesses against him."

The Sixth Amendment right that "the accused shall enjoy the right to a speedy and public trial" can be discerned in Ecclesiastes 8:11, "Because the sentence against an evil deed is not executed quickly, therefore the hearts of the sons of mankind among them are fully given to do evil." Today, a speedy trial is meant to protect a defendant from being held in custody for an extended period of time. Ecclesiastes 8:11 has a different connotation that we should fear God and his judgement when mankind is not being held accountable for their evil actions in a timely matter.

Due process protection from being put on trial more than one time for the same crime (double jeopardy) can be discerned in Romans 7:14. Romans 7:14 reads, "For we know that the Law is spiritual, but I am fleshly, sold into bondage to sin." In Romans 7:14, Saint Paul indicates anyone who is punished for sins of the flesh cannot be punished for similar sins of the spirit. If the law and the Constitution are, indeed, divinely inspired by God, then one can rationalize the law is spiritual and includes both the flesh and the spirit of man. The human body is referred to as the flesh in the Bible. Every person has basically the same body or vessel to house the soul and spirit. The soul is defined as the human personality. The spirit is a subset of the human personality or soul which defines our connection with God. Thus, sins of the soul and spirit include our thoughts, whereas sins of the flesh include our actions. People who act on sinful thoughts of the soul and spirit commit crimes and sins of the flesh. Those people punished for crimes or sins of the flesh are also being punished for sins of the spirit which inspired the crime. Similarly, the Founding Fathers prohibit a person from being put on trial for the same crime more than one time. More specifically, a person cannot be found innocent and then convicted of the same crime at a later trial. The Double Jeopardy Clause is found in the Fifth Amendment of the United States Constitution which states, "No person shall ... be subject for the same offense to be twice put in jeopardy of life or limb…"

Protection from excessive punishment for a crime is found in Exodus 21:24, which notes retribution must be an "Eye for an eye, tooth for a tooth, hand for a hand, foot for a foot." The preceding verse is often thought to be one of revenge, but the revenge definition is not true, the verse is asking the judicial system to seek equal punishment for crimes. The Eighth Amendment of the United States Constitution protects citizens from excessive punishment for a crime, "Excessive bail shall not be required, nor excessive fines imposed, nor cruel and unusual punishments inflicted." For instance, a person should not face life in prison for shoplifting a pack of chewing gum.

When Jesus was put on trial, Matthew 26:63 declares, "Jesus kept silent" in his defense. Remaining silent is the same as the due process principle which protects defendants from being compelled to incriminate themselves. A person accused of a crime does not have to say anything in their defense. When people are arrested, police officers are required by law to read the accused their Miranda rights which reads, in part, the accused "have the right to remain silent." Since the accused is innocent until proven guilty, the onus is on the justice system to prove the accused is guilty beyond a reasonable doubt. The right against self-incrimination is found in the Fifth Amendment of the Constitution, "nor shall [the defendant] be compelled in any criminal case to be a witness against himself." People compelled to testify in front of Congress will sometimes plead the Fifth Amendment and not answer any questions. Of course, the accused has every right to tell their side of the story if their lawyer believes their testimony is the best strategy for them to earn an acquittal.

The Trial by Jury Clause has its roots in Numbers 35:24 when Moses proclaimed that "the congregation shall judge" the accused. Trial by jury protects the accused in many ways. First, trial by jury takes the government out of the decision-making process by placing the responsibility with the community. In other words, the accused is judged by a jury of their peers—a jury whose members are from the same community as the person on trial. Trial by jury is a check and balance to prevent the government or judicial system from becoming too corrupt by sending political adversaries to prison for absolutely no reason. Second, trial by jury requires a unanimous decision from all twelve jurors to find the accused guilty. If a jury member holds biases, opinions, or prejudices against the defendant, their guilty vote may not matter because it takes all twelve jury members to convict a defendant. The entire purpose of trial by jury is to level the playing field by removing potential biases held by the government, the judicial system, and even individual citizens who may sit on the jury. Trial by jury is defined in the Seventh Amendment of the United States Constitution. The Seventh Amendment reads, "In suits at common law, where the value in controversy shall exceed twenty dollars, the right of trial by jury shall be preserved, and no fact tried by a jury, shall be otherwise reexamined in any court of the United States, then according to the rules of the common law."

The entire purpose of every clause that makes up the Sixth Amendment is for the accused to have a fair and impartial trial. Acts 24–26 not only details the first arrest of Saint Paul, but the story highlights the importance of many fair trial clauses outlined in the Sixth Amendment. Paul was charged by the Jewish high priests and elders with a crime detailed in Acts 24:5 suggesting Paul was "a public menace and one who stirs up dissensions among all the Jews throughout the world, and a ringleader of the sect of the Nazarenes." Furthermore, the revenge minded priests and elders sought an unreasonable death sentence for Paul's minor crimes (Acts 25:15). Paul feared he could not receive a fair and impartial trial from the Jewish leaders and, therefore, wished for trial in front of the Roman Emperor (Acts 25:10). A Roman, Festus, however, referred Paul's case to Jewish King Agrippa. Festus informs King Agrippa in Acts 25:17: "For it seems absurd to me in sending a prisoner, not to indicate the charges against him as well." Acts 25:17 establishes the importance of the Sixth Amendment right of the accused to be "informed of the nature and cause of the accusation." A fair trial for Saint Paul was the inspiration for Acts 25:16 (New Living Translation Version) when Festus informed King Agrippa, "I pointed out to them [elders] that Roman law does not convict people without a trial. They must be given an opportunity to confront their accusers and defend themselves." The elders and priests did not provide Festus with any charges against Paul because his charges amounted to no more than a misdemeanor that did not warrant prison time let alone a death sentence. Since Paul did not know the charges against him, he was not provided any opportunity to prepare for his defense. King Agrippa verified Paul's innocence in Acts 26:31, "This man is not doing anything deserving death or imprisonment."

The Sixth Amendment's fair trial clauses also include the accused having a right to a lawyer and a process to obtain witnesses to testify on their behalf. Deuteronomy 16:18–20 best explains the impartial trial process in the Bible, "You shall appoint for yourself judges and officers in all your towns which the LORD your God is giving you, according to your tribes, and they shall judge the people with righteous judgment. You shall not distort justice, you shall not show partiality; and you shall not accept a bribe, because a bribe blinds the eyes of the wise and distorts the words of the righteous. Justice, and only justice, you shall pursue, so that you may live and possess the land which the LORD your God is giving you."

Another justice right found in the Constitution is a prohibition on bills of attainder. A bill of attainder is when a person or group of people are convicted of a crime without a trial. The prohibition on bills of attainder is found in Article I, Section 9, Clause 3 of the Constitution which reads, "No Bill of Attainder or ex post facto Law shall be passed." Article III, Section 3, Clause 2 of the Constitution also reinforces prohibitions against bills of attainder. It was not uncommon for some governments around the globe to convict people of a crime or deny them of their inheritance when their only wrongdoing was being related to person who committed a crime. The process of convicting blood relatives was referred to as "corruption of blood" by the Founders. Thus, Article III, Section 3, Clause 2 prohibits the corruption of blood laws and reads, "The Congress shall have Power to declare the Punishment of Treason, but no Attainder of Treason shall work Corruption of Blood, or Forfeiture except during the Life of the Person attainted." Prohibitions against bills of attainder and corruption of blood laws have their origins in Ezekiel 18:20, "The person who sins will die. A son will not suffer the punishment for the father's guilt, nor will a father suffer the punishment for the son's guilt; the righteousness of the righteous will be upon himself, and the wickedness of the wicked will be upon himself."

In Romans 3:28–31, Paul silences arguments that gentiles and Jews should be governed under different laws. Paul says, "Do we then nullify the Law through faith? Far from it! On the contrary, we establish the Law."

Prohibitions on ex post facto laws is also found in Article I, Section 9, Clause 3 of the Constitution. An ex post facto law is a retroactive law that criminalizes behavior before it was a crime. Paul understands a two-tiered system of law complicates the justice system and opens people up to unlawful prosecutions perhaps by inventing new laws to prosecute what were once legal actions. Thus, laws must be applied to everyone equally.

The Right to Marriage and to Raise a Family

Genesis 2:24 introduces marriage to society, "For this reason a man shall leave his father and his mother and be joined to his wife; and they shall become one flesh." Marriage and raising a family are the cornerstone of any society. Although these rights are not mentioned in the Constitution, the Supreme Court has protected these rights as well as many other rights in cases such as *Pierce v. Society of Sisters* and *Meyer v. Nebraska.* In Meyer, Justice James McReynolds opined,

> The Court has never attempted to define, with exactness, the liberty guaranteed by the Fourteenth Amendment. Without doubt, it denotes not merely liberty from bodily restraint but also the right of the individual to contract, to engage in any of the common occupations of life, to acquire useful knowledge, to marry, establish a home and bring up children, to worship according to the dictates of his own conscious, and generally to enjoy those privileges long recognized at statutory law as essential to the orderly pursuit of happiness by free men.

In Pierce, Justice McReynolds wrote, "Under the doctrine of *Meyer v. Nebraska,* we think it entirely plain that the Act of 1922 unreasonably interferes with the liberty of parents and guardians to direct the upbringing and education of children under their control."

The Ninth Amendment in the United States Constitution protects what are called unenumerated fundamental rights. The Ninth Amendment reads, "The enumeration in the Constitution, of certain rights, shall not be construed to deny or disparage others retained by the people." Unenumerated fundamental rights are those rights which are not listed or enumerated in the Constitution and Bill of Rights (the first ten amendments). The right to marry and raise a family are examples of unenumerated rights.

The Right to Self-Defense for the Purpose to Protect Oneself, Their Family, and Their Property

Self-defense has its basis in Exodus 22:2: "If the thief is caught while breaking in and is struck so that he dies, there will be no guilt for bloodshed on his account." Exodus 20:15 prohibits people from stealing and Deuteronomy 5:21 commands people not to covet their neighbors' possessions. Exodus 22:2 is self-explanatory and affords people the right to protect themselves, their family, and their property because Exodus 20:15 and Deuteronomy 5:21 prohibits people from violating the property rights of their neighbors. Self-defense is widely considered to be implied in the Second Amendment's right to bear arms. The Second Amendment reads, "A well-regulated Militia, being necessary to the security of a free State, the right of the people to keep and bear

Arms, shall not be infringed." The Founding Fathers placed gun ownership rights in the Constitution so the people could protect themselves not only from criminals, but from an intrusive government. After all, the tyrannical actions of English King George III, which resulted in the American Revolutionary War, were fresh on the Founders' minds when they drafted the Second Amendment. Furthermore, guns used for the purpose of self-preservation is also warranted. Self-preservation is a form of self-defense. For instance, hunting is a form of self-preservation because food is essential for survival and reinforced in Genesis 1:26. Genesis 1:26 reads, "Then God said, 'Let Us make mankind in Our image, according to Our likeness; and let them rule over the fish of the sea and over the birds of the sky and over the livestock and over all the earth, and over every crawling thing that crawls on the earth.'"

The Right to Buy and Sell Property and the Right to Privacy Within One's Home

Jeremiah 29:5 establishes the principle of property ownership, "Build houses and live in them; and plant gardens and eat their produce." Jeremiah 29:5 reinforces the principle that people are allowed to do as they wish with their property to ensure their survival or self-preservation. Property owners are allowed to neglect their private property so long as their actions do not violate the rights of their neighbors. Property and privacy rights are protected in the Third Amendment of the United States Constitution which prevents the government from quartering troops in the homes of citizens. The Third Amendment reads, "No Soldier shall, in time of peace be quartered in any house, without the consent of the Owner, nor in time of war, but in a manner to be prescribed by law." Furthermore, the Fourth Amendment protects citizens from warrantless searches and seizure of their property. The Fourth Amendment reads, "The right of the people to be secure in their persons, houses, papers, and effects, against unreasonable searches and seizures, shall not be violated, and no Warrants shall issue, but upon probable cause, supported by Oath or affirmation, and particularly describing the place to be searched, and the persons or things to be seized." Additionally, the Fifth Amendment's Takings Clause prevents the government from confiscating private property without just compensation. The Takings Clause reads, "private property shall not be taken for public use, without just compensation."

In *Calder v. Bull (1798)*, Justice Samuel Chase enforces the sacred principle of property ownership when he wrote the government should enforce no law "that takes property from A and gives it to B." The Civil Rights Act of 1866 was drafted following the Civil War to provide African Americans equal rights. The Civil Rights Act of 1866 clearly acknowledges many rights including property ownership and emphasizes that all people have a right

> To make and enforce contracts, sue, be parties, and give evidence, to inherit, purchase, lease, sell, hold, and convey real and personal property, and to full and equal benefits of all laws and proceedings for the security of person and property, as is enjoyed by white citizens, and shall be subject to like punishment,

pains, and penalties, and to none other, any law, statute, ordinance, regulation, or custom, to the contrary notwithstanding.

The Third, Fourth, and Fifth Amendments as well as Calder and the Civil Rights Act of 1866 not only protect property but also implicitly protect privacy rights. Privacy was first provided constitutional protection in the 1965 Supreme Court case, *Griswold v. Connecticut.*

The Right to Obtain Knowledge, Understanding, and Wisdom

The right to obtain knowledge, understanding, and wisdom was discussed by King Solomon in Proverbs 24:3, "By wisdom a house is built, and by understanding it is established; and by knowledge the rooms are filled with all precious and pleasant riches." Educational rights or the right to obtain knowledge and wisdom have long been protected in American society. Although never mentioned in the Constitution, the right to obtain knowledge was specifically protected in the Supreme Court case *Meyer v. Nebraska.* Two years before the Constitution was written, Congress passed the Northwest Ordinance of 1787. Article 3 of the Northwest Ordinance states, "Religion, morality, and knowledge, being necessary to good government and the happiness of humankind, schools and the means of education shall forever be encouraged."

The Right to Make Legal Choices to Pursue Life, Liberty, and Happiness [114]

Free will is the ability for people to make choices or decisions without any interference from God. 2 Corinthians 5:10 explains people have the liberty to make their own decisions (free will), but ultimately, everyone will be judged for those choices. 2 Corinthians 5:10 reads, "For we must all appear before the judgment seat of Christ, so that each one may receive compensation for his deeds done through the body, in accordance with what he has done, whether good or bad."

The unalienable rights to pursue life, liberty, and happiness are established in the Declaration of Independence, "We hold these truths to be self-evident, that all men are created equal, that they are endowed by their Creator with certain unalienable Rights, that among these are Life, Liberty, and the pursuit of Happiness." Unalienable rights are those rights which are so important that without these rights all other rights become obsolete. For example, without life, other rights do not exist. Without liberty to pursue our fundamental rights, then other rights become hollow. And without happiness, then other rights become meaningless. The Constitution's Fifth Amendment declares no person shall "be deprived of life, liberty, or property, without due process of law." Notice the pursuit of happiness was replaced with property in the Fifth Amendment. However, the Founding Fathers equated happiness with property ownership. Furthermore, property had a broad meaning during the founding era to include not only tangible belongings, but people owned their actions, decisions, and choices. Thus, property is also an unalienable right because without property ownership then people no longer control their liberty to make free will choices to pursue life, liberty, and happiness.

The Right to Travel

The right to travel as well as other fundamental rights were established in *Corfield v. Coryell*. Corfield declares people have a right to

> Protection by the Government; the enjoyment of life and liberty, with the right to acquire and possess property of every kind, and to pursue and obtain happiness and safety; subject nevertheless to such restraints as the Government must justly prescribe for the general good of the whole. The right of a citizen of one State to pass through, or to reside in any other State, for purposes of trade, agriculture, professional pursuits, or otherwise; to claim the benefits of the writ of habeas corpus; to institute and maintain actions of any kind in the courts of the State; to take, hold and dispose of property, either real or personal; and an exemption from higher taxes or impositions than are paid by the other citizens of the State.

Similarly, the Bible constantly reminds us that the Lord travels with us and watches over us. For instance, in Psalms 23:3–4 (New Century Version) King David wrote, "He gives me new strength. He leads me on paths that are right for the good of his name. Even if I walk through a very dark valley, I will not be afraid, because you are with me. Your rod and your shepherd's staff comfort me."

The unenumerated right to travel is important in the United States. While most people regard the right to vote as the most powerful political right, the ability to travel is truly the most powerful political right. The United States is truly amazing because America contains fifty individual republics (states) within one united nation. If Americans do not like the laws in one state, wise citizens choose to vote with their feet and move to a state of their liking. Federalism is what allows each individual state to have unique laws governing their citizens. Federalism is joint power sharing between the federal and state governments and is protected by the Tenth Amendment. Federalism is a check and balance to prevent the federal government from becoming too powerful and is what makes the United States truly unique and unlike any other nation in the world. The Tenth Amendment reads, "The powers not delegated to the United States by the Constitution, nor prohibited by it to the States, are reserved to the States respectively, or to the people." In other words, any powers not expressly provided to the federal government in the Article I, Section 8 of the Constitution are reserved for each individual state and their citizens to enforce.

The Right to Enter into Agreements or Contracts

The responsibility of entering financial contracts is clarified in Proverbs 22:26–27, "Do not be among those who shake hands, among those who become guarantors for debts. If you have nothing with which to repay, why should he take your bed from under you?" Namely, only people who can repay their debts should enter in financial agreements. The Constitution's Contract Clause appears in Article I, Section 10 and reads, "No State shall... pass any... Law impairing the Obligation of Contracts." The Contract Clause's purpose is to protect lenders from citizens defaulting on their debts. Today, the Contract Clause is regularly violated because modern laws not only protect borrowers from predatory lenders, but many laws often protect borrowers from reasonable contracts. Thus, if a judge deems a lender's contract is unreasonable, the judge may rule a person has a right to breach or not honor their contract obligations. That said, contract rights of citizens are clearly identified as protected fundamental rights in the passages provided earlier in this book for *Meyer v. Nebraska* and *Corfield v. Coryell.*

The Right to Vote, to Sit on Juries, to Consent to be Governed, and to have Representation in Government

These rights are referred to as our political fundamental rights by law scholars. Exodus 18:21 establishes the right to vote, consent to be governed, and to be represented in government when Moses declared that the Israelites "shall select out of all the people able men who fear God, men of truth, those who hate dishonest gain; and you shall place these over them as leaders of thousands, of hundreds, of fifties, and of tens." Moreover, Deuteronomy 1:13 makes a similar suggestion as Exodus 18:21. The right for all non-felon American citizens over the age of 18 to earn voting privileges was established with both the passage of the Fifteenth Amendment in 1870, and the Nineteenth Amendment that provided women with the right to vote in 1920. The Fifteenth Amendment reads, "The right of citizens of the United States to vote shall not be denied or abridged by the United States or by any State on account of race, color, or previous condition of servitude." The Nineteenth Amendment reads, "The right of citizens of the United States to vote shall not be denied or abridged by the United States or by any State on account of sex." The right for the United States citizens to be represented in the federal government is granted in Article I, Section 2, "The House of Representatives shall be composed of Members chosen every second Year by the People of the several States..."

The right for citizens to sit on juries was established earlier in this text when discussing the due process right to have a trial by jury. In Numbers 35:24, "the congregation shall judge" the accused covers two purposes. The accused has both the right to a jury trial as well as receiving a jury of their peers. The right to sit on a jury was established in the Civil Rights Act of 1957 which reads, "Any Citizen of the United States who has attained the age of twenty-one years and who has resided for a period of one year within the judicial district, is competent to serve as a Grand or petit jury." The Civil Rights Act of 1957 finally permitted all non-felon American citizens above the age of 18 the privilege to sit on juries. In early American history only white men could sit on juries, vote, and partake in the political process. Unfortunately, nearly two centuries passed before women and African American citizens obtained equal political rights.

The Right to Work, Profit from One's Labor, and Enjoy an Equal and Fair Tax System

The necessity of working a lawful profession was established in 2 Thessalonians 3:10, "If anyone is not willing to work, then he is not to eat, either." In Proverbs 14:23, King Solomon again provides us with his wisdom: "In all labor there is profit." Moreover, in the parable of the Ten Minas in Luke 19, Jesus reminds us how the ability to profit from one's labor is a common good to be enjoyed by all citizens. God's message is clear in the above three verses. First, all those who can work should do so and second, people should profit from their work. The right to work is not enumerated in the Constitution, but the rights of workers was protected in *Meyer v. Nebraska* and *Corfield v. Coryell*. The only conceivable way for American citizens to profit from their labor is if there is a fair tax system which is outline in Article I, Section 8 of the Constitution and clearly indicates taxes should be equal and uniform. The principle of equal and uniform taxes complies with Founding Father, Thomas Jefferson's statement, "There cannot be a stronger natural right than that of a man making the best profit he can." In other words, minimal, equal, and reasonable tax rates to profit from one's labor is a fundamental right to be enjoyed by all citizens.

The Right to Equality or Equal Application of All Laws

The right to equality can be discerned from Saint Luke when he wrote in Acts 10:34, "I most certainly understand now that God is not one to show partiality." Again, in Romans 2:11, Saint Paul wrote, "For there is no partiality with God." If God is not partial, then He must regard all His servants equal regardless of race, religion, gender, socioeconomic status, or ideology. Similarly, the Equal Protection Clause of the Fourteenth Amendment reads, "nor shall any State ... deny to any person within its jurisdiction the equal protection of the laws." In other words, everyone is equal and not only born with the same fundamental rights, but everyone is also responsible for upholding the law which protects those same fundamental rights of our fellow citizens. Equality means race, gender, ideology, and economic status do not matter when considering fundamental rights. In Martin Luther King's famous "I have a Dream" speech he said, "I look to a day when people will not be judged by the color of their skin, but by the content of their character." Justice John Harlan's famous dissent in the case *Plessy v. Ferguson* echoes Acts 10:34, Romans 2:11, and the Equal Protection Clause. In Plessy (1896), the Supreme Court erroneously decided segregating people based on race was constitutional. Justice Harlan was the only one of nine justices to object. Justice Harlan would later be vindicated when Plessy was overruled in *Brown v. School Board* in 1954. When Plessy was overruled, Justice Harlan's dissent became the majority opinion and law of the land. Justice Harlan wrote:

> But in view of the constitution, in the eye of the law, there is in this country no superior, dominant, ruling class of citizens. There is no caste here. Our constitution is color-blind, and neither knows nor tolerates classes among citizens. In respect of civil rights, all citizens are equal before the law. The humblest is the peer of the most powerful. The law regards man as man and takes no account of his surroundings or of his color when his civil rights as guaranteed by the supreme law of the land are involved. It is, therefore, to be regretted that this high tribunal, the final expositor of the fundamental law of the land, has reached the conclusion that it is competent for a State to regulate the enjoyment by

> citizens of their civil rights solely upon the basis of race. In my opinion, the judgment this day rendered will, in time, prove to be quite as pernicious as the decision made by this tribunal in the *Dred Scott* case.

The right to equality should not be confused with societal classifications, which are required for physical limitations. For example, age and gender classifications in athletics and the grade system in education levels the playing field to compensate for obvious strength and maturity differences. Classifications pertain to a specific reason, whereas segregation is a social policy that prohibits certain groups of people from interacting for many unrelated and discriminatory reasons. Segregation was ruled unconstitutional in *Brown v. School Board*.

Chapter 5: Protecting Fundamental Rights and the Role of the Statutory Law and Natural Law in United States History

Ninth Amendment [115]

Unenumerated rights are protected through both the Ninth Amendment and the Privileges and Immunities Clause of the Fourteenth Amendment (discussed next). The Founders felt it was futile to define all the fundamental rights or liberties that humanity may pursue because there are hundreds of fundamental rights, such as the right to brush your teeth or shower. Thus, many Founders objected to a Bill of Rights because they feared unenumerated rights (or rights not listed in the Bill of Rights) would not be protected or protected as vigorously as those rights enumerated in the Constitution. [116] To resolve this conundrum, James Madison proposed the Ninth Amendment, which reads:

> The enumeration in the Constitution, of certain rights, shall not be construed to deny or disparage others retained by the people.

The Ninth Amendment is synonymous with liberty and is the most magnificent and ingenious twenty-one words of the Bill of Rights and Constitution. The Ninth Amendment is so magnificent it could have been used as a vessel to end slavery and support women's suffrage. That is right; there was no reason to pass the Thirteenth, Fourteenth, Fifteenth, and Nineteenth Amendments since they are encompassed in the Ninth Amendment.

Unfortunately, legislatures and courts very rarely use or rely on the Ninth Amendment for two reasons. First, many law experts claim that they need help understanding the amendment or they are uncertain of the true meaning behind the amendment. The uncertainty claim is nonsense since the amendment is self-explanatory, and information explaining why James Madison included it in the Bill of Rights is readily available. Second, many jurists are afraid to open Pandora's box because they are uncertain of how the other side will use the amendment. For example, liberals and conservatives alike may use the amendment to protect things that are not fundamental rights. Those fears have already been realized when the Supreme Court protected abortion without the use of the Ninth Amendment. Of course, this apprehension or fear of how the amendment would be used could easily have been averted. Legislators and courts could simply define the properties a fundamental right must possess to be elevated to constitutional protection through the Ninth Amendment. Many properties a fundamental right should possess were highlighted in the previous chapter, such as being undisputed, equal, non-political, non-controversial, and deep-rooted in American culture and history.

An amendment to protect all rights seems intuitive, but if the Ninth Amendment was intuitive, then legislators and courts would not ignore its brilliance. Resolving both natural law and quantum physics has become a difficult task because they pose interesting paradoxes. For example, the thought-provoking quantum mechanics experiment "Schrödinger's cat" leads scientists to believe a cat placed in the closed box can be both alive and dead because of the uncertainty surrounding subatomic particles. Similarly, the uncertainty surrounding the Ninth Amendment's use or meaning leaves many rights in limbo, neither protected or unprotected. Until courts and legislators resolve the Ninth Amendment paradox they manufactured, the fundamental rights of citizens will suffer significantly as the scope and mission of the federal government expand. Likewise, until scientists resolve the uncertainty regarding subatomic particles, humanity may never understand the true nature of the universe and human reality.

Fourteenth Amendment

Section 1 of the Fourteenth Amendment reads:

> Section 1: All persons born or naturalized in the United States, and subject to the jurisdiction thereof, are citizens of the United States and of the State wherein they reside. No State shall make or enforce any law which shall abridge the privileges or immunities of citizens of the United States; nor shall any State deprive any person of life, liberty, or property, without due process of law; nor deny to any person within its jurisdiction the equal protection of the laws.

The Fourteenth Amendment was not only passed to protect newly freed slaves, but it was also a repudiation of *Barron v. Baltimore*. Chief Justice Marshall held in Barron that the Bill of Rights did not apply to the states. Section 1 of the Fourteenth Amendment clearly states that no *state* shall abridge the privileges and immunities (fundamental rights) of citizens which would include those rights found in the Bill of Rights such as free speech and religious liberty. [117]

A vast majority of law scholars correctly argue cases such as *Bradwell v. Illinois (1873)*, *The Slaughter-House Cases (1873),* and *United States v. Cruikshank (1876)* were incorrectly decided. It was argued that these cases were decided incorrectly by circumventing the spirit of the newly passed Fourteenth Amendment in 1868. The *Slaughter-House Cases* denied butchers the right to work and in Cruikshank the Court failed to hold states accountable for upholding the Bill of Rights. [118] In Cruikshank, peacefully assembled black Republicans were viciously attacked and as many as four hundred were killed! Bradwell upheld an Illinois law that denied women the right to work as a lawyer. In each case, the Court failed to hold states accountable for denying the right to the work (Bradwell and *Slaughter-House Cases*) and the right to peacefully assemble and carry arms (Cruikshank). The *Slaughter-House Cases* was probably the most harmful decision because it essentially redacted the Privileges and Immunities Clause from the Fourteenth Amendment which has never been corrected.

Justice Samuel Miller wrote a convoluted majority opinion in the *Slaughter-House Cases*. Miller held a very narrow reading of the Privileges and Immunities Clause to imply the sole focus of the amendment was for equal rights for freed slaves, but not equal rights for white men or women denied the right to work in the *Slaughter-House Cases* or Bradwell. Furthermore, Miller erroneously denies that the Privileges and Immunities Clause protects citizens from states infringing on any of the rights outlined in the Bill of Rights. Justice Miller elaborated that the Fourteenth Amendment only protected privilege and immunities for national citizenship, but not rights specific to state citizenship such as those rights outlined *Corfield v. Coryell*. Justice Miller is clearly wrong because there should not be any distinction between the rights protected by both national and state citizenship. The Citizenship Clause of the Fourteenth Amendment states, "All persons born or naturalized in the United States and subject to the jurisdiction thereof, are citizens of the United States and of the State wherein they reside." I read this clause to suggest state and national citizenship are synonymous. [119]

To compensate for the egregious error in the *Slaughter-House Cases*, a flawed doctrine called Substantive Due Process is used to protect fundamental rights. Substantive Due Process uses the Due Process Clause of the Fourteenth Amendment instead of the redacted Privileges and Immunities Clause. The purpose of the Privileges and Immunities Clause was intended to identify fundamental rights. The purpose of the Due Process Clause was to enforce and protect all fundamental rights. The purpose of the Due Process Clause was never intended to both identify and protect fundamental rights.

Cruikshank would take over a century to correct. Although Cruikshank was never overturned, the Court went through a process called "incorporation" to apply the Bill of Rights to the states. It was a slow and controversial process for several reasons. First, incorporation incorrectly used Substantive Due Process to protect enumerated rights. Second, it was done on a case-by-case basis applying one Bill of Rights clause at a time. The *Slaughter-House Cases*, Cruikshank, and Bradwell stunted gender and racial equality, inhibited the protection of fundamental rights, and further muddled the definition of privileges and immunities and fundamental rights.

To summarize, the entire way Congress and the courts go about protecting rights needs to be clarified. While the Fourteenth Amendment applied to the state governments, the Ninth Amendment applied to the federal government. It seems preposterous to make such a distinction, but Justice Miller's opinion in the *Slaughter-House Cases* clearly fails to repeal *Barron v. Baltimore*. If this is not confusing enough, both the Ninth Amendment and the Privileges and Immunities Clause of the Fourteenth Amendment have basically been redacted from the Constitution. The latter in the awful *Slaughter-House Cases* (1873) and the former from lack of use and precedent. Despite these setbacks, social reform was and is possible using other constitutional methods, such as Substantive Due Process (more on this in Chapter 7). For instance, in *Griswold v. Connecticut (1965),* the right to privacy was elevated to constitutional status to protect family rights via Substantive Due Process. Congress and the courts have made the process of protecting rights much more complex than needed. [120]

Accommodation Laws [121]

The most challenging conflict between fundamental rights to resolve, in my opinion, is how to resolve business controversies. In particular, resolving the dispute when a business owner denies service to a customer. Accommodation laws attempt to resolve this conflict. For instance, the Civil Rights Act of 1875 held that hotels, restaurants, and movie theaters were prohibited from denying anyone service based on race. The Civil Rights Act of 1875 was later found unconstitutional but has been supplanted with the Civil Rights Act of 1964, which prohibits the denial of any service because of discrimination. Both civil rights acts were enforced by the Fourteenth Amendment. That sounds rational and seems to follow the rule of right (discussed later in the chapter). Unfortunately, it is not that simple since the Fourteenth Amendment clearly proclaims it can only prohibit acts of discrimination committed by state governments, not those committed by private citizens. Moreover, store owners should have the fundamental right to associate and contract with whomever they please and, therefore, should be able to deny services for any reason. Additionally, the fundamental right of property includes the protection of business property. Thus, businesses should be able to control, maintain, and handle their business affairs without government interference. Protecting contracts, associations, and business property rights are precisely why the Civil Rights Act of 1875 was found unconstitutional in the *Civil Rights Cases in 1883.*

No one should discriminate, but any civil society must be able to tolerate offensive viewpoints; otherwise, the cornerstone of any free society – the right to conscious thought and free speech – will perish. Furthermore, not every instance of a business denying service is an act of discrimination. For example, a baker who declined to make a gay couple a wedding cake on religious grounds was vindicated by the Supreme Court. In fact, the Supreme Court has protected artistic professions, such as bakers, from accommodation laws (more on this Chapter 8).

Law scholars Randy Barnett and Evan Bernick defend accommodation laws in their book, *The Original Meaning of the Fourteenth Amendment*. To make their argument, Barnett and Bernick argue that there are three realms in society: Government, business, and citizen. They theorize that one purpose of the Fourteenth Amendment was to prevent both state governments and businesses from discriminating. They admit private citizens are free to discriminate so long as their discrimination does not involve physical harm to another person. They even recognize in the book's introduction that the business realm of their theory is "slippery." Bernick and Barnett are correct to suggest that Justice Joseph Bradley's majority opinion in the *Civil Rights Cases* was flawed because he suggests the Fourteenth Amendment does not protect fundamental rights when the state government fails to act and implement laws that would protect rights. However, I am afraid I must disagree with Barnett and Bernick that Bradley's opinion was wrong to suggest that regulating who has access to a business was outside the scope of government reach. [122]

Justice John Harlan was the lone dissenter in the *Civil Rights Cases* and presented a convincing argument to suggest that access to public accommodations is a fundamental right and businesses, therefore, have an obligation, responsibility, and duty to society to serve customers. I also take these obligations of businesses that Justice Harlan refers to include taking care of employees, customers, shareholders, the community, and the environment. However, how are these business obligations any different than what a private citizen owes to their spouse, family, friends, neighbors, community, and environment? If obligations are the same for businesses and private citizens, then why are treated differently? [123]

It is also argued by Barnett and Bernick that customers are different from those persons that are associations such as friends or those permitted in one's inner circle. I genuinely do not believe this to be the case for most small businesses whose customers include friendships. Nevertheless, business owners compelled to serve customers with a controversial value system could persuade some customers to conduct their business elsewhere. Even if I concede the point customers and associations are different, Barnett and Bernick do not address government regulation of private property to influence the contract and conscience rights of business owners that may conflict with those values held by some customers. [124]

Barnett and Berwick's argument hinges on the premise that the Equal Protection Clause of the Fourteenth Amendment is unlike all other clauses in the Constitution that are, for the most part, prohibitions against the government. In their view, the Equal Protection Clause is applied to both the government and businesses. Does it make sense for the Fourteenth Amendment to defend the rights of customers more vigorously than the rights of store owners? When rights favor one group of people over another group, I refer to them as one-way rights. One-way rights defeat the whole purpose of both the Privileges and Immunities and Equal Protection clauses of the Fourteenth Amendment, which were written specifically to defend the fundamental rights of everyone equally. I agree that the government cannot discriminate for any reason, but suggesting businesses can be treated both like a citizen (taxes) and government entity is slippery indeed. I do concede there are two exceptions when the federal government can interfere with state inaction to protect citizens from discriminatory practices of businesses. The first exception is that any businesses or other entities that accept government funding or bailouts can undoubtedly be compelled by the federal government to adhere to strict discrimination guidelines if state inaction fails to enforce them. Businesses such as museums, parks, schools, and mass transit fit under this umbrella. The stipulation that companies receiving government-issued licenses and franchises should also be included under this umbrella is, however, incorrect. The government could use license and franchise agreements to pressure companies to comply with antidiscrimination laws. Compelling businesses to purchase a license or franchise agreement so they can be regulated could easily be viewed as coercion. [125]

Barnett and Bernick point to the Ku Klux Klan Act, passed in 1871, as evidence the federal government can regulate both the state and people for discriminatory practices. In the reconstruction era following the Civil War, Southern states allowed the practice of not only discrimination but the intimidation of black citizens by assaulting them with force. Therefore, the Ku Klux Klan Act could very easily be deemed necessary and proper. Today, it is less likely that states will not do everything in their power to enforce laws to prevent or prosecute racial assaults. Sure, racial assaults happen, but it is very rare that the state will turn a blind eye to such events. The preceding explanation leads to the second exception; the federal government can step in and enforce antidiscrimination laws from state inaction if the discrimination results in physical harm to citizens. Discrimination must be accompanied by a crime such as assault. Discrimination committed by private citizens or businesses that does not result in physical harm is not a crime. [126]

I will stress this point again because it is important: A civil society must tolerate hateful and evil thoughts and nonviolent actions that do not result in harm. Why? The backbone or cornerstone of American society is the protection of the First Amendment right to conscious thought and expression. When people are jailed for their ideas, then no one is safe from confinement, and America is no longer a free society. After all, it is easy to extrapolate discrimination thoughts to criminalize things that may be merely offensive speech. Nor should the federal government feel compelled to interfere in local matters that the state has under control. Every state has laws to prosecute assault.

Barnett and Bernick conclude that the *Civil Rights Cases of 1883* set back reconstruction and allowed Jim Crow laws to flourish. Perhaps, it is impossible to know for sure. Unfortunately, what we do know is that the accommodation laws were the beginning of federal government enforcement overreach (discussed later). For instance, the federal government uses an unconstitutional expansion of the Interstate Commerce Clause to enforce hate crimes. The distinction between crime and hate crime to gain access to local crimes is ridiculous because I am unaware of any crime committed out of love. Hate crime statutes are obviously a gross overreach of power allowed by antidiscrimination civil rights laws. The distinction between crime and hate crime is not needed to hold criminals accountable. Although Republicans nearly unanimously voted in favor of the accommodation laws in the Civil Rights Act of 1875, they ignored that, for fundamental rights to be protected, the federal government should only have limited powers. The Republicans ventured on a slippery slope to solve a specific dire crisis, but they set a precedent for a huge federal government expansion of power that is now weaponized to enforce the majority party's opinion, bias, and conjecture. Now, the federal government has control over any crime they deem necessary and proper and will interfere even when the ends do not justify the means. [127]

To summarize the enforcement limits of the Equal Protection and Due Process clauses of the Fourteenth Amendment are fourfold. First, the clauses can be enforced by Congress and the federal courts. Second, the clauses protect citizens from all forms of state and federal government discrimination. Third, the clauses can prohibit state and federal inaction to prevent all forms of discrimination by government entities and private entities that receive government taxes and subsidies. Finally, the clauses can prohibit state and federal inaction when a citizen or a private business's discriminatory practices result in physical harm to another citizen.

The above four-prong solution I propose is comprehensive. For instance, it would correct the error in *Deshaney v. Winnebago* (1989), where the court failed to hold state social services accountable for its inaction to protect a four-year-old boy from abuse that resulted in his death. The principle to arise from Deshaney is that state officials have no-duty to protect citizens, and it was upheld in *Castle Rock v. Gonzales* when the police refused to enforce a restraining order leading to the death of three children. The whole reason for government agencies such as child protective services and the police is to secure the fundamental right for citizens to have protection and security from harm. Providing protection and security is the primary responsibility of the government. Barnett and Bernick suggest that Deshaney and Gonzales were decided incorrectly to protect government institutions from expensive liability and litigation. They propose the solution to the problem is to create a liability protection fund that is subsidized by government officials. I agree and believe their plan should include limiting litigation costs through tort reform to make injurious claims reasonable. If claims are reasonable, then the court would not have to protect government institutions for not doing their job. [128]

The Scholarly Theories [129]

Defining a specific list of privilege and immunities or fundamental rights was the biggest shortcoming of the drafters of the Fourteenth Amendment, courts, Congress, and scholars. Why is it so difficult to come to a consensus? First, the definition or criteria for fundamental rights is vague. I address this shortcoming in the preceding chapter. Second, most lists are a subset of natural, civil, political, economic, personal, social, civil, enumerated, and unenumerated rights. To overcome this shortcoming, I do not distinguish between natural, political, economic, personal, social, civil, enumerated, and unenumerated rights. Finally, in some circles, there is an incorrect distinction between national and state citizenship.

There are at least six scholarly theories with some credence, and for the most part, they are all a subset of my definition of privileges and immunities or fundamental rights. The theory proposed by Barnett and Bernick is highlighted in this text because it is the closest to my theory. That said, their list of privileges and immunities includes few political and economic rights, and it would also exclude enumerated rights that are not personal. That means their theory would exclude economic rights such as the right to profit or protection from welfare taxes, and exclude political rights, such as the right to vote, sit on a jury, and hold public office. However, Barnett and Bernick emphasize that once political rights become civil rights they can be elevated to privileges and immunities such as the right to vote via the Nineteenth Amendment. Their theory may also exclude enumerated rights such as the establishment of religions and protection from bills of attainder or ex post facto laws. Remember, Barnett and Bernick incorrectly label many enumerated justice rights as procedural actions such as trial by jury, protection from bills of attainder or ex post facto laws, or protection from excessive fines and punishment.

Other even less inclusive theories consist of the Slaughter-House guideline theory that privilege and immunities are restricted to those federal government protections outlined by Justice Miller's decision. For example, Miller's decision distinguishes between national and state citizenship and excludes enumerated rights. The enumerated theory has two schools of thought. First, privileges and immunities include those rights found in the Bill of Rights, and second, privileges and immunities include those rights uncovered in the Bill of Rights and in the Constitution. The equality theory only includes those privileges and immunities found in the Civil

Rights Act of 1866. The equality theory restricts the number of rights by labeling potential rights as mere benefits. The static theory states that privileges and immunities only include those rights that were identified prior to the passage of the Fourteenth Amendment in 1868. Those rights uncovered after 1868 are excluded from privilege and immunity status. The static theory would inexplicably exclude the right to vote as being a fundamental right. The variable theory suggests that privileges and immunities not only have a hierarchical standing, but rights can also be added or subtracted. For instance, the right to work established by the courts in the dissent of the *Slaughter-House Cases* and in future cases such as *Lochner v. New York* would not be protected because it was, in my opinion, erroneously rescinded in cases such as *West Coast Hotel v. Parrish.* Thus, this theory erroneously argues that there is no longer a right to work a lawful profession protected as a privilege and immunity. Just because a majority eliminates a right does not necessarily mean their decision was correct. United States history is plagued with majoritarian failures.

My theory is different from the previously mentioned theories in many regards. First, it establishes its floor of rights as those rights that can be discerned in the Bible that have been federally enshrined in historical documents. Second, it is much more inclusive and comprehensive. Law scholars believe natural rights or those God-given rights are limited to life, liberty, pursuit of happiness, safety, and property or those rights defined as unalienable rights by natural law theorists and the Founders. That said, natural law philosophers and the Founders' definition of natural and inalienable rights was broad. Thus, natural rights include social, political, personal, economic, and civil rights. For example, the natural law definition of property includes both tangible property and the personal liberty to pursue other fundamental rights. In other words, anyone losing property rights lose the liberty to pursue all fundamental rights. Furthermore, unlike Barnett and Bernick, I maintain that the Founders meant for liberty to have a broad meaning which is addressed in Chapter 6. Third, my theory does not define national and state citizenship differently, nor does it define enumerated or unenumerated rights any differently. Finally, and most importantly, my theory suggests that privileges and immunities must follow the laws of science. For instance, privileges and immunities are symmetrical and equal and therefore, there is no hierarchical standing of privileges and immunities. Furthermore, although new rights can be uncovered, rights cannot be improved, altered, or abolished. My theory is the only theory to go beyond constitutional law to include the Bible and the laws of science and human nature for construction. Following the laws of human nature, for instance, would prohibit the inclusion of some enumerated rights in my theory while discarding others since they are all equal.

Therefore, it is safe to assume, law scholars would dispute many of the fundamental rights identified and the criteria used to identify a fundamental right outlined in the prior sections. For example, it can be disputed political rights did not exist until governments instituted them which would exclude them from being a fundamental right since they did not come from God. On the contrary, the right to vote, sit on jury, hold public office, and due process rights were the basis to form a government. Therefore, political rights existed before the formation of any government and the only reason governments were formed was to enshrine and protect political rights. The Bible clearly identifies political rights came from God through Moses in the Old Testament. Thus, I view political and natural rights to be one in the same. It was already demonstrated in the last chapter, that the entire Bill of Rights and the civil laws of society originate from the Bible including voting, due process rights, and jury rights. Famous English jurist Sir William Blackstone also considers natural or civil rights to be synonymous with political rights. [130]

A Reasonable Infringement of Fundamental Rights

Law scholars distinguish between political and natural rights because the Privileges and Immunities Clause of the Fourteenth Amendment protects *citizens,* whereas the Due Process and Equal Protection clauses protect *persons*. Thus, the Due Process and Equal Protection clauses do not protect political rights, whereas the Privileges and Immunities clause does protect political rights. For example, citizens can vote, run for Congress, and sit on juries whereas non-citizens are denied those privileges. [131] Denying non-citizen aliens the right to vote or sit on a jury is not because they are not important or valued in society, it is for national security reasons. Political rights require citizenship so the political process is not influenced by an influx of aliens wishing to change the outcome of elections for the benefit of a foreign country. Non-citizen aliens need to assimilate to United States customs, understand English, and gain knowledge of the United States law system to gain citizenship and political rights. Citizenship has its privileges. The information in this book deals primarily with the rights of citizens of the United States.

According to Locke, there are many reasonable explanations as to why the fundamental rights of some, such as for criminals, may be denied in civil society. [132] Fundamental rights may be abridged if there is a compelling reason such as an emergency to protect the safety of other citizens. The government should use the least evasive method to achieve its objective to protect citizens when abridging rights. During the Covid-19 pandemic, the right to travel, work, go to church, enjoy recreational activities, and meet friends was curtailed to protect the safety of the entire population. Government overreach happens when emergency powers turn permanent or last longer than is necessary. Rights are abridged for other reasons, such as for prisoners, non-citizen aliens (discussed in the prior paragraph), or children. Anyone who is convicted of violating the fundamental rights of others will have their rights mitigated, such as facing imprisonment. Many rights of children are mitigated until they reach maturity, which is usually 18 to 21 years of age. For example, people must be 18 or 21 years old to marry, vote, or to have the right to choose to smoke or drink. In fact, rights are restricted based on state citizenship. For instance, I cannot vote in a state where I do not reside.

Conflicting Rights [133]

The rule of right is a natural law principle coined by John Locke that suggests politicians should use wisdom and commonsense to resolve conflicts between fundamental rights. The objective of the rule of right is for the government to use the least evasive method to achieve its constitutional objective. The Bible refers to the rule of right as knowledge, understanding, and wisdom. Proverbs 24:3–4 states, "By wisdom a house is built, and by understanding it is established; and by knowledge the rooms are filled with all the precious and pleasant riches." Knowledge is understanding the facts, and wisdom is understanding what conclusion to draw from the facts. Knowledge is useless without understanding and wisdom. As more facts are uncovered, over time, our wisdom and common sense can evolve about what conclusions to draw. [134] [135] The rule of right is a common-sense approach to protect the fundamental rights of each American citizen equally regardless of race, sexual orientation, ethnicity, gender, religion, socio-economic status, and intellect.

The law would refer to the rule of right as (1) determining the original meaning or intent of the law (knowledge) and (2) construction or drawing conclusions from the original meaning of the law (wisdom) to resolve controversies in the spirit of its original meaning. For example, the Fourth Amendment provides for protection from illegal warrantless searches. Construction would be determining that using thermal imaging to identify a marijuana farm inside a residence or tracking the GPS location of a cell phone without a warrant to solve a crime would defeat the letter and spirit of the Search and Seizure Clause. Construction without considering the original meaning of the law is an incorrect method used by lawyers and judges who interject bias, opinion, and conjecture into the Constitution's meaning. Construction of the law by applying the original meaning of constitutional text is referred to as originalism and construction of the law with no regard to the original meaning of the Constitution is called the living constitution. A living constitution is one that evolves and changes to keep up advancements in society. That said, an evolving Constitution knows no boundary and provides judges with an opportunity to inject bias and opinion into decisions. [136] [137]

Americans have a wealth of knowledge and truths at their fingertips. Yet most of us are ignorant, prejudiced, biased, opinionated, presumptive, and short-sighted. Lack of knowledge exists because we first rely on knowledge and information from one source that fits our specific narratives. Second, we use emotion and passion instead of reason to draw conclusions (wisdom) from knowledge (facts and truths). Third, our knowledge, understanding, and wisdom lack diversity from free speech and open debate. [138]

Natural Law

Natural law, according to C.S. Lewis in *Mere Christianity,* is the same as moral principles or the law of right and wrong or the law of human nature. I refer to moral principles and natural law as God's law. For example, in Exodus 34:7, God refers to forgiving those who violate "His Law." Moreover, in Leviticus 18:4, God said, "You are to perform My judgments and keep My statutes, to live according to them, I am the LORD your God."

The Declaration of Independence reads in part: [139]

> When in the course of human events, it becomes necessary for one people to dissolve the political bands which have connected them with another, and to assume among the powers of the Earth, the separate and equal station to which the *Laws of Nature* and of Nature's God entitle them, a decent respect to the opinions of mankind requires that they should declare the causes which impel them to the separation.
>
> We hold these truths to be self-evident, that all men are created equal, that they are endowed by their Creator with certain unalienable Rights, that among these are Life, Liberty, and the pursuit of Happiness.
>
> That to secure these rights, Governments are instituted among Men, deriving their just powers from the *consent of the governed*—That whenever any Form of Government becomes destructive of these ends, it is the Right of the People to alter or to abolish it, and to institute new Government, laying its foundation on such principles and organizing its powers in such form, as to them shall seem most likely to affect their Safety and Happiness.

Jefferson copied the above principles directly from John Locke's natural law philosophies. There are several things of importance to point out in the above quote:

- Note the reference to the laws of nature I italicized. William Blackstone, a famous English jurist, wrote there is a difference between natural law and the laws of nature. The laws of nature are written by God in the Bible, whereas natural law is how people may interpret the laws of nature. Specifically, natural law is how people interpret and incorporate God's law into the statutory law. Since people are imperfect, they could incorrectly construe the laws of nature into the nature law. Despite the fallibility of people, the terms are used interchangeably in this text because Thomas Jefferson goes on to explain in the above quote from the Declaration of Independence, that the laws of nature or our inalienable rights are self-evident. [140]
- The Declaration of Independence and Constitution are forever linked. The Declaration of Independence is a social contract between the government and the people (God refers to social contracts as covenants in the Bible), whereas the Constitution outlines the framework from which the government can write the statutory law. The two documents are assumed to be mutually exclusive, but does one exist without the other? No, the Declaration of Independence is the foundation for the United States constitutional republic to protect "life, liberty and the pursuit of happiness." If the United States declared its independence without writing the Declaration of Independence, it is highly debatable if the Constitution would share any resemblance to the current document.

- Since government legitimacy hinges on the consent of the governed (italicized in the Declaration of Independence quote above), we need to determine what is meant by consent. A society is defined by a social contract between a government with limited constitutional powers and those who consent to be governed. How people consent to a social contract is sometimes difficult to conceptualize. Our Founders signed the Declaration of Independence and Constitution, but no future generations signed on to any of these documents. So how do Americans consent to be governed by the social contract that is written in the Declaration of Independence and the statutory laws that are written from within the framework of the Constitution? Natural law philosopher, John Locke, proposes that there is tacit or implied consent to be governed. People who own property or use government resources such as the Post Office, roads, and expect protection from the police, fire department, and military tacitly consent to be governed by the laws of that society. [141] The act of voting for government officials is also perceived as tacit consent. Military personnel, immigrants who become citizens, lawyers, and other public officials who take an oath to uphold the Constitution consent to be governed.

Statutory Law [142] [143]

The statutory law is the written law of society enacted by legislators within the framework of constitutional guidelines. The statutory law may be interpreted from the Bible, English law, or prior precedent.

Governments and the statutory law are essential because man is sinful and fallible and therefore, does not always follow God's moral principles and develop Godly virtues. Natural law philosopher, John Locke, explains that people are willing to give up some of their fundamental rights to join society and consent to be governed for several reasons. First, the statutory law is to act as both a deterrent and protection from sinners who may violate the rights of their fellow citizens. Second, the statutory law attempts to garner justice and retribution for those citizens whose rights have been violated. Third, the statutory law seeks punishment for those who violate the rights of others in society. Finally, the statutory law is to be impartial and applied to every citizen *equally* regardless of their demographic makeup, economic status, or ideological belief system. Thus, safety and protection are the primary reasons why people decide to move from a state of nature and consent to live in a society governed by a set of laws. [144]

Although statutory law punishment for violating any of the Ten Commandments is widely varied, each law is on equal footing. Some may argue from Mark 12:28–34 that Jesus claims the two commandments to love God and thy neighbor are the most important commandments. That is true, but what Jesus was saying is that if we follow those two commandments, then it is nearly impossible to break the other commandments. For instance, if you love God, you will not use his name in vain, and if you love your neighbor, then you will not steal from them, murder them, or covet their belongings.

Locke explains that there are limits to what the civil laws of society can protect. For instance, civil laws do not protect people who do harm to their own property. People have every right to neglect oneself by being unhealthy, poor, and uneducated. In Locke's exact words, laws "do not guard them against the negligence" they may inflict on themselves. [145] In our present-day society, most instances of self-destructive behavior are not against the law, and in fact, some people may pursue happiness through drugs, alcohol, pornography, unhealthy foods, smoking, and other addictions. Laws protecting people from self-destructive behavior fail common sense, wisdom, and the rule of right because everyone is a sinner and guilty of self-destructive behavior. Today, the law still prosecutes some self-destructive actions such as prostitution or drug possession.

There are several differences between moral principles and our present-day criminal code or the statutory law. First, moral principles are much more stringent than our modern-day criminal code. Similarly, there is a difference between ethical and legal behavior. If something is unethical, it is not morally acceptable, but the reverse is not necessarily true. Not all tolerable behavior is morally acceptable. People may tolerate bad manners, but it is not morally acceptable. [146] Second, moral principles primarily police oneself, whereas the modern criminal code primarily protects everyone collectively from harm or having their rights violated by other people in society. Hence, it is possible to break God's law and not violate the criminal code. That said, it may not be a crime to boast about oneself, have bad manners, and be selfish, but the behavior is divisive and polarizing. That is why following God's moral principles are so important. If we follow them, then we live in a society with low crime. Furthermore, we live in a well-mannered society that is less polarized and politically charged. Thus, moral principles promote civility, unity, and tranquility by treating each other with dignity and respect. A nation divided and polarized can only happen if most of its citizens are neglecting God's moral principles.

In Galatians 2:21, Paul writes, "I do not nullify the grace of God, for if righteousness comes through the Law, then Christ died needlessly." Furthermore, in Galatians 3:11, "The righteous one will live by faith." Moreover, in Philippians 3:9, "not having a righteousness of my own derived from the law, but that which is through faith in Christ, the righteousness which comes from God on the basis of faith." Finally, in Galatians 3:24, "Therefore the Law has become our guardian to lead us to Christ, so that we may be justified by faith." Living a righteous life comes from following faith (moral principles) and not just the criminal law.

The Higher and Maximum Standard

In the preceding section it was pointed out that following moral principles are more difficult than following the statutory law and therefore, moral principles have been coined the higher maximum standard. The best evidence to support the existence of God is the maximum standard that God's laws and His moral principles define. Not only are these laws universally defined throughout the many cultures of the world, but they were defined at a time when these cultures could not communicate with each other. Since no one can measure up to

God's maximum standard (other than Jesus), it seems preposterous to assume anyone other than God could have defined these moral principles and commandments. No ordinary person would define principles that they could never achieve or live up to, right? Man is too flawed, stubborn, selfish, irrational, and opinionated to have created moral principles or the laws of human nature. In fact, our national and global polarization suggests we are more apt to violate God's moral principles than follow them.

Part III: The Progressive Coup d'état to Mitigate and Remove Fundamental Rights [147]

Chapter 6: The Regression of Constitutional Principles [148]

How is it possible that the United States can be so dramatically transformed in two hundred years without radically altering the Constitution? I argue that the progressive movement has been a non-violent coup d'état. Most scholars suggest that progressivism began in the 1890s, but it started much sooner in the George Washington administration when federalism and anti-federalism views began to take hold over the national bank issue. [149] In this chapter, I explain the damaging evolution of constitutional principles that the Founders enshrined in the Constitution.

The next three chapters describe how the progressive coup d'état regresses constitutional principles, eliminates natural law, and removes fundamental rights. However, why the government, individuals, and organizations mitigate fundamental rights, natural law, and constitutional principles is open to debate. I theorize it serves two purposes. First, it achieves the objective of funneling more power from the common man to influential organizations and individuals as well as the federal government. Second, if fundamental rights are truly God-given, then the objective of any government agency, individual, or organization wanting to rewrite the history of the United States as a secular nation must include downplaying the God-given fundamental rights of Americans.

Constitutional Republic versus a Democracy

A democracy was referred to by American Founders as "mob rule" or "mobocracy." John Adams would declare, "Remember, democracy never lasts long. It soon wastes, exhausts, and murders itself. There never was a democracy yet that did not commit suicide." A republic is defined as a nation governed by laws, not people. Conversely, a democracy is a nation governed by people and what the majority dictates. A democracy is defined similarly in Judges 17:6 when it suggests "everyone did what is right in his own eyes." Everyone includes politicians who seek power and control instead of protecting the fundamental rights of all their constituents equally. [150]

James Madison writes in Federalist Paper 10 that the Founders were afraid majority factions would rule supreme over minority factions. Thus, the whole purpose of the Constitution and establishing a republic, as Madison put it, was to curb the power of majority factions and to "restrain some of the worst impulses of man." [151] Similarly, many philosophers, such as Aristotle, point out that democracies are far from being ideal because they promote selfish motives. According to Aristotle, a democracy pits the selfish rich against the selfish poor, providing both groups of people with motive and incentive to be unjust. [152]

State governments instituted democracies following American Independence. Most state constitutions allowed for a governor, a state supreme court, and two houses of legislators with the lower house elected by the people. Since the definition of a democracy was for the people to consent to be governed, almost all power in state governments resided in the lower house which was composed of elected representatives. The upper house of the legislature, governor, and supreme court almost had no power in state governments.

Madison feared state democracies would violate the rights of citizens because too much power resided in one house of government. Hence, he wanted the federal government to have the power to void unconstitutional state laws, but that power was denied. However, in *Marbury v. Madison,* decided in 1803, Chief Justice John Marshall ruled the Supreme Court had the right to judicial review. Hence, the Supreme Court granted itself the power to nullify state laws if they were unconstitutional. Later, the passage of the Fourteenth Amendment also provided the federal government with the authority to review and overturn state legislation that did uphold the fundamental rights of citizens. [153] Unfortunately, judicial review and the Fourteenth Amendment did not always prevent democratic majorities from denying minority groups of its rights: Slavery, imprisonment of socialists, internment of Asian Americans, segregation, eugenics, sterilization, and denying territories, such as Guam and Puerto Rico, the same rights as residents in the homeland are a few egregious examples.

A constitutional republic is, in many respects, like a democracy. The primary difference is a constitutional republic has built in protections to prevent majorities from imposing their will on minority factions. Those protections include checks and balances such as the separation of powers between the branches of the federal government (legislative, judicial, and executive) and between the federal and state governments (federalism). The Founders' objective was to prevent tyranny by limiting the power that any one branch of government may possess.

Many believe the Bible supports socialism over democratic or republican forms of government. Socialist proponents point to Acts 2:44 which suggests the people were sharing their belongings, "And all the believers were together and had all things in common" or Acts 4:32–33 when the people "claimed that anything belonging to him was his own, but all things were common property." However, Acts 5:1–4 illustrate what happens in a socialist state when Ananias "sold a piece of property, and kept back some of the proceeds for himself". Therefore, the Bible teaches us a socialist society is one that promotes deceit, greed, and laziness; instead, the Bible promotes individualism over community, such as in 2 Thessalonians 3:10, "If anyone is not willing to work, then he is not to eat, either." In fact, these were John Smith's words to his congregation at the first American settlement, Jamestown, established in 1607. With death, starvation, and disease rampant among the new colony, Smith emphasized the only way to persevere was through a strong work ethic and that no more laziness and idleness would be tolerated. America and capitalism were founded on 2 Thessalonians 3:10. Smith understood that without a change in direction, the colony would have perished. [154] Compare the simple but brilliant principle posed in 2 Thessalonians 3:10 to the current welfare policies that plague the United States. For example, student loan forgiveness rewards idleness and laziness at the expense of hard-working citizens. Most Americans are generous and willing to help their neighbors who are sick, disabled, or those who want to help themselves. The problem with the American welfare system is that citizens are compelled to help anyone including those who abuse the system or are lazy.

The most influential colonial document in support of the Revolutionary War and a republic form of government was Thomas Paine's book *Common Sense*. Although Paine was probably the least religious of the Founders, one quarter of the book is dedicated to the significance of the verses that make up 1 Samuel 8. The story in 1 Samuel 8 explains that the people of Israel insisted they should be governed by a king instead of by judges. Paine successfully argues to his fellow American citizens that God's response to the Israelites demand for a king demonstrates how much He detested kings and monarchies. [155]

During the pre- and post-Revolutionary War period there was much discussion over the type of constitution to ratify. The problem with this period that continues to persist and plague America today is that a republic and democracy are incorrectly thought to be one of the same. To be sure, early American Puritan democracies lasted as long as the consenting public allowed that trust. Democracies were not permanent fixtures because they were not immune to tyranny. The people had the power to dissolve democracies that became corrupt. A republic tries to resolve this issue or temptation of government to become corrupt by incorporating checks and balances. Governments not being permanent fixtures was important because the Puritans soon realized dissolving a sinister government was not always easy to accomplish since those in control do not like to relinquish their power. Since a republic is defined as a nation of laws and not of people, a republic attempts to eliminate fallible, power hungry, and corrupt politicians from the equation of government. The Founders went far out of their way to remove as many democratic principles as possible from the Constitution. Checks and balances to prevent corruption and tyranny included equal state representation in the Senate, federalism, separation of powers, the electoral college, and requiring supermajorities to pass certain legislation and confirm important cabinet posts.

In sum, over the past 230 years checks and balances have been gradually stripped away from the Constitution. Now the United States more closely resembles a true democracy. While a republic protects the fundamental rights of everyone equally, a democracy only protects the ideology of the majority. Thus, fundamental rights are often abridged in democracies and many of these government indiscretions are highlighted in the Chapter 8. [156] [157]

Liberty versus Freedom and Fundamental Rights

What is the difference between liberty and freedom? Why do Americans have the "right to life, liberty, and happiness" and not life, freedom, and happiness? Liberty is defined as the capacity for citizens to exercise their fundamental rights protected by non-arbitrary laws from a government with limited power that is bound and controlled by a constitution. Freedom is a democracy principle. More specifically, the freedom for citizens to practice certain fundamental rights can be revoked by a majority or those in political power. Liberty is a republican principle because it is an unalienable right from our creator that protects all legal actions of citizens to pursue fundamental rights which cannot be taken away by a government or a majority. The more liberty citizens possess then the more freedom they have to pursue fundamental rights. Thus, fundamental rights can encompass hundreds of legal actions that citizens have the liberty to pursue each day and in their lifetimes. When the United States government denies or limits fundamental rights, they are in direct violation of the Constitution which protects liberty above freedom. [158]

Why is the federal government failing to protect liberty and fundamental rights? This may be best explained by three Bible verses. First, Exodus 18:21 explains the desired qualities of elected officials. Exodus 18:21 states the populous must "select out of all the people able men who fear God, men of truth, those who hate dishonest gain; and you shall place these over them as leaders of thousands, of hundreds, of fifties, and of tens." Second, Deuteronomy 1:13 similarly suggests citizens should "Obtain for yourselves men who are wise, discerning, and informed from your tribes, and I will appoint them as your heads." Minister, Thomas Hooker, would emphasize the above verses to his Connecticut congregation very early in American history (1638). For this reason, Hooker is incorrectly identified in history books as the father of American democracy, but instead, as we have learned, he should be known as the father of the American constitutional republic. Finally, Judges 9:8–15 explains that good political candidates do not want to be part of any corrupt and broken political system. Thus, we are stuck with uncivil, corrupt, and power-hungry politicians who are intent on destroying American constitutional protections and limiting fundamental rights for personal gain. Unfortunately, it is difficult to name one current politician in Washington who upholds liberty and the Constitution and defends the fundamental rights of everyone equally. [159] [160]

Standard of Liberty

Since liberty is often considered a secular political term, it is widely believed it has no biblical connotation. The school of thought that liberty being a secular term is erroneous. In the Book of Mormon Alma 46:12 Captain Moroni defines the title (standard) of Liberty to his soldiers that they should fight "In memory of our God, our religion, and liberty, and our peace, our wives, and our children." The above Mormon verse sounds very similar to Nehemiah 4:14, "Do not be afraid of them. Remember the Lord, great and awesome, and fight for your brethren, your sons, your daughters, your wife, and your houses." Furthermore, there are three important Bible passages which prove unequivocally that liberty is also spiritual. First, Psalms 119:45 of the Bible reads, "And I will walk at liberty, for I seek Your precepts." Second, Galatians 5:1 tells us, "It was for freedom that Christ set us free." Finally, Leviticus 25:10 which inspired the inscription placed on the Liberty Bell declares, "Proclaim liberty throughout all the land to all its inhabitants." [161]

There is a fine line between spiritual, political, and personal liberty. They are basically one in the same, one cannot exist without the other. The political problems that confound the United States today can only be resolved through a renewed spiritual liberty. The above scripture verses would resonate in all realms of American culture. Founding father John Witherspoon would write, "God grant that in America, true religion and civil liberty may be inseparable." Founding era Pastor Jonas Clark taught his congregation about personal, civil, and religious liberties all within the same sermon. Pastor Israel Evans would refer to the standard of liberty in a sermon in New York following the American victory in the Revolutionary War. In that sermon, Evans would correctly prognosticate the greatness that will bestow the newly formed United States in achieving a new standard of liberty. [162]

Politics and war were a necessity to secure personal and spiritual liberty. Nehemiah 4:14 would reverberate with political and spiritual leaders alike. In a George Washington address to Canadians on September 14, 1775, he stated, "We have taken up Arms in defense of our Liberty, our Property; our Wives and our Children. We are determined to preserve them or die." Tennessee pastor Samuel Doak, would rally nearby congregations to fight the British in North Carolina, "Go forth then in the strength of your manhood to the aid of your brethren, the defense of your liberty, and the protection of your homes." Patrick Henry, in one of the greatest speeches ever told at a Virginia congregation said, "Is life so dear, or peace so sweet, as to be purchased at the price of chains and slavery? Forbid it Almighty God, I know not what course others may take, but as for me, give me liberty or give me death." Founding era Pastor Jonathan Parsons told his congregation, "If it should be so that our natural and constitutional liberties cannot be recovered or maintained without repelling force with force, who could hesitate for a moment about the propriety of taking up arms!" Similarly, in Jeremiah 6:14 the profit challenges Israelites to fight for their liberty, "They have healed the brokenness of my people superficially, saying, 'Peace, peace,' but there is no peace." Jeremiah understands that peace comes at a price, it is not free, it must be earned and sometimes that means through conflict. [163] What the above quotes from Washington, Doak, Henry, Parsons, and the profit Jeremiah reveal is that both spiritual and personal liberty are connected and to maximize personal and spiritual liberty, political liberty needs to play a role in achieving that objective.

The Structure of Government

Natural law philosophers such as John Locke, Charles de Montesquieu, and Thomas Aquinas provided the framework or model for the United States government that the Founders enshrined in the Constitution. The Constitution emphasized Locke's principles for government and Aquinas' and Montesquieu's structure for government.

Locke's theories were vague and lacked wisdom when it came to the structure of government. The primary feature of a Locke government was that the people should elect a legislative branch of government and it should garner the most power. [164] Locke's suggestion of placing most government power in a duly elected legislature was a mistake. Empowering legislatures, elected by the people, is a democratic principle with no checks and balances to prevent legislators from going rogue. Thus, Locke's structure of government principles falls short of emphasizing protective checks and balances to reign in government power. Although Locke suggests that governments can agree to supermajorities to pass legislation, he errs because he does not make it a requirement of the government. Supermajorities would limit the power of the legislative branch because it forces political parties to work together to pass legislation. [165]

While Locke had a basic understanding of the separation of powers to mitigate government power, government institutions and their structure were secondary to Locke because his principles focused on consent, property, and the laws of nature. Consequently, so long as people consent to be governed by a body with limited powers, then, according to Locke, the structure of the government is not as important. [166]

Checks and Balances

The Founders placed many checks and balance protections in the Constitution such as equal state representation in the Senate regardless of population. Equal Senate representation protects the political interests of smaller states from being drowned out by larger states. It also explains why a Presidential candidate who garners the most votes may lose the Electoral College. Hence, some would argue that the Electoral College should be abolished. However, there are sound republic principles and checks and balances that support the Electoral College. First, it increases the chances that the winner of the Presidential election will win most of the states. The Electoral College prevents a few heavily populated states from imposing their will on the many less populated states. Second, the Electoral College not only protects the rights of smaller states, but it ensures that every person's vote has more impact. My vote counts more when it decides the outcome of a state with 5 million people than when my vote is deciding the outcome of a national election with over 150 million voters. My voting power is essentially reduced by a magnitude of 30! Finally, it is also reasonable to assume election fraud can be better prevented and monitored locally than nationally. Thus, the Electoral College increases personal rights by increasing the impact of a person's vote, protects the integrity of elections, and balances the sovereign interests between large and small states.

The role of juries is an overlooked example of a check and balance marginalized in modern America. In early American history, juries had the power to determine if a law was reasonable and they were therefore, also privy to all the information regarding a case. That is no longer the situation. Judges dictate to juries what information they need and are instructed they must apply the case to the law as it is written. For instance, juries in *Nebbia v. New York* could not exonerate the grocer who sold a quart of milk for under nine cents (discussed in more detail in Chapter 7). Even if the jury viewed the law as an obvious infringement on the grocer's right to contract or to work, they had to apply the case to the misguided law. Sovereignty has been wrestled away from "We the people" at the expense of more judiciary and legislative power. A vital check and balance to prevent the judicial and legislative branches from an obvious overreach of power has been rescinded. [167]

Separation of Powers

The principle for the separation of powers between the executive, legislative, and judicial branches of government originated in Isaiah 33:22 "For the Lord is our judge, the Lord is our Lawgiver, the Lord is our

King." Since God is perfect, He can handle all the duties of the executive, legislative, and judicial branches, but since humans are fallible and partial to corruption these functions must be separated. The Bible was a constant reminder to the Founders about the imperfections of humanity, such as in Jeremiah 17:9, when the profit Jeremiah warns that man cannot be entrusted with power because "The heart is more deceitful than all else and is desperately sick; who can understand it?" Moreover, philosophers, such as Charles de Montesquieu, warned the Founders about the dangers of when the branches of government are not separated or entrusting government power in a single person. Montesquieu said, "When the legislative and executive powers are united in the same person .... there can be no liberty." Montesquieu added that, "there is no liberty if the power of judging is not separated from the legislative and executive powers." Similarly, Thomas Aquinas thought the best form of government would be to take the benefits found in the three primary forms of government (separation of powers): Monarchy, aristocracy, and democracy. The monarchy represents the president or executive, the aristocracy represents the Senate, and the democracy embodies the House of Representatives. [168]

In 2021, Democrats considered packing the Supreme Court so their party could control all three branches of government. Of course, the purpose of such a stunt is to avert the separation of powers in the Constitution. Finding ways to circumvent the Constitution has become a curse and has infected most affiliated Republicans and Democrats in this great country. Packing the Court may sound great to liberals, but once conservatives are in power, then they, too, will add more conservatives to the Supreme Court to change the balance of the Court in their favor. Where does it end? Using an executive order is another tool the President uses to circumvent separation of powers to bypass Congress. For instance, all appropriation legislation must originate in Congress, but Biden signed an executive order for student loan forgiveness that will cost the federal government 400 billion dollars. Hopefully, the Supreme Court will void this stunt.

The 2023 election process for Speaker of the House was very intriguing. Although I believe that the twenty Republicans stalling the effort did not have a united voice and some of their motivations may have been disingenuous, the principle of trying to wrestle away power from a few leaders has merits. The Founders did not want a select few in the House to hold all the power. Separation of powers is also important not just *between* the branches of government but *within* the branches of government to prevent tyranny. There are 435 House members, and the power should not be concentrated in a few leaders and a select few who head important committees. The Founders' intention was clear, they disliked power and therefore, they felt power should be shared by as many people as possible to take the corrupt tendencies of humans out of the equation of government. [169] The NY Post reports that the agreement between the twenty Republicans and speaker elect Kevin McCarthy include a guarantee to vote on a balanced budget amendment and term limits for Congress. New rules concessions include making legislation focus on one issue instead of multiple issues loaded with pet projects and thousands of pages of "pork," a 72-hour window to read the bill before a vote, an inflation score on appropriations, and a promise to refuse another debt ceiling hike. [170] These all make sense and are solid republic principles.

Federalism

The Constitution embodies a unique feature of government structure called federalism or shared power between the state and federal governments. A common error made by most Americans is to refer to federalism as states' rights. States have limited powers that are restricted by the constitution of each state. Only people have rights. Thus, the correct nomenclature would be to refer to federalism as states' powers. The Tenth Amendment provides that all grants of power not assigned to the federal government in the Constitution fall to the states. Unfortunately, a closer look at the present scope, power, and objectives of the federal government clearly demonstrates that they control much more than the grants of power permitted by the Constitution. Discussed in more detail in Chapter 7, the federal government power grab to control, for example, education and agriculture (Department of Education and Agriculture) is a good example of increased federal power. Both education and agriculture were important issues at the time of the drafting of the Constitution, but the Founders saw no need to provide the federal government any control over these important aspects of American society and culture. Control over education and agriculture should be in the hands of local and state governments. Another example discussed in more detail in Chapter 7 is how the federal government has expanded its authority to fight crime and inject itself into local police matters by expanding the Interstate Commerce Clause. These are just a few of the many far-reaching policies of the federal government.

As the progressive movement has gradually eroded many constitutional protections, more power funnels to the federal government at the expense of the state governments and the people. For example, the Sixteenth Amendment to legalize an income tax and the Seventeenth Amendment to allow for senators to be elected by the citizens of each state. Both amendments provide the federal government with more coercive powers over each state. For instance, for states to recoup federal taxes paid by their constituents, they are coerced to go along with laws they do not agree with. A state may not agree with welfare legislation, but state officials understand that their citizens' taxes will fund the welfare agenda even if they do not want to be part of the program. Henceforth, states may feel compelled to sign on to the legislation to prevent tax dollars from their state being funneled to other states to support the federal welfare initiative. Similarly, eliminating senator appointments from state legislators and empowering that trust with the people made it more difficult for states to maintain federalism. In the above welfare example, a senator appointed by state legislators would represent the state by opposing the welfare legislation, whereas a senator appointed by the people may be inclined to support the welfare legislation to buy votes.

Sovereignty

Sovereignty is defined as "the notion that there must reside somewhere in every political unit a single, undivided, final power, higher in legal authority than any other power, subject to no law, a law unto itself." During the colonial struggle for independence from England, loyalists reasoned that since parliament was sovereign in the English political system, the colonies had to obey their laws including to pay their taxes. [171] Parliamentary sovereignty became a tough argument for colonists to contest. After all, in the English governmental system since 1689, there was no higher power than parliament. [172]

To overcome the conundrum of parliamentary sovereignty colonists argued that the above definition of sovereignty was not entirely correct, and sovereignty can be shared between political institutions and the people. Sovereignty sharing is a republican principle that ensures the fundamental rights of the people were maintained. For example, in the American Constitution, federal government sovereignty is shared between the three branches of government. Additionally, federal government sovereignty is shared with the state governments (federalism). And a fact that is often ignored, federal and state sovereignty is shared with "We the people."

Over the years, there is no question that the federal government has garnered much more power than state governments and the people, but that is not how this great country was founded. In fact, it was easy to surmise at the founding that the people had the most power (sovereignty) followed by the states and federal government in that order. In the Supreme Court case *Chisholm v. Georgia* (1795), Chief Justice John Jay said sovereignty rested entirely with the people, not the government. Sovereignty residing with the people makes sense for several reasons. First, grants of federal government power are confined to the 4,500 words of the Constitution while the state governments control all power not designated to the federal government (Tenth Amendment). That said, state government power is also confined to the individual state constitutions. And a point that is often forgotten, state and federal constitutions are a prohibition against the governments, not the people. Second, the governments confer no rights, only restricted powers. Finally, both state and federal governments were formed for the sole purpose of protecting the fundamental rights of all citizens, and any law that violates any fundamental rights should be nullified. It is easy to conclude, "We the people" are the most sovereign entity in the United States government system.

The constitutional sovereignty sharing model has led to a 230-year power struggle in American history. The power struggle between the branches of government and between nationalism and states' powers has slowly eroded the safeguards to protect the sovereignty of the people and their fundamental rights. Nevertheless, the ongoing struggle for power does suggest the Founding Fathers' task to prevent too much power or sovereignty to any one entity has had some degree of success.

Erasing History

Why is history important? Patrick Henry said, "I know of no way of judging the future but by the past." Thomas Jefferson pronounced that understanding history makes the people "judges of the actions and design of men …. to know ambition under every disguise it may assume; and knowing it, to defeat its views." [173]

Similarly, the Bible teaches the importance of history:

> Please inquire of past generations, and consider the things searched out by their fathers. For we are only of yesterday and know nothing, because our days on Earth are as a shadow. Will they not teach you and tell you, and bring forth words from their minds? (Job 8:8–10) Remember the days of old, consider the years of all generations. Ask your father and he will inform you, your elders, and they will tell you. (Deuteronomy 32:7)

Erasing history and failing to learn the lessons of the past is dangerous because history can repeat itself. Any attempt, for example, to remove slavery from our checkered past would be erroneous. Ecclesiastes 1:9 explains the phenomenon of why historical blunders are repeated, "What has been, it is what will be, and what has been done, it is what will be done. So there is nothing new under the sun."

We live in dangerous times. The 1619 Project is interesting in that it teaches history solely from the narrative that America is bad. Although the 1619 project teaches factual aspects of America's checkered past, it conveniently omits all the good that America has achieved. The 1619 Project gives rise to cancel culture and its objective to erase the stains of American history. [174] Americans should never forget the mistakes of its past. What is worse, cancel culture objectives can go much deeper by demonizing those who own different opinions to dismantle free speech. Furthermore, cancel culture is used to punish political enemies for mistakes they made decades earlier. The implications of erasing history is explained best in Mormon 9:31 when Captain Moroni explains that people should learn from the "imperfections" of prior generations.

Evolution of the Law

If individuals and society evolve, then shouldn't the Constitution and the statutory law also evolve? The answer to this is both yes and no. Fundamental rights and moral principles are God-given and do not evolve. Therefore, fundamental rights are not open to interpretation from biased and opinionated jurists and legislators. Philosopher John Locke would write, "Human laws must be made according to the general laws of nature and without contradiction to any positive law of Scripture, otherwise they are ill made." Founding Father and the United States' first Chief Justice, John Jay, explained moral law "Being founded by infinite wisdom and goodness on essential right, which never varies, it can require no amendment or alteration." Although society has evolved and majorities have found, for instance, that adultery is not a crime, it is still in violation of God's moral code. Society and majorities may evolve, but moral principles and fundamental rights do not. Thus, it begs to reason the Constitution needs no evolutionary updates to protect fundamental rights. [175]

That said, criminal or statutory laws can change to keep up with societal changes to protect fundamental rights. For example, when cars were introduced to society, traffic laws were necessary to protect citizens from harm. Moreover, changes to the law are not evolutionary when Supreme Court justices such as Evan Hughes write, "the Constitution is what the judges say it is" or Benjamin Cardozo proclaims that "judge-made laws are one of the existing realities of life." Hughes and Cardozo's belief system describes how a few influential unelected, egotistical, and power-hungry judges inject bias, opinion, and prejudice into the law, which has nothing to do with evolutionary changes in society. [176]

The Role of the Judiciary

There are five fallacies about the United States judicial branch of government. First, Americans universally assume that all three branches of government are equal. Quite the contrary, Alexander Hamilton writes in Federalist Paper 78 that the judicial branch was designed to be the weakest branch of government because they have no legislative powers nor any power to enforce their rulings. Second, it is widely accepted that the judicial branch is independent to act. Again, that is false because no branch of the United States government is independent to act as they wish. All branches of government are accountable to the most sovereign entity in the United States: "We the people." Third, it is broadly recognized that justices have lifetime appointments. Article III, Section 1 of the Constitution reads, "The Judges, both of the Supreme and inferior Courts, shall hold their offices during good behavior." Hence, judges can be impeached for bad behavior and that may include actions that are not a crime such as drunkenness. Judges with a history of circumventing the Constitution by using bias, opinion, social data, statistics, current affairs, and inventing balancing tests are in contempt of the law and should be impeached. Similarly, Ezra 7:25 instructs leaders to appoint judges who would uphold law. Fourth, it is commonly agreed that the Supreme Court has the final say about the constitutionality of legislation. If this were true, then the Court would be more powerful than the legislative and executive branches. Judicial review, granted in *Marbury v. Madison* in 1803, did not intend for judges to become lawmakers or final arbiters of the law, but to provide legal advice to legislators within the narrow scope of the Constitution's 4,500 words. Finally, it is often recognized that the Supreme Court has the power or jurisdiction to enforce its rulings. Enforcement of law is the duty of the executive branch. [177]

Government Power

Locke defined tyranny as the use of government power that is beyond its authority. Thus, a tyrannical or corrupt government is no longer following the original meaning of the Constitution. Abuse of government power or corruption can also be defined as a select set of people who control facets of human life beyond their scope. Moreover, it is common for government power to progressively increase over time. Governmental power was and is aggressive, knowing no boundaries when in the hands of humans; such power was defined during the American Revolution very similarly by dozens of literary protestors of the time. [178]

There were two primary objectives of the United States constitutional republic. First, to limit government power and require the mutual consent of those to be governed. Second, to limit the powers of individuals in government to eliminate the temptation of humans to become corrupt. Abuse of power becomes an ill perceived fundamental right to those who have it. For this reason, the social contract in the Declaration of Independence says it is a right of the people to abolish and replace a corrupt government. The event on 1-6-2021 was an insurrection, but the way both parties in Washington abuse their power and mitigate the rights of citizens would be considered just as much an insurrection and dereliction of duty by the Founders. The difference between 1-6-2021 and government abuse of power is that 1-6-2021 was one very bad day, and government abuse of power is a daily event. [179]

Chapter 7: Government Techniques That Eliminate Natural Law and Alter Fundamental Rights [180] [181] [182]

Today, everyone has an agenda and wants to change moral principles to meet their personal standards and not the standards of God. Most government policies are a classic example of doing harm to natural law or moral principles and fundamental rights. Government techniques or practices such as changing the meaning of words, canceling or erasing history, political correctness, changing the meaning of the Constitution, identity politics, critical race theory, and diversity are all misguided attempts to improve, mitigate, or remove moral principles and fundamental rights. The primary issue centers around the belief that advancement in modern society calls for updating the moral principles, fundamental rights, and the Constitution. The belief the Constitution can evolve is wrong and has led to a 230-year power struggle that has resulted in increased federal government authority at the expense of the states and people. Increased federal government power has been what I have labelled a non-violent progressive coup d'état that has slowly eroded away republic constitutional protection enshrined by the Founders. The coup d'état has resulted in a democracy that has forever mitigated and removed the fundamental rights of citizens.

Fearmongering [183]

The federal government uses national emergencies such as wars, pandemics, depressions, and catastrophic climatic events to encroach on the fundamental rights of the populous. Cases such as *Wickard v. Filburn*, *Nebbia v. New York*, and *Carolene Products v. United States* are classic examples of how the government used a national emergency, the Great Depression, to increase its power by changing the meaning of the Interstate Commerce Clause in the Constitution. The Founders' definition of commerce was trade; today, it covers everything economic, including crime, manufacturing, and labor laws. More troubling, these awful decisions are still valid laws defended by most law scholars. In Wickard, the Court held the federal government could dictate how much wheat a farmer can produce, and growing any excess to feed his family and livestock was prohibited. In Nebbia, the Court caved to the powerful dairy lobby and jailed a store owner for selling milk for under 9 cents a quart. During the Great Depression, people were desperate and starving, but the objective of the New York law, upheld in Nebbia, was to help the dairy lobby fix milk prices to inflate their profits. In Carolene Products, filled milk was banned from interstate commerce because it was sold for 3 cents less a quart than natural milk. Again, the dairy lobby won at the expense of the starving public and small businesses. As people lived in fear, wondering how they may survive without work and food during the Great Depression, politicians used it as an excuse to expand the scope and power of the federal government to protect the affluent at the expense of the poor.

Fear during World War I led to placing restrictions on First Amendment free speech liberties that were considered a "clear and present danger." In *Schenck v. United States*, Schenck was arrested for writing a pamphlet that disagreed with the draft and war effort. Although only a few pamphlets were distributed, it was decided Schenck violated the newly passed Espionage Act and was not only denied his free speech rights but was jailed. In *Debs v. United States* and *Abrams v. United States*, fear of communism led to the Court rejecting the First Amendment rights of those partaking in the socialist movement. Fear of persons with learning disabilities, the disabled, the sick, the poor, immigrants, and minorities drove the concept of eugenics which supported abortion, sterilization, and anti-immigration policy in the 1920s. In the infamous case *Buck v. Bell*, Justice Oliver Wendall Holmes would write, "Three generations of imbeciles are enough," as he ordered the sterilization of a young woman. Fear during World War II led to Japanese Americans' internment (*Korematsu v. United States*).

Consider another example, the 1873 *Slaughter-House Cases,* which were discussed earlier. The Supreme Court held that the city of New Orleans could produce a law that would monopolize the butcher industry to prevent cholera cases. That sounds reasonable, the Court wanted to protect the safety and wellbeing of citizens from the unhealthy butcher practices of dumping waste into the drinking water. However, does providing one butcher company a monopoly choose the least evasive method to achieve its goal of public safety? No, closer inspection and commonsense would lead one to think the city did not have to eliminate the right of dozens of butchers to work a lawful profession. Instead, a law that outlines proper methods for disposing of waste would make more sense than removing the livelihood of hundreds of people. Again, a local emergency allowed a local government to use fear to garner more power by allowing them to needlessly reduce the rights of individuals and workers. The *Slaughter-House Cases* are a classic example of fear leading to irrational problem-solving.

In *The Book of Revelation,* William Anderson summarizes why fear dominates society: "Evil causes fear and fear invokes interest." [184] Unfortunately, goodness and kindness do not invoke the interest that fear does. Fear is a strong negative emotion that invokes other strong negative emotions and sensations like anger, hate, and pain, taking people out of their natural state of rational thought. In a natural state, human beings are incredibly analytical. However, in an unnatural state, rational thought is replaced by irrational thinking, so our critical reasoning skills tend to suffer. One message I have taken from the Bible is that life is about confronting our adversities and fears to become better people for the greater good of society. Instead, fear polarizes and divides Americans into demographic factions with different political ideologies. Thus, fear is the most effective way to influence the populous by having our educational system, corporations, and the media fill our minds with their narrative and versions of the truth.

Downplaying the role of Natural Law in United States History [185]

Most arguments contrary to natural law are not intuitive. Opponents to natural law believe that the pursuit of pleasure and emotions may resolve justice or that evil is acceptable if the outcome may result in good. In other words, in the name of pleasure and emotions, it is acceptable to riot and destroy businesses to achieve social justice, abort an unwanted baby, steal from the rich and give it to the poor, or protect an endangered fish at the expense of the livelihood of a human being. When this happens, there are no clear laws or rules for society; instead, we are governed by opinions, bias, and conjecture.

Some opponents to natural law argue that its principles vary and lack consistency and therefore, a vast majority of people do not believe natural law exists. True, natural law theories fluctuate, but the basic principles of natural law are consistent. It is normal to have opposing theories about any abstract subject, such as fundamental rights. Moreover, all people know more about natural law and moral principles than they think they know. For instance, everyone knows they should respect their neighbors; it is common sense. In fact, most atheists practice natural law whether they know it or not. For example, most people do not assault or injure another human being because they know it is wrong. In James 4:17, "So for one who knows the right thing to do and does not do it, for him it is a sin."

Some opponents argue natural law cannot exist because people regularly choose to ignore moral principles. Given that we all sin, even good people who believe in natural law routinely violate it. The purpose of moral principles is to strive to be better people, not that we are perfect and do not sin. Some breaches of natural law may happen because people are ignorant or repress certain moral principles. For example, those people who show remorse for their actions prove they understood natural law but repressed or ignored it. Women who have depression following an abortion are probably expressing remorse because they know what they did conflicts with natural law and the sanctity of life.

Some opponents insist natural law does not exist because people are constantly creating new values or rights. When that happens, the building blocks of new values and rights must come from those basic natural law principles defined by the Bible. If new values are not derived from natural law dictated by the Bible, then the new values are misguided principles. Gay marriage is considered a new value that is built on the moral principle of treating everyone equally. That is true, but since gay marriage is a sin, it is not a new moral value, but a self-destructive behavior that should be a tolerated action since it does not harm other people in society. Since abortion is controversial and violates the right to life, abortion is also a misguided right. Other, more ridiculous, arguments against natural law are that its philosophers are dead, and they were only a product of their time. Natural law being outdated is a very shallow argument considering natural law was the basis for the United States Constitution and Declaration of Independence. The same argument can be used to say democracy is outdated.

One fallacy about natural law is one must believe in God to believe in natural law. Yes, natural law philosophers believe natural law is connected to God, but I challenge the atheist to tell me which of the fundamental rights in Table I they would discard. We can have faith that love is better than hate, and the right to travel is better than being confined without having faith in God.

Most historians suggest that Locke's principles about society and government are outdated and old-school liberal. Opponents of Locke's theories of government state his beliefs are "too static, too mechanical, and too rational." To say Locke's principles are too rational makes it sound as if rationality is wicked. Rationality and reason are better than a government dictated by partisanship, bias, opinion, groupthink, irrationality, and emotion. True, Locke's theory of government was static since fundamental rights do not change over time. That said, Locke's theories were not too static since he suggests governments should have some flexibility to act in the event of emergencies (natural disasters, war, economic calamities) to deny fundamental rights for the common good.

Another historian argues that the government "is the product of many centuries of almost unconscious development." For instance, natural law has had no impact on the unconscious development of social justice. Locke's theories certainly encompass social justice. My definition of social justice is equal rights for everyone, which is certainly supported by the Constitution and Locke's principles. The Equal Protection Clause of the Fourteenth Amendment is straight from Locke's principles, and it has been the basis for social justice reforms such as overturning segregation in *Brown v. School Board (1954)*. Yes, it is true, however, that natural law and the Bible do not account for the liberal definition of social justice which includes income, gender, and racial equity. Another fallacy is that natural law philosophers, such as John Locke, support both slavery and capital punishment. Slavery and capital punishment are not part of natural law theory, but a retribution penalty created by society for certain crimes that violate the fundamental rights of others.

Some opponents argue that fundamental rights are not absolute and have exceptions. However, this is true of all our fundamental rights outlined in the Constitution. Free speech includes liberty of expression, but it does not include acts of violence, nor would the second amendment include persons who are violent criminals. Citizens have the right to only work lawful jobs and any crime committed in the privacy of a home would not be a protected right of privacy. Using wisdom and common sense (rule of right) indicate when exceptions to a fundamental right are required. Similarly, when rights and or moral principles conflict, it should be resolved using common sense and wisdom. What happens when hate speech collides with the moral principle to show love and kindness? Civil society must learn how to tolerate offensive things. Hurt feelings are not a reason to abridge free speech. Moral principles and virtuous traits such as duty, self-control, selflessness, tolerance, and fairness must take root to resolve these disputes for the greater good of society.

Finally, some opponents argue that Locke's concept of a social contract no longer has any relevance. The social contract is no longer relevant is false because Locke's social contract principles (our Declaration of Independence) have been renewed throughout American history, such as for women's suffrage, the abolition of slavery, Martin Luther King's "I have a Dream" speech, and even Newt Gingrich's "Contract with America."

The Lockean effect on United States history is immeasurable. First, Locke's influence explains why the colonies fought both the American Revolutionary and Civil Wars. Second, Locke's principles are forever embedded in both the Declaration of Independence and the Constitution. Finally, Locke's influence explains why other British colonies, who did not have access to Locke, tolerated English tyranny. In these regards, Locke was not only important in American history, but the United States probably would not exist without his influence.

Creating False Narratives

Below are the ways people may manipulate an argument to set a false narrative: [187] [188]

- If the person is not an authority on the subject. For instance, taking political advice from ignorant athletes and Hollywood stars. [189]
- The argument is an illegitimate appeal to fear (emotion). For example, Covid-19 on going restrictions use fear mongering tactics to insist the pandemic is still a threat. [190]
- The argument is an illegitimate appeal to shame. For instance, arguments about police arrest tactics may encompass race-baiting to shame the police. [191]
- The argument is an illegitimate personal attack against the other party. Unfortunately, most debates devolve into personal attacks.
- The argument draws false conclusions. One example is that only white men can be racist and sexist. [192]
- The argument consists of false consequences. One common false consequence is when the president receives credit for any national economic conditions shortly after taking office.
- The argument compares parts with the whole. For example, when politicians fail to realize that education and social problems are vastly different in New York and a small Midwest farming community than from the nation as a whole. [193]
- The arguments are generalizations. For example, all persons of color are liberals, or all Evangelicals are conservative.
- The argument makes exceptions. Politicians commonly make exceptions by splitting hairs, such as Trump's travel ban for Covid-19 was wrong, but Biden's travel ban was acceptable or vice versa. Trump and Biden having classified documents in their possession is a great example. Both sides try to split hairs and argue that, for instance, Biden's infringement of the law was less severe. [194]
- The argument is a claim that the other side does the same thing. If something is wrong, then it is wrong regardless of who carried out the action. If Trump's travel ban was wrong, then it was wrong when Biden implemented a travel ban. [195]

Most arguments encompass one or many of these errors. For instance, illegitimate arguments attempt to distract people from believing in God and religion by asking the inevitable questions about the Bible, which were addressed in Chapter 3.

Changing the Meaning of Constitutional Clauses and Amendments

Although the Constitution's original meaning is only supposed to change by amendment, it is routinely altered by legislation and controversial court decisions. Originalism is a philosophy followed by some jurists and maintains that the meaning of the Constitution's text is fixed. However, the living constitution philosophy is followed by many other jurists who suggest the meaning of the Constitution changes to keep up with changes in modern society. If natural law, fundamental rights, and moral principles remain unchanged and the principal purpose of the Constitution is to protect those fundamental rights, then there should be very little reason to alter the document. When the original meaning of the Constitution is not used in the construction of the law, the meaning changes. One example, discussed in more detail throughout the text, is the expansion of the Interstate Commerce Clause to include manufacturing, intrastate trade, labor laws, and crime. The expansion of the Constitution's Necessary and Proper Clause is discussed in Chapters 10 and 11 when the Court upheld the constitutionality of the national bank. More examples are provided in Chapter 8 such as changing the meaning of the Takings Clause and the introduction of progressive tax rates.

Changing the Meaning of Words

The right to equality protects everyone the same regardless of the situation. Unfortunately, the right to equality has been replaced with the right to equity. Equity is not defined the same as equality. Equity introduces social measures such as demographics into the equation for equality. For example, employment hiring practices and college entrance procedures that factor race and gender into its admission guidelines are following equity, not equality. The best qualified person is not always selected once other equity measures are considered, which creates a system where fundamental rights are replaced with the bias, opinion, and conjecture of bureaucrats. Equity violates the Equal Protection Clause of the Fourteenth Amendment: "…nor shall any State...deny to any person within its jurisdiction the equal protection of the laws." Equity is also destructive because it expands government control over more aspects of society outside its constitutional authority, equity fails to hold people accountable for their decisions, and equity dissolves the merit system by punishing hard work, achievement, and excellence.

Not Defending Fundamental Rights Equally

Prout v. Starr held that all constitutional clauses and amendments have equal weighting. Justice George Shiras wrote, "The Constitution of the United States, with the several amendments thereof, must be regarded as one instrument, all of whose provisions are to be deemed of equal validity." Since the primary purpose of the Constitution is to protect fundamental rights, then one can conclude that fundamental rights must also have equal intrinsic value. Since *Prout v. Starr* is not considered a landmark decision, it is prudent to evaluate an example of how the Courts violate Shiras' jurisprudence of equality or symmetry between constitutional clauses and amendments. According to Shiras, the Ninth Amendment is equal to all the other amendments and therefore, one may conclude that unenumerated rights protected by the Ninth Amendment are on equal footing with enumerated rights. Hence, one may deduce that decisions such as *Carolene Products v. United States (1938)* and its infamous Footnote 4, encroach upon the sound jurisprudence put forth by Justice Shiras. Footnote 4 provides four instances when the Supreme Court's practice of judicial restraint may be ignored. Judicial restraint is the Supreme Court's practice of upholding state laws and allowing states to experiment with legislation. One instance of importance noted in Footnote 4 is when the Bill of Rights (first eight amendments) is violated. Thus, Footnote 4 implies, for instance, that the right to free speech (First Amendment) has more importance than rights not found in the Bill of Rights (unenumerated). The preceding sentence is true since Footnote 4 allows states to experiment with unenumerated rights such as the right to work a lawful profession, the right to obtain knowledge, or the right to travel. Courts often rely on flawed jurisprudence set forth in Footnote 4 to decide the fate of laws.

I often wonder what would have happened if the first eight amendments, that protect the most obvious rights (self-defense, speech, religion, property, and justice) of citizens, were never added to the Bill of Rights and the Founders felt the masterful language of the Ninth Amendment was sufficient to protect the liberty of each citizen. Technically, if the first eight amendments were omitted then the Ninth Amendment language should protect those rights. Under such a scenario, would unenumerated rights have more protection, or would all fundamental rights, including those omitted in the first eight amendments, have limited protection? Would the Ninth Amendment be taken more seriously, or would it continue to be ignored?

As it stands, courts protect enumerated fundamental rights with more vigor than those unenumerated fundamental rights. The practice of protecting enumerated rights over unenumerated rights not only violates the Ninth Amendment; it violates the equality property that fundamental rights should possess. Unfortunately, the Founders fear of a two-tiered system of rights has come to fruition primarily due to decisions such as Carolene Products and Footnote 4. Even more troubling, Footnote 4 led directly to the Supreme Court standard set by Justice William O. Douglas in *Williamson v. Lee Optical* to deny the right to work a lawful profession in 1954 that businesses such as Lens Crafters perform today. In Lee Optical, Douglas suggested that if the Court found any conceivable or hypothetical reason for a law, it would be held constitutional. What law, no matter how intrusive, would not pass this standard? Proponents for the scrutiny levels defined in Footnote 4 and the low bar for legal legislation set in Lee Optical will argue these standards were a necessity to limit lawsuits that are a burden on the judiciary. The number of lawsuits can be properly addressed by better defining fundamental rights and the criteria necessary for fundamental rights to earn constitutional protection. It is not acceptable, however, to protect the workload of the judicial system in lieu of protecting the fundamental rights of the public. [196] [197]

Chapter 8 provides many more examples describing how equality of rights is denied to certain populations. Examples include how voting power favors urban centers over rural areas, how antidiscrimination laws tend to discriminate, and how some groups garner more free speech protection over other groups.

Inventing Constitutional Doctrines

The best example of inventing a new constitutional doctrine is the notion of Separation of Church and State. The Separation of Church and State doctrine was discovered in a benign letter between Thomas Jefferson and a Connecticut pastor. Justice Hugo Black introduced the Separation of Church and State doctrine in *Everson v. Board of Education* decided in 1947. Although the case was correctly decided and allowed tax dollars to bus parochial students to school, it opened the door to use the doctrine in the future. Separation of Church and State is not in the Constitution, yet many courts would use the Separation of Church and State doctrine to determine the fate of the Establishment Clause in the First Amendment. The original meaning and purpose for the Establishment Clause was to end the practice of colonies establishing religions. Specifically, some colonists were compelled to pay taxes to support established religions even if they were not members of the church. Compelling non-members to pay taxes was taxation without representation, the same reason why the colonists fought the Revolutionary War. [198]

The concept of Separation of Church and State was first recognized in Genesis when Moses led the government and his brother, Aaron, led the spiritual aspect of society. Most societies have Separation of Church and State. Unfortunately, the Establishment Clause of the First Amendment has been used in conjunction with the Separation of Church and State doctrine to ban parking in government parking lots for vehicles sporting a religious sticker, prayer at a graduation ceremony, vouchers from being used for parochial schools, scholarships for theology, grammar school students praying before lunch, senior citizens praying at community centers, a librarian wearing a cross, college students conducting Bible study in their dorm rooms, a third grader wearing a shirt referring to Jesus, students praying at a football game, students doing research papers on religious topics, a choir singing religious songs, and having a Bible in a classroom. In other words, the Separation of Church and State doctrine can be used to ban this book on public grounds since it suggests God is a logical reason for the formation of the universe and life on Earth. [199]

Some of the most damaging Supreme Court cases that enforced some of the above restrictions include *Zelman v. Simmons-Harris, Locke v. Davey*, and *Lee v. Weisman*. In *Zelman v. Simmons-Harris*, the Court held educational vouchers could not be used to send children to parochial school. In *Locke v. Davey,* the Court held a scholarship could be withheld from students studying theology. In *Lee v. Weisman,* the Court held that prayer at a graduation ceremony was unconstitutional. In Lee, the Court essentially rescinded religious liberty to protect a newly invented right to prevent people from feeling uncomfortable when forced to listen to prayers. With all that in mind, the Separation of Church and State doctrine has nothing to do with the exclusion of God. In fact, the Establishment Clause of the First Amendment pertains to prohibitions against the government, it is not a restriction against the Church or the individual to pursue their religious beliefs. [200]

Another example of an invented constitutional doctrine is called Substantive Due Process. The modern view of Substantive Due Process probably took hold in *Adamson v. California* in 1947 and is used from time to time to protect unenumerated rights instead of the Ninth Amendment or the Privileges and Immunities Clause of the Fourteenth Amendment. The doctrine is flawed and controversial because it incorrectly uses the Due Process Clause of the Fourteenth Amendment to both identify and protect rights. The controversy surrounding the Substantive Due Process doctrine could be averted by eliminating the doctrine in favor of the Ninth Amendment and better defining the properties of a fundamental right. Another option would be to overrule the *Slaughter-House Cases* to reinstate the Privileges and Immunities Clause of the Fourteenth Amendment. Instead, Congress and the courts elect to make identifying and protecting rights much more difficult than necessary. Although Substantive Due Process corrects a prior error, it must be corrected, clarified, and debated. It is a slippery slope when the Court invents flawed doctrines. Substantive Due Process has, after all, been used to protect the right to abortion.

Defining New or Altering the Meaning of Fundamental Rights [201]

One technique to mitigate rights is to pass laws with the purpose of making rights better. Take, for example, the progressive push for a 15-dollar minimum wage. Good pay for an honest day's work appears as if it makes the right to work stronger. What would be the overall result of a 15-dollar minimum wage? Sure, many will benefit, but there will be negatives. First, it will result in the loss of jobs because employers will not be able to afford to have as many employees. Second, the cost of higher-paying jobs will be passed on to the consumer to absorb the higher costs. The rights of some will be enhanced, but the rights of others will be denied.

Another way governments violate moral principles is to create new moral principles. For example, one new moral principle suggests we need to leave the planet a better place than when we inhabited it. Saving the planet sounds reasonable, but it also violates the rights of citizens. The problem is not so much the principle of protecting our environment, it is how government policies attack the problem of protecting the planet? Whether we realize it or not, humans are, by nature, carbon-emitting resource-consuming waste machines. Thus, it is an impossible moral principle to follow especially if China and India do nothing to curb their emissions. Furthermore, government solutions to the problem violate fundamental rights. For example, government regulations to cut carbon emissions violate the fundamental rights of people and companies because:

- Certain jobs that are bad for the environment are eliminated (eliminating fossil fuel jobs via the closing of coal mines and shutting down the Keystone Pipeline). These policies violate the right of people to work a lawful job.

- Subsidizing some companies and people for making green improvements over people who are unable to pay the high cost of upgrades. These policies violate the right to equality.
- Subsidizing some green energy sector companies over others allows the government to pick winners and losers in the industry. These policies violate the right to equality.
- The exorbitant costs of green policies add to the national debt, which is a tax on future generations who have no say in the process. These policies violate the right to be represented in government.
- Compelling people to buy products they do not want such as expensive green cars or cars that are lighter and less safe to meet mileage regulations. These policies violate the rights of people to contract and choose products they want to purchase.

The moral principle of leaving the planet a better place simply cannot coexist with other moral principles using current government policies. Instead of violating the rights of citizens, it makes more sense to let the private sector focus on carbon capture techniques. If the United States can capture carbon emissions instead of trying to reduce carbon emissions, then both the rights of citizens are protected, and it resolves the problem of China and India refusing to curb their emissions. Carbon capture is beyond the scope of this writing, but it is a technique that has been used with some success.

Climate and pollution are a real concern that should be addressed in the free market system. The federal government should have no place in the solution. Furthermore, more productive results from climate change activists would be helpful. Activists earning science and engineering degrees to help solve the problem is much more helpful than protesting and suggesting more should be done. Additionally, climate activists are their own worst enemy when their protests use bad behavior to get their message across. Many young and ambitious people truly want to make a difference but are, unfortunately, part of the problem rather than part of the solution. It is one thing to bring attention to an issue, it is another thing to do something of significance to solve it.

Limiting How much an Individual may Pursue a Particular Fundamental Right

Is there a limit to how much a person may use a specific liberty to pursue a fundamental right? No, there are no limits, and it is up to each person to decide how aggressively they wish to pursue certain fundamental rights. One person may have three jobs and therefore, they use their right to work a lawful job a bit more than others. A person who contributes large sums of money to a charity or to political campaigns uses their freedom of expression more than others. Not long ago, the government incorrectly intervened to limit how much money a person or organization could contribute to political campaigns. Although that error has been corrected, the government continues to place many erroneous guidelines to discourage large amounts of money from being donated to political campaigns. These guidelines include, for instance, the mandatory disclosure of donations. Some people may choose to never pursue a fundamental right. Atheists may refuse to use their religious liberty.

That said, free speech and religious liberty also encompasses the right to conscious thought, which would protect the belief system held by atheists.

Society's Role in Mitigating Rights

Why do people violate moral principles? The answer is simple: Comfort and ease. To follow moral principles requires hard work and can take people out of their comfort zone. Many biblical stories of success happen when persons are taken out of their comfort zone – Abraham (moved from his home), Joseph (sold into slavery by his brothers), Moses (exiled), Ruth (moved to a new country), and Mary (the immaculate conception). The comfort and pleasure principles reveal that, given a choice, people will choose comfort and pleasure over things that may be uncomfortable and unpleasant. The same is true for the government. For instance, it is easy to borrow from future generations for the pleasure and comfort of the current voting base. Technology is one-factor driving comfort and pleasure in humans. For example, it is easier to take an elevator than walking up the stairs; or it is easier to watch TV instead of reading a book or exercising; or it is certainly easier to play video games than to play outside. The comfort and pleasure principles also lead to something called the present principle. The present principle theorizes people will choose comfort and pleasure even though they understand the long-term consequences of their actions will be bad. For example, eating unhealthily can lead to long-term health issues, and forgoing knowledge to watch TV or play on a smartphone can lead to ignorance and social disorders. If the objective of moral principles is to guide us to be better people for the greater good, the pleasure, comfort, and present principles counteract that objective. [202]

Life is hard, and it involves dealing with adversity. It is through adversity that we perfect ourselves and become better human beings. However, the more we stay in our comfort zone, the less equipped we are to follow moral principles and deal with adversity and suffering. If we choose a life of taking the easy way out, then we can expect to struggle with moral principles, adversity, suffering, and pain. If rising disability payrolls are any indication of our inability to deal with adversity, more people are likely to be a burden on their families and society. Disability and other forms of government dependency enable the comfort and pleasure principles while punishing hardworking taxpayers to care for those taking advantage of the system. [203]

The futile principle happens when there are more people requiring assistance than there are people to support those needing help. In other words, futility happens when there are more people taking from government programs than there are people financing the programs. The futile principle suggests that humanity is on a trajectory toward extinction. C.S. Lewis was correct when he stated in *Mere Christianity* that it was a myth that living things are always improving and getting better. If the populous is moving further away from God but more attached to technology, comfort, pleasure, and ease, the imperfection of humans will multiply. [204]

Civilizations evolve to rationalize or invent ways to justify evil habits and customs. Today, wokeness has little tolerance for political debate and different opinions. Why? Wokeness is used to a drive social and racial justice wedge between different demographic classes whose objective is to erase history, promote political correctness, and foster victimization (critical race theory). Wokeness is trying to rewrite history by erasing history and quelling the speech of its adversaries. It is no longer acceptable to say, "all lives matter," but only "black lives matter." Wokeness is no different than plantation owners rationalizing "only white lives matter" or the KKK declaring "whites should receive preferential treatment." I am not comparing slavery to what is happening today, but merely suggesting that the thought process that brought about slavery and white supremacy is no different than the dangers and unreasonable concepts that lurk behind woke principles. History has a way of repeating its errors from the past, and right now, the movement of wokeness is in its infancy, but it is gaining traction. The longer the perverse movement exists, the more it may become an evil habit, custom, or passion. Just as the United States has justified sterilization, abortion, the internment of a race of people, slavery, discriminatory immigration and territorial laws, prohibitions against women, and other infringement of rights, it may become the new norm to have a completely fictitious history of the United States. Similarly, virtue signaling is another common trait portrayed by many people that adversely affects society. Virtue signaling is when people aim to demonstrate their moral superiority, but it is all talk, as they take no actions supporting their claims. Society is better off with anonymous acts of kindness instead of artificially satisfying one's ego.

The United States is the most successful government ever formed, but the trend to undermine our Founders' genius is real. Over the centuries, there has been an alarming trend to remove many of the protections our Founders placed in the Constitution to protect the fundamental rights of the people. This topic will be elaborated on further in the next chapter.

Expanding Federal Government Power

The creation of dozens of bureaucratic federal agencies is the best example of the national government garnering a massive expansion of power at the expense of both individual and state sovereignty. During the founding period, agriculture and education were important aspects of society. Furthermore, agriculture in the colonies was adversely affected by the Revolutionary War. For instance, certain crop markets became obsolete and, what is worse, many farms were destroyed by the war effort. During the war, crops and livestock were not only stolen, but property and dwellings were trampled and burned to the ground. Farmers needed help following the war, but they evolved and grew new crops and restored their farms without government interference. Founding father and the father of education, Noah Webster, asked those attending the Constitutional Convention for patent and copywrite protections in the Constitution (Article I, Section 8, Clause 8). Although Webster supported protecting inventors and innovation, he never calls for any federal control or regulation of education. Thus, the Founders failed to provide the federal government with any power over agriculture and education because they felt states could not only monitor their food production but their educational needs. Today, there are federal government agencies in charge of agriculture (USDA) and education (DoE) and dozens of other federal agencies controlling fields of expertise that the Constitution fails to mention. [205]

This expansion of power comes from the Necessary and Proper Clause – now called the Elastic Clause for its broad reaching powers. That said, for something to be necessary and proper, the government needs to use the least evasive method to achieve its constitutional objective. Cases such as *Whitman v. American Truckers (2001)* and *Chevron v. Natural Resources Defense Council (1984)* provide government agencies with power that cannot be justified by any originalism construction of the Constitution. In Whitman, the Court held the Clean Air Act properly delegated legislative power to the Environmental Protection Agency. In Chevron, the Court held that lower courts must defer to administrative agency interpretations of the authority granted to them by Congress (1) where the intent of Congress was ambiguous and (2) where the interpretation was reasonable or permissible. The budget for the USDA and DoE in 2022 was nearly one half a trillion dollars in 2021. If that is the least evasive method to help farmers and educators, then Americans are being duped. Moreover, the Constitution was never amended to account for this huge expansion of federal government control. Since the federal government has taken over education, there has been a steady decline in United States performances in reading, writing, and especially math. Furthermore, rural America, controlled by the USDA, has the highest rates of poverty and uneducated. [206] [207] [208]

Obviously, the federal government is not helping the education and agriculture aspects of society despite their oversight. Thus, it is apparent these departments fail to meet not only the least evasive condition of the Necessary and Proper Clause, but it can be argued if they are necessary and proper at all. The federal government solution to everything is to throw money at the problem and ignore the other variables that can be improved without money. For instance, in education it may be more prudent to address non-monetary issues such as the culture between administrators, teachers, parents, and students. Moreover, eliminating analysis paralysis such as the constant focus on test scores as well as reforming curriculum and changing the focus and approach taken to education should be considered before raising taxes. There is a complete and utter lack of wisdom in Congress to generate creative and practical solutions. When everything in society is considered necessary and proper and requiring federal regulation and financing, it is no wonder the United States is over 32 trillion dollars in debt.

Federal Law Enforcement Expansion [209]

How do federal enforcement agencies stack the odds in their favor if they decide to prosecute a company or individual? There are many tricks at their disposal to mitigate the rights of citizens and companies:

- Federal law enforcement agencies write vague, ambiguous, confusing, and incoherent statutes that can be interpreted to cover a wide range of issues. This practice allows federal prosecutors to invent crimes to pursue by making up the law on the fly. Furthermore, vague and incoherent statutes confuse juries more likely to be sympathetic with government agencies they believe are operating in good faith.

- Federal law enforcement writes statutes covering topics they do not understand such as laws regulating technical products, finance, insurance, and the medical industry.
- Federal law enforcement writes statutes covering topics they have no grants of power to enforce in the Constitution. For instance, federal law enforcement uses the Interstate Commerce Clause of the Constitution to broaden the scope of its jurisdiction. The Founders' purpose for including the Interstate Commerce Clause in the Constitution was to regulate trade between the states. Now, the scope of the clause is so broad it is used to regulate anything including manufacturing, crime, gambling, insurance, business activities, finance, intrastate commerce, and labor laws.
- Federal enforcement agencies have mastered the art of inventing crimes without victims. For instance, in most cases where people are charged with conspiracy, perjury, and obstruction, they have not infringed on the rights of anyone.
- Federal law enforcement writes statutes that are viewed favorably in the public eye. The federal government's war on drugs and cracking down on securities exchange violations are viewed favorably even though the federal government has no authority in the Constitution to pursue such measures.
- Federal law enforcement agencies attempt to force innocent individuals and companies to accept plea deals to avoid long and arduous trials that may bankrupt them.
- Federal law enforcement uses incentives to conjure up false witnesses. For example, whistleblowers receive a percentage of the fines obtained from defendants. Additionally, some witnesses receive immunity if they agree to testify against someone higher on the political or corporate ladder. In other words, whistleblowers and those provided blanket immunity have incentive to lie to receive cash rewards or keep from going to prison.
- Since the United States government has a massive national debt, they are always seeking ways to increase their revenues. Thus, federal enforcement agencies have motive and incentive to conjure up phony cases against companies and wealthy individuals that may result in large fines to help finance government operations.
- Companies and citizens are now guilty until proven innocent under the new federal system of crime enforcement.

There is a simple litmus test for Congress and the courts to follow: If the law does not protect the fundamental rights of citizens equally and falls under the umbrella of federal grants of powers permitted by the Constitution – it must fail. One reason to explain the decline in fundamental rights is the outlandish overreach of federal enforcement agencies. The federal government has grants of power in the Constitution to police counterfeiting, piracy, crimes against the nation, treason, and slavery. A strong argument can be made that the federal government also has the power to enforce national security measures and protect the fundamental rights of citizens. But that is it! Now consider that there are over 5000 federal statutes and over 400,000 federal regulations that carry criminal penalties. If that does not sound outrageous consider the United States has only been a nation for fewer than 90,000 days. The amount of federal interference in crime is mindboggling because it means that even the best citizens have probably unintentionally violated several of these laws or regulations. One book, *Three Felonies a Day*, details how even the most noble citizens unknowingly commit three felonies every day. Any American can be jailed if the government decides to go after you. No one is safe! [210] I estimate that well over 90% of federal laws fail the simple litmus test posed at the beginning of this paragraph.

Chapter 8: Examples of Mitigating Fundamental Rights in United States History [211]

Understanding our Rights

This chapter provides historical examples of how the government has violated, infringed upon, and mitigated the God-given fundamental rights of American citizens. Most citizens are unaware of their rights and, therefore, obliviously accept a vast majority of any government infringement of our rights. The government has been slowly chipping away at our rights and we need to take notice and voice our concerns. What is important to note, it is no coincidence that constitutional grants of power are expanding, whereas at the same time constitutional provisions protecting fundamental rights are dwindling.

Equality and Voting Rights [212]

One modern example of applying the law unfairly is how voting power is concentrated in urban centers at the expense of rural areas. In fact, I have never seen this obscure injustice covered in any law books. Let us delve into the details.

Article IV, Section 4 of the Constitution reads:

> The United States shall guarantee to every State in this Union a Republican Form of Government and shall protect each of them against Invasion; and on Application of the Legislature, or of the Executive (when the Legislature cannot be convened) against domestic violence.

There is no mincing of words, the above section of the Constitution clearly indicates states should have republican forms of government. However, democracy principles were forced onto the states in *Baker v. Carr (1962)* and *Reynolds v. Simms (1964)* or better known as the One Person, One Vote cases.

In Baker and Reynolds, the Supreme Court decided that districts for both state legislative houses must be evenly divided based on population. The United States Senate does not follow the standard decided in Baker and Reynolds because each state has two senators regardless of population. Baker and Reynolds provide all the voting power within states to urban areas. Rural regions are now at the mercy of big-city politics. There is no good reason why one of the two state house chambers cannot have equal representation for urban and rural regions. According to the Department of Agriculture, per capita data suggests rural areas are more poverty-stricken and less educated than inner cities. [213] Considering how state and federal tax money is appropriated, that finding should not be a shock. Those with greater representation receive the most benefits. There are no dirt roads in cities, urban teachers make more money than rural teachers, many rural areas have limited internet and cell phone coverage, and state constitutional amendments are dominated by urban centers. The purpose of Baker and Reynolds was to stop the disenfranchisement of minority voters, but instead, it displaced subjugation to rural areas. One solution would be for one house in the state legislature to be divided equally among urban and rural counties, for example providing each county of the state with one representative.

Present-day issues regarding voting rights are centered around voter identification (ID) laws. The reason for voter ID laws is to verify that only legal citizens residing in a particular municipality vote no more than once per election cycle. Fraudulent votes dilute the votes of legal voters, mitigating their voting rights. Voter ID laws are frowned upon because they are viewed as disenfranchising minority voters, but most voter ID laws are reasonable. Identification is required to do anything in the United States, and proper identification should not be a burden to maintain the integrity of elections. The United States uses Covid-19 passports or identification cards to identify vaccinated persons so they can go back to work, travel, and regain other rights. If the United States can impose proof of Covid-19 vaccinations on the populous, then there is no reason the government cannot issue a national citizenship card. It simply should not be a burden for anyone to possess a state or national government-issued identification for voting purposes. If the government cannot correct this simple problem, then how can they be entrusted to solve any problem?

The Right to Work a Lawful Profession [214]

Contract rights for workers was an important reason to end slavery and led to the drafting of the Civil Rights Act of 1866 and the Fourteenth Amendment. Asian racial discrimination in the workplace was ended using the right to work in cases such as *Wick Yo v. Hopkins*. Ending racial discrimination was primarily accomplished by protecting labor rights in early American history. The right to work was powerful. Today, unions and social legislation mitigate the importance of the right to work or the right for the employer and employee to reach contract agreements without government interference.

The right to work is no longer a fundamental right fully embraced by the federal government. Employer and employee rights are routinely diminished by the expansion of the Interstate Commerce Clause to pass harmful legislation. For example, regulations dictate minimum wages and maximum daily and weekly hour limits. Other regulations prevent minors under the age of 16 from joining the workforce. Unions interfere with free labor by dictating useless regulations including fees that are imposed on those who do not wish to be part of the union. If exempt employees (salary) can negotiate their wages and work hours, then why can't hourly workers have the same liberty? These regulations may sound reasonable but there is a misconception that employers are always trying to take advantage of their employees. In a right to work society, those that take advantage of workers will lose them. Furthermore, the minimum wage does not always guarantee employers will receive a higher wage. If businesses had to compete for employees, then the free market would generally dictate better wages. Limiting hours is unfair to those who require more work hours to support their family. Moreover, people needing additional money to support their family are generally forced to get another job to circumvent hour restrictions. Cases such as *Nebbia v. New York*, *Carolene Products v. United States,* and

Wickard v. Filburn, discussed earlier, illustrate how the right to work and contract were weakened through regulations permitted by the expansion of the Interstate Commerce Clause.

The Right to Religion [215]

In the previous chapter the Separation of Church and State doctrine was discussed and how it is used in conjunction with the Establishment Clause to mitigate religious liberty. In this section, the Free Exercise Clause of the First Amendment is explored. The Free Exercise Clause prevents Congress from creating any law abridging religion. Congress and courts circumvent the Free Exercise Clause by distinguishing between beliefs and behavior. In *Human Resources of Oregon v. Smith*, the Court struck down the Native American ritual of using peyote during religious ceremonies. Drug use may be beyond western religious norms, but the government must have a compelling reason to deny these practices. Furthermore, all questionable religious behavior is not treated the same. For example, Jewish and Catholic rituals, which allow minors to drink alcohol have not been restricted by the courts and Congress. Opinion and bias are used to dictate what is acceptable religious behavior.

The Court was in damage control mode to correct past mistakes interpreting the Free Exercise Clause in *Sherbert v. Verner*. In this case, the Court held an employer could not force or compel a person to work on Saturdays (the Day of Sabbath). Likewise, in the *Church of Lukumi Babalo Aye v. City of Hialeah,* the Court held hallucinogens were legal for some religious rituals. Similarly, in *Gonzales v. O Centro Espirita Beneficiente Uniao Do Vegetal,* the Court held that animal sacrifices were legal for some religious rituals. Justice Anthony Scalia feared that people would hide behind the guise of religious liberty to legitimize criminal behavior. That said, in all Supreme Court cases regarding religious behavior, there has never been anyone trying to use religion to benefit financially or to commit a crime. Religious behavior that does not harm others should be tolerated. For example, drug use that only harms the user and does not harm others should be tolerated behavior. Again, Locke and natural law explain that the purpose of statuary law was not to protect individuals from self-destructive behavior, but to protect individuals from violating the rights of others. Crimes without victims have no place in the criminal justice system.

Family Rights and the Right to Friendships

In *Pierce v. Society of Sisters* (1925) the Court wrote that it was a right "of parents and guardians to direct the upbringing and education of children under their control." Similarly, natural law holds that the governing of families belongs to the parents, and it is separate from politics and the governing of communities, states, and nations. Family rights or parental rights received considerable attention in 2021. A *New York Times* article title, *Republicans Seize on Schools as a Wedge Issue to Unite Party,* clearly believes parental rights are a fabricated liberty. The article was about how parental rights are "stoking white resentment and tapping into broader anger at the educational system" because parents are concerned about what is being taught to their children. [216]

For instance, some parents are concerned that critical race theory may promote different values than what they expect from their children. Critical race theory correctly teaches students how American institutions have historically had a negative impact on minorities. Unfortunately, the theory in some schools has evolved to be more divisive by attaching race to benign subjects and placing blame on white students. Race shaming is one technique used by some teachers whose purpose is to bring about white guilt. White guilt has many young, non-racially motivated students apologizing for being white. What modern critical race theory incorrectly attempts to promote is that race relations have not changed for the better since the antebellum era nearly two centuries ago. Without question, the discriminatory past of United States history should be highlighted in civic classes. However, it is polarizing to reintroduce racial segregations concepts, racial universalism, racial stereotyping, and victimization at the core of modern American society. Modern critical race theory fails to highlight any progress in race relations. The concepts behind modern critical race theory, unfortunately, will regress race relations. [217]

The First Amendment right to friendships (liberty of association) has, for the most part, garnered mixed reviews. Liberty of association was protected in cases such as *DeJong v. Oregon (1937)* and *Bates v. Little Rock (1960)*. In Bates freedom of association was protected for African Americans during the process of school integration. In DeJong, the Court allowed for the peaceful assembly of Communists. That said, the right to friendships is not considered as sacred as family or marriage rights. That may explain why the right to association was initially denied to socialists in *Debs v. United States* and I also contend this right is currently being denied in accommodations laws upheld by *Katzenbach v. McClung* and *Atlanta Motel v. United States* (Katzenbach and McClung will be addressed in more detail later in the text). Aristotle would agree and frown upon government intervention for things like urban renewal (eminent domain) that can displace friendships or the glue that holds society together. The power of friendships in society should not be marginalized because it is what fosters charity and economic growth. [218]

The Bible stresses the importance of friendships. The entire story of Jesus is not about family or marriage, but it encompasses His many sacred friendships that grow Christianity. In fact, it is my impression that the Old Testament is more about family (the want to conceive children), whereas the New Testament is more about friendships (other than the immaculate conception). The story of Ruth and Naomi, in the Book of Ruth, is the best Old Testament example of friendship and its importance. [219]

Gun Rights

Although gun rights have remained protected by the Court, most decisions that protect gun rights such as *Heller v. DC* and *McDonald v. Chicago*, have unfortunately opened the door to significant regulation. Guns should not be in the hands of unstable persons, mentally ill persons, or persons with a criminal background. Nevertheless, courts have too much flexibility (bias and opinions) to decide where to draw the line between sanity and mental illness to carve out any exception to gun rights. [220] Some exceptions include bans on certain types of guns and ammunition limits despite there being no such distinction in the Second Amendment.

There are actions that both sides can take to provide better protection to gun owners and victims of gun crimes. What if people owned smart guns? Smart guns are guns that can only be fired by the owners of the gun and provide data such as the location of the gun, time of a discharge, height of the gun at the time of a discharge, direction of the bullet, angle of the bullet, speed of the bullet, and so forth. Smart guns could be a form of gun control and police reform. The police can use the data from smart guns to solve crimes and track guns. Smart guns are a 24/7 background check on gun owners. There are smart guns on the market, but they are not as sophisticated as they should be and have many issues to resolve – including backlash from the NRA. The NRA knows if smart guns gain traction, then non-smart guns will come under legislative assault. [221] [222] In return for Republican support for smart guns, Democrats could back legislation that protects non-smart guns from confiscation. Additionally, legislation may abolish laws prohibiting the use of guns for self-defense, gun types, magazine types, and concealed carry so long as the weapon is a smart gun. Smart guns can improve the proficiency of users, help solve crimes, prevent the police from abusing their power, and prevent crimes. It will never happen, but there is middle ground to resolve controversial political issues if politicians get out of the mindset that solutions must be binary without middle ground.

The Right to Obtain Knowledge

Every family should have the right to choose where their children go to school from kindergarten through twelfth grade. Furthermore, the family's tax money should follow their child to the school of their choice. Citizens pay property and local sales taxes for this privilege. The government should not dictate where children go to school to meet, for example, their diversity objectives. A free choice educational system will enhance competition and make schools better. Ideally, the federal government would play no role in education at all. Instead, these responsibilities should fall to state and local municipalities. For a better educational system, it is essential to eliminate redundancy and red tape associated with layers of government regulation. Education should focus on teaching all subjects instead of concentrating on a few subjects that require standardized tests. It would also be prudent for education to not only include training for higher education, but trade school options for children not wanting to go to college. Education is the great equalizer in society. That means if everyone is provided the same access to an education, then everyone has the same chance to have an unfettered start in the race of life.

Free Speech Rights

First Amendment rights saw their constitutional protection begin to wane with the passage of the Alien and Seditions Act during the John Adams presidency. The Alien and Seditions Act criminalized false and misleading statements made against the government. As discussed earlier, these rights would be further mitigated in *Schenck v. United States, Debs v. United States,* and *Abrams v. United States*. In *McCullen v. Coakley,* the Court held that some speech should garner more protection than other types of similar speech, such as pro-abortion speech is more meaningful than prolife speech. In McCullen, the Court held a law restricting prolife protestors from being within 35 feet of an abortion clinic was unnecessary, but the law was considered content neutral. In other words, the law was not considered by the Court as discriminatory although no other organization receives the same First Amendment protection as abortion speech. Prolife organizations are routinely attacked but they receive no preferential protection. [223] It is not clear if McCullen overruled or just narrowed a similar law in *Hill v. Colorado*, but the bottom line is that McCullen does not preclude governments from passing similar laws to protect abortion clinics. [224]

Today, there is a push by the Biden administration to form a disinformation governance board. [225] It is never a good idea for one political party to decide which information is factual and which information is disinformation. A disinformation board is a very dangerous power grab and describes precisely how governments become propaganda institutions. Russia and China are classic examples of one party pushing one narrative. To justify war, the narrative in Russia is that Ukraine is a genocidal nation. I would hope the Supreme Court would rule the disinformation governance board is unconstitutional, violating our free speech privileges.

The Right to Pursue Health

Just as everyone has a right to pursue happiness, every citizen has a right to pursue health. Pursuing happiness and health does not mean everyone is guaranteed happiness or a healthy life. In fact, these rights routinely conflict. A person may find happiness eating junk food and not pursuing a healthy lifestyle. We all make choices and often Americans succumb to the comfort and present principles. What unhealthy people fail to realize is that they are part of the problem of rising healthcare costs in the United States. A healthier country means lower premiums for everyone. The distinction between pursuing health and health insurance as right is discussed later in this chapter.

In *Gonzales v. Raich,* the Court held that a California citizen, following state law, could not grow medical marijuana for cancer pain relief. Jurists felt it was more important to protect the Interstate Commerce Clause power attained from *Wickard v. Filburn* than allow a citizen the right to use medical marijuana. Raich is a perfect example of the government failing to do its job to protect the rights of citizens. People should have the right to pursue a health treatment option that makes them pain free. In Raich, both the right to choose and pursue health were denied. [226]

The Right to Property

The Constitution's Takings Clause (Fifth Amendment) provides that the government may take private property only for public uses and with just compensation. The government may take property to build public roads if the owner is properly compensated for the confiscated property. The decline in property rights began in the 1954 case *Berman v. Parker*. In this case, the Court held that "blighted" property may be taken for public benefit instead of for public use. Property rights were further stripped in the 2005 case *Kelo v. New London*. Here, the Court held that taking well maintained property for both public and private benefit was also permissible. In Kelo, the Court reasoned the public could benefit from both job creation and increased tax revenue by removing homes in favor of new businesses. If Kelo is the standard, then no one's property is safe from government confiscation. Of course, just compensation is needed, but even then, the government routinely violates this obligation. In both *Penn Central v. New York* and *Sierra-Tahoe v. Tahoe Reginal Planning Association* the Court denied the expansion of a private business and the building of a home on private property respectively, without compensating the owners. [227]

Conflicting Rights

Accommodation laws, discussed extensively earlier, were reintroduced in the Civil Rights Act of 1964 and where upheld in *Atlanta Motel v. United States* and *Katzenbach v. McClung*. These cases held places of business cannot deny customers service for discriminatory reasons. To overcome stare decisis protecting the liberty of association and contract rights of business owners decided in the *Civil Rights Cases of 1883*, the Court reasoned that people were commerce that could be regulated by the ever-expanding Interstate Commerce Clause. Since these rulings in the 1960s, courts have been using opinions, bias, and balancing tests to decide which exceptions are permissible to deny customer service. In *Masterpiece Cakeshop v. Colorado*, a baker refused to make a gay wedding cake for a customer. In this case, the Court upheld the baker's First Amendment artistic freedom right to deny service. [228]

Masterpiece Cakeshop demonstrates that it becomes convoluted to determine what exceptions are acceptable for denying service and which are not. Although it is odd that in Masterpiece Cakeshop the Court did not protect religious liberty, but instead artistic liberty. Regardless of the reason, it does not change the fact that all lawful professions are equal and have the same intrinsic value. Providing artistic professions more liberty violates the laws of symmetry and henceforth, common sense to treat everyone and all businesses equally. Why should someone working in a non-artistic profession be compelled to serve a customer who is wearing an offensive t-shirt that depicts Jesus or Allah in an unfavorable manner or displays any offensive message that conflicts with the values held by the store owner? Why should Facebook and Twitter be compelled to promote free speech and protect conservative speech that is different from their values? It should be noted that discriminatory speech is not against the law unless it incites "imminent lawless action" (*Brandenburg v. Ohio, 1969*).

Organizations, churches, and schools have the right to deny admittance of certain groups of people into their inner circle. Nothing precludes schools and organizations catering to, for instance, the intelligent, those with rare diseases, or women. The same should be true for businesses when it comes to selecting who they want to serve. It should also be pointed out customers routinely leave businesses without purchasing anything. Perhaps the customer's reason for declining to purchase anything was because the clerk looked ungroomed, or they sported a turban. We do not know the customers' thoughts, but the point is they are allowed to discriminate if they wish. Again, why are customers treated differently than business owners? [229]

Consider these five cases: Poor persons are denied service at a country club; a person is denied service at a restaurant because of their political ideology; a person is denied service at a bakery because of their sexual orientation; Facebook denies free speech to Christians and conservatives; and a person is denied service because of their skin color. Which of the five cases are discriminatory and which are not? Technically, they are all discriminatory, but they are not all treated the same. High membership fees to keep out the poor and denying Trump officials service in a restaurant or on Facebook may seem acceptable to some people. Those same people may find it offensive that a baker would deny making a wedding cake for a gay couple or for any business to deny service because someone is Hispanic or Black. That is the problem with so-called antidiscrimination or accommodation laws, they are not consistent, and everyone is treated differently. If everyone has equal rights, then in the five examples listed above everyone should be treated the same, not differently. When people are treated the same, they cannot argue, but when they are treated differently, problems arise. Treating people differently is how conflicts arise between races, genders, and other classes of people. Accommodation laws do not unite, but instead polarize and fuel identity politics. My point is this, we are making the world more complicated than it needs to be. Let the free-market system play out by letting businesses pick their customers and to hire who they deem are the most qualified.

Turning away business under any circumstance does not make sense but people have different principles, values, and priorities in life. Under most circumstances it is best for people to sort out their differences or respectfully part ways. Unfortunately, Americans tend to get offended much too easy and escalate conflicts that are best to resolve, for instance, by going to the baker around the corner. Regrettably, politics, polarity, power grabs, biases, opinions, and other poor critical thinking skills escalate simple conflicts into major disputes.

Why should discriminatory businesses get off scot-free and face no penalty? Society will judge those businesses that discriminate and consequently they will lose business. Those businesses that discriminate will forfeit some of their fundamental rights (contracts and friendships) for their bigoted decisions. In the present day 24/7 social media environment, discriminators can no longer hide.

Homosexuality Rights

Romans 1:26–27 is clear that homosexuality is "contrary to natural" and a sin, but it is not up to me or you to judge another person's character or orientation. Just because homosexual behavior is outside my norm, it does not mean I am not obligated to love, accept, and treat homosexuals as any other human being. When judging homosexuality, it would be prudent for Christians to remember John 8:7, "He that is without sin among you, let him be the first to throw a stone at her." Christian historical author, David Barton, condemns homosexuality and claims that higher rates of HIV and venereal disease in the homosexual community are Godly interventions punishing those to reap what they sow. Barton's rhetoric is purely speculative. For example, no one views sickle cell anemia as a Godly curse on the African race. Barton argues that God does not create people to have homosexual feelings. Barton reasons that same-gender attraction is a choice. Perhaps Barton can explain why some people are born with multiple genitalia? The Bible never says anything about God creating persons who may be both male and female. Yet, it happens, and it is not a personal choice, so why is so improbable to think that God created homosexuality? Homosexuality may be God's way of testing heterosexual people to not only accept and tolerate, but to treat homosexuals equally. If evolution is part of God's plan to satisfy His want for diversity and uniqueness, then homosexuality may very well be part of God's plan. [230]

Barton's critical mistake is to imply homosexuality is a crime. Barton bases his assumption on prior laws that banned the practice of sodomy. Sodomy was a crime in various states until those laws were ruled unconstitutional by the Supreme Court in *Lawrence v. Texas* in 2003. Where Barton's logic goes awry is when he fails to understand the difference between immoral actions that result in victims and immoral actions that do not result in victims. Immoral actions that result in victims should be the sole focus of the justice system. Yes, God holds people responsible for the health and wellbeing of their body. Most people forget that the body is considered a sacred vessel to house their spirit (2 Timothy 2:21 and 1 Corinthians 6:19–20). That said, natural law philosophy is clear that people can do what they wish with their property. Moreover, according to natural law, the human body is both property and owned by the person occupying it. Defiling or doing harm to oneself may be a sin and crime against God, but these actions should not be a prosecutorial crime because everyone commits self-destructive sins. If homosexuality is criminalized, then everyone belongs in prison. For example, who is not guilty of eating unhealthy foods, watching mind numbing TV, cursing, lying, playing violent video games, watching pornography, having premarital sex, defiling oneself sexually, gambling, getting tattoos, getting drunk, smoking tobacco or marijuana, disrespecting their parents, doing drugs, and so on. For the justice system to be fair and consistent, then any criminal law that prosecutes people without a victim needs to be rescinded. Immoral behavior toward others, including bad manners, is more destructive to society than immoral behavior committed against oneself. [231]

Civil Unions should be tolerated for a few reasons. First, if people follow moral principles, then homosexuals should be treated no different than any other person. Second, marriage has been expanded to include gay couples, and although that holding was partially correct, the decision in Obergefell v. Hodges to protect gay marriage rights was atrocious. Obergefell was not about love and marriage; instead, it was about government entitlements. Obergefell was about why government tax laws treat single persons differently than married couples. The government discriminates against single people by providing married couples favorable tax rates. Obergefell was about gay couples legally expecting the same favorable tax rates provided to married couples.

Perhaps if the government stops discriminating and violating the rights of single persons, then many gay and straight couples may see no benefit in the institution of marriage and decline to get married. That will, ultimately, make marriage about love and conceivably reduce the high divorce rate. That said, like store owners, religions can deny service to anyone they wish. Hence, they cannot be compelled or forced to marry gay couples if it violates their belief system.

Equal Tax and Profit Rights

Article I, Section 8 of the Constitution provides the government with the power and lay taxes, "but all duties, imposts, and excises shall be uniform throughout the United States." The preceding clause complies with Deuteronomy 14:22, "You shall surely tithe all the produce from what you sow, which comes out of the field every year." A tithe was equivalent to a 10% tax of what each person would produce. Article I, Section 8, and Deuteronomy 14:22 imply that every person shall be taxed equally regardless of their income. A progressive or variable tax rate did not become the norm until the passage of the Sixteenth Amendment (income tax) in 1909 and the repeal of *Pollock v. Farmers Loan and Trust* (1895). That said, the Sixteenth Amendment may allow the government to tax income, but it does not allow them to tax citizens at different rates. Furthermore, it does not allow the government to use revenues collected from taxes for anything outside its grants of power in the Constitution. [232] A good solution to resolve the problem of unequal tax rates is to repeal the Sixteenth Amendment, abolish the Internal Revenue Service (IRS), and establish a fair tax. A fair tax is a national sales tax placed on all goods and services. In other words, with a fair tax people are taxed equivalently on what they consume. Keep in mind that although the national sales tax maintains a uniform tax rate, those who buy and consume more will pay more in taxes.

Moreover, it is a fundamental right for people to profit from the fruits of their labor. The parable of the Ten Minas in Luke 19 is clear, Jesus is endorsing profitable behavior, which should not be penalized with excessive tax rates. The Founders agreed, explaining profits promote hard work and higher production. Thomas Jefferson said, "There cannot be a stronger natural right than that of a man making the best profit he can." Similarly, in the 1874 case *Loan Association v. Topeka*, the power to tax was described as the power to destroy. [233] The Bible and the Founders wanted a system of government that taxed citizens both equally and at low rates.

The Right to Consent to Government

The right to consent to government is a subject that is often ignored since it is widely assumed that every citizen consents to be governed by the laws of society at birth. That is not true. As discussed earlier, most people tacitly consent to the Declaration of Independence social contract and to be governed by the Constitution. However, what happens when the government breaks its vow to uphold the social contract and Constitution?

Our government has failed to protect the rights of all citizens equally because of partisan politics. The United States borders are not secure and protected from undocumented immigration that threatens the rights of citizens. Increased crime is a growing issue even though it is the primary responsibility of the government to protect people and their property. [234] Some people no longer have faith in the security and integrity of their elections. The United States federal government is coercive and violates citizens' rights by spending their tax dollars on unenumerated projects. Expansion of power in all three branches of the government is also a threat to constitutional principles. For example, presidential overuse of executive orders, voided legislative supermajorities to approve Supreme Court justices and important government officials, and the Supreme Court power to not only legislate, but to enforce their rulings. All the above abuses violate both the social contract (Declaration of Independence) and Constitution. The United States may be more divided today since the Civil War. What politicians forget is that no one in the United States has consented to any government action that is outside the scope and mission of the Constitution and Declaration of Independence.

The Declaration of Independence suggests that people have the right to overthrow the government when it abuses its power. I am certainly not suggesting force to overthrow the government. What I am suggesting is a state constitutional convention to propose amendments to the Constitution per Article V of the Constitution. Using this method of amending the Constitution, the states can bypass Congress to reinstate federalism and sovereignty for the people. In Chapter 1, I suggested several amendment proposals to regain the original meaning of the Constitution.

Fictitious Rights

The term fictitious rights explain the many unconstitutional rights that have garnered popularity in recent history. The fictitious rights discussed in this section are all ill-conceived government created rights. Although some citizens will benefit from fictitious rights, a vast majority of citizens will find many of their God-given fundamental rights are infringed by any fictitious right.

Welfare Rights

The Bible is clear; charity should come from the community, not the government. For example, in Deuteronomy 15:11, God is asking the community to help the poor, "For the poor will not cease to exist in the land; therefore I am commanding you, saying, 'You shall fully open your hand to your brother, to your needy and poor in your land.'" Deuteronomy 15:11 never suggests the government is responsible for the charity. In fact, the Bible explains that the government must be impartial regardless of the socioeconomic status of individuals. For example, Exodus 23:3–6, Leviticus 19:15, and Proverbs 29:14 specifically inform Christians that the poor should receive no preferential treatment. Practically speaking, the United States government has proven itself to be a woefully inefficient charity since less than 30% of its revenue earmarked for welfare makes it to the nation's poor. Any charity with the government's efficiency would surely never last very long in the private sector. [235]

In Deuteronomy 24:19–21 God spells out how poverty should be addressed. Deuteronomy 24:19–21 instructs farmers to leave a portion of their crop unharvested, which should be earmarked for the poor. That said, it was the duty of the poor to work the fields and collect any remaining provisions, which is reinforced in 2 Thessalonians 3:10, "If anyone is not willing to work, then he is not to eat, either." The Founders, such as Ben Franklin, similarly believed "the best way of doing good to the poor is not making them easy in poverty but leading or driving them out of it." Ben Franklin, Thomas Jefferson, and George Washington explain the obvious, that no one will get out of poverty through "idleness" or "laziness." The Bible and Constitution do not support welfare or the concept of people receiving a benefit for doing nothing. [236]

Charity is a common subject in the Bible. In 2 Corinthians 8:13–14, "For this is not for the relief of others and for your hardship, but by way of equality – at this present time your abundance will serve as assistance for their need, so that their abundance also may serve as assistance for your need, so that there may be equality." This Bible verse suggests that money (property) is not the only form of charity to achieve equality. Everyone has something of abundance to offer in return for charity such as labor skills. If there must be welfare, the mission of the government should be to promote temporary workfare instead of permanent welfare. Workfare requires individuals to provide labor for the greater good of society in return for their welfare checks.

The Takings Clause of the Fifth Amendment does not allow welfare policies. The antiwelfare constitutional standard was also set in *Calder v. Bull (1798)*. Justice Samuel Chase in Calder held the government should enforce no law "that takes property [money] from A and gives it to B." Collecting tax revenues (money is property) from private citizens and giving that money to other private citizens violates the Takings Clause. Although James Iredell dissented in Calder, his opinion was in the slim minority during the nineteenth century. Cases such as *Vanhorn's Lessee v. Dorrance, Fletcher v. Peck, Dartmouth v. Woodard, Wilkinson v. Leland, Terrett v. Taylor,* and *Taylor v. Porter and Ford* support Justice Chase's view. Judge Greene Bronson echoed Justice Chase in Porter and Ford that legislatures could not "take the property of A, with or without just compensation, and give it B." Due process of the law requires that life, liberty, and property cannot be abridged and welfare not only violates a constitutional provision but its ends do not achieve a constitutional outcome. Citing the Supremacy Clause is the go-to argument to defend unconstitutional legislative power such as welfare. Alexander Hamilton wrote in Federalist Paper 33 that the Supremacy Clause "expressly confines this supremacy to laws made pursuant to the Constitution." In other words, only federal laws made in pursuant of the Constitution are the "Supreme law of the land." [237]

The Sixteenth Amendment affords that the government can levy an income tax overruling *Pollock v. Farmers Loan and Trust*, but the amendment does not empower the federal government to use tax money for anything outside the legislative grants of power enumerated in the Constitution. For example, income tax revenues should be restricted to financing the military, infrastructure, and post offices. There are no grants of power in the Constitution to afford the federal government the authority to spend tax revenues on welfare or to legislate welfare. Charity should be the responsibility of the community.

Since the inception of welfare, the number of people living in poverty has remained about the same – 15% of the population. [238] The United States spends over 550 billion dollars annually on poverty (10 years ago). That is enough to give each person in poverty over 11,000 dollars annually. Hence, a family of four would earn nearly 50,000 dollars. There should be no poverty. The problem is that poverty dollars come from dozens of bureaucratic agencies with excessive overhead costs. There are food stamps, housing vouchers, Medicaid, school vouchers, and multiple other redundant revenue sources. If the government is only 30% efficient, then only 165 billion of that 550 trillion reach the poor. Of course, this does not include welfare funding from state governments or the billions that come from charity. The number of dollars thrown at poverty is much closer to 1 trillion annually today. [239] Thus, it is easy to conclude that the government's war on poverty has been an utter failure to lift more people out of poverty. No one objects to temporarily helping those in need, but when welfare becomes a permanent fixture in the lives of some citizens, then welfare is a failure. Besides, citizens addicted to government dependency is the catalyst for government expansion to garner more power.

One important thing to note about welfare – it divides the populous because it promotes selfishness and pits the rich against the poor. The poor expect their neighbors, the wealthy, and corporations to pay for their benefit. The rich, of course, want to hang onto their hard-earned dollars. Polarity, selfishness, and failing to mind our own business violate the true purpose of charity. Furthermore, welfare is not seen as a charity, but an entitlement. Most who receive welfare do not view it as a gift nor do they believe they are accountable or responsible for any revenue they receive. At the same time, those who receive a gift from charity may be more inclined to appreciate and value that money, especially if it is not a continuous cash stream. Americans are among the most generous people in the world and if they were able to hang onto more of their hard-earned dollars with lower taxes, then more efficient charities could benefit and play a bigger role in ending poverty. [240]

Legal and Illegal Immigration Rights

Undocumented immigration is a controversial subject. Most historians failed to recognize the humanitarian crisis of slavery for causing the Civil War. Similarly, undocumented immigration is a humanitarian crisis as thousands flock to the United States looking for asylum and a better life. Joe Biden is on record saying that the one million legal immigrants the United States accepts each year is peanuts and the United States should absorb as many as three million immigrants annually. The "per year" is a key element of Biden's statement. [241] Absorbing 1% of the population each year adds up very quickly. In a mere decade that would amount to a 10% population increase from immigration alone. The strain that will have on not only the immigration system, but the entire United States economy would be massive. The United States economy does not create three million new jobs annually (aside from recession recoveries). In fact, in the past 30 years the United States economy only added thirty million new jobs. [242] Without question, there are millions of people suffering around the globe and it would be fantastic to help them all, but that is unrealistic. Most of us do not realize it, but we won the lottery when born in the United States. I understand the eagerness of others wanting to pursue their dreams by coming to the United States. Sources on the subject are very volatile but suggest that the United States pays anywhere from 54 to 116 billion annually for illegal immigration. Since illegal immigration exploded under Biden those estimates are too small and do not factor in state finances to support illegal immigration. It is a fairly conservate estimate that families pay anywhere from 1 to 2 thousand dollars annually to fund illegal migrants. [243] [244] [245] [246]

If an undocumented immigrant violates the rights of one American citizen by for instance, criminal activity, carrying a contagious and deadly illness, replacing citizens in the workforce, diluting the votes of citizens, displacing persons wanting to immigrate legally, injuring citizens by accident, or accepting tax money without contributing to society, then it should be the objective of the government to end the practice. It would be great to help everyone, but where do we draw the line? If the United States knowingly allows entry to one undocumented immigrant, then technically, they cannot deny anyone with credible hardships amnesty and illegal entry into the country.

Healthcare or Health Insurance Rights

We can pursue health, but healthcare or health insurance is not a right for many reasons. First, rights are not created by the government, second rights do not need money for their creation, and finally, rights do not need the support of other citizens for one to garner the privilege. The individual controls pursuing fundamental rights such as the right to health, whereas the economy, private sector, and government dictate health insurance, which is mostly out of the individual's control. Therefore, while pursuing health is a right, there is, however, no fundamental right to healthcare or health insurance.

Is providing health insurance to citizens the central problem regarding healthcare? No, the problem is the cost of the healthcare. Nothing is being done to curb medical costs. As alluded to, American citizens are not helping the situation by living unhealthy lifestyles. If the government wants to protect the right of people to pursue health, then they should focus on finding ways to reduce healthcare costs. For example, health insurance costs can be reduced by incentivizing a lower premium for those living a healthy lifestyle, tort reform, and researching cures for devastating diseases and finding cheaper and more effective diagnostic testing methods. For instance, in home treatment and diagnostic testing is cheaper than if these tests or procedures were done at a clinic or hospital.

One issue with government subsidized healthcare such as Medicaid is that no restrictions are placed on people who receive the benefit. Should people who take taxpayer money be forced to use that gift responsibly and maintain some health standards? People have the right to eat junk food, but should they retain that right once they get government subsidized health insurance? People who receive welfare should be held accountable for that gift. Charity should never be taken for granted. Furthermore, why should healthy persons who eat right, exercise, sleep eight hours per day, get vaccinated, and use sun screen be obliged to pay for the healthcare of irresponsible persons?

I was born with a deficit immune system and consequently, I developed several autoimmune diseases with debilitating and severe neurological symptoms. Should the government be responsible for researching autoimmune diseases since we know very little about them? No, it is not the responsibility of the government to improve my life. The private sector should be responsible for finding answers if they want to pursue that research. Only charitable and private sector research is acceptable, not taxpayer research.

Abortion Rights [247]

The wonders of human life are best explained in Psalms 139:13–16:

> For You created my innermost parts; you wove me in my mother's womb. I will give thanks to You, because I am awesomely and wonderfully made; wonderful are Your works, and my soul knows it very well. My frame was not hidden from You when I was made in secret, and skillfully formed in the depths of the Earth; your eyes have seen my formless substance; and in Your book were written all the days that were ordained for me, when as yet there was not one of them.

English judge and writer, Sir William Blackstone, and Supreme Court justice, James Wilson, wrote "life begins when the infant can stir." Of course, this was before sonograms, but notice at the first instant a baby was felt, it was considered a human life deserving constitutional protections. [248]

Remember, for an action to be a fundamental right it needs to be unanimously accepted, it cannot be controversial, and it cannot oppose other rights (right to life). Abortion infringes on all the principal requirements for an action to be considered a fundamental right. That is why abortion rights advocates suggest they protect the right to choose, the right to privacy, or reproductive rights instead of defending abortion rights. The right to choose and privacy are fundamental rights, but they are predicated on the condition: The choice or action done in private does no harm to another person. Here, again, abortion fails. Reproductive rights are just another way to say abortion rights. There is no such thing as cardio pulmonary, respiratory, or nervous system rights. We only have the right to pursue health. Hence, if a mother's life is in jeopardy from a pregnancy, an abortion to protect her health should be permissible. Additionally, if a mother's mental health is jeopardized from being raped then abortion may be rationally argued. Mental health from a non-crime pregnancy should not be a reason for an abortion. The mental health of most women is altered from a pregnancy. For example, postpartum depression is quite common.

Some pro-abortion advocates have described pregnancy as making women slaves to their bodies. It is also reasoned that pregnancy is unfair since men do not have similar experiences. There is no doubt pregnancy is a rough and painful experience, but there are many things that men must endure that are just as difficult.

Around the same time *Roe v. Wade* was being decided, men were drafted to fight in the Vietnam War. The draft was also like being a slave since the military stripped men of most of their rights. Drafted military men were deprived of seeing their family and friends, traveling, free speech, religious practice, recreation, and in some cases to life by no choice of their own.

Abortion proponents claim that a fetus is a human life at no stage during a pregnancy; therefore, the fetus's rights are never denied. A new Colorado law states a fetus has no rights during pregnancy. Common sense acknowledges that a fetus is a baby once viable and can survive outside the womb. Viability happens around 20 weeks into the pregnancy. Furthermore, the rights of a fetus can be defended even if it is not considered a human life. The Supreme Court has protected animals such as upholding a treaty with Canada to protect migratory birds from hunting (*Missouri v. Holland*, 1920). The Environmental Protection Agency has laws and regulations protecting nature (The Clean Air Act). United States laws (wills) protect the dead. If all the above is true, that courts can protect non-living things and non-human life, then it is not too farfetched for courts to protect a fetus or a group of cells that will form a human life?

I explained how liberal justices have worked tirelessly over the years expanding the federal government's control over commerce. The Constitution's Interstate Commerce Clause was meant to control trade between the states. The Supreme Court has expanded the meaning to include controlling or regulating manufacturing, intrastate commerce, and anything that may have a minute impact on commerce. For example, in *Atlanta Motel v. United States* discussed earlier, the Court expanded the Interstate Commerce Clause to include the regulation of people. It is easy to surmise that any reduction in population through abortions would also impact economic commerce. The argument regarding people as commerce could be disputed on the grounds of ripeness or mootness since it is impossible to understand the effect a potential child would have on the economy. Perhaps, but in *Wickard v. Filburn* (discussed earlier), the government was granted control over anything that may minutely affect commerce. Thus, aborting a fetus violates the Interstate Commerce Clause because it would have a minute effect on the economy, including changing parents' buying habits and denying a future taxpaying consumer and worker in the United States economy.

My point is that abortion (reproductive rights) or a woman's right to choose an abortion are not fundamental rights. A person should have the right to do whatever they want to their own body so long as it does not violate the rights of others. A person can eat unhealthy foods, drink, and do drugs but abortion involves more than just the mother. Abortion involves the fetus and father, and they have rights. A fetus can have rights even if it is not considered a human life (but a fetus is a life at conception). Sure, rational arguments can be made to defend abortion to save the mother's life or if the pregnancy was the result of a crime, but these cases are very rare and account for less than 3% of all abortions. [249] The entire purpose of the law is to protect the fundamental rights of everyone, especially those who may not be able to speak for themselves: Children, the dead (wills), the incapacitated, those with disabilities, victims of crime, and the unborn.

With all the above arguments stated, prolife advocates can do more to break down barriers or reasons why women get abortions. Pregnancy centers are a good start, but life does not end at birth. Churches and communities need to help scared and financially strapped mothers with counseling, daycare, and pediatric medical care. Moreover, more needs to be done to improve the adoption process. I get it, care must be taken to ensure kids are placed in the right hands, but it should take only a short time. What is more, adoptions can be pricy. The adoption process should be a target of reform so families can adopt children in the United States instead of choosing foreign-born children because it is easier.

Diversity Rights [250]

Martin Luther King's *I Have a Dream* speech stresses equality when he demanded that Americans should judge a person based on their character and not by the color of their skin. *Galatians 3:28* emphasizes the need for societal impartiality and equality when Paul writes, "There is neither a Jew nor Greek, there is neither slave nor free, there is neither male nor female, for you are all one in Christ Jesus." Americans are reminded daily of their equality by the Latin phrase written on United States currency, which reads, "*E Pluribus Unum.*" The phrase can be interpreted to mean that the citizens of America are united. The phrase reminds Americans that they are not to be categorized or divided based on their demographic composition or ideological beliefs. Americans are equal, and no government partiality should be used to polarize and divide the populous.

Diversity and affirmative action policies establish racial and gender criteria used by employers and schools to determine the qualification of candidates for entrance into a business or school. Diversity and affirmative action qualification for a job and school were upheld in *Grutter v. Bollinger* (2003). Diversity policies are wrong for several reasons. First, diversity policies usually only consider gender and race. As we learned earlier, this is a very narrow definition of diversity since everyone is unique based on their exclusive environmental experiences. Second, any quota system that provides an opportunity to a less qualified candidate will, at the same time, deny a suitable candidate the right to work or obtain knowledge. Making up for past gender and racial injustices by violating the rights of an innocent bystander makes little sense. Diversity should be replaced with educational reforms by empowering families to select the school of their choice for their children. Education is the great equalizer of society, not diversity. Third, antidiscrimination laws tend to discriminate. For example, age antidiscrimination laws may protect older people in the workforce while preventing job opportunities for younger, more qualified, and more diverse candidates. Remember, younger populations in the United States are more diverse in terms of race. Accommodation laws, discussed earlier, discriminate because they are not applied equally between businesses and between owners and customers. Also as previously discussed, affirmative action discriminates against more qualified candidates. Antidiscrimination laws tend to alienate and polarize citizens because they discriminate.

Preferred classes of people and social justice strip the rights of some to protect others. We all belong to one type of people: United States citizens. Any identity politics to pit races, genders, and socioeconomic classes against each other should be censored if it is intended to polarize and divide. Creating polarization and division encroaches upon the Constitution's preamble to "insure domestic tranquility." Modern diversity policies are not much different than the thought process of slave owners. No, diversity policies are not as barbaric as slavery, but denying rights to one group of people while elevating the rights of another group is eerily similar and is an evil habit that needs to be corrected before it becomes an evil custom.

Part IV: The United States History of Fundamental Rights [251]

Chapter 9: The Revolutionary War Background Information

The Significance of the Revolutionary and Civil Wars

The American Revolution and the Civil War were the two most influential and important events shaping the Constitution and protecting fundamental rights. [252] [253] The American Revolution and Civil Wars were the two most deadly wars in American history based on per capita data. Twenty-five thousand Americans died in the American Revolution, or nearly 1% of the population. 655,000 Americans died in the Civil War—about 2.1% of the population. [254] To put that in perspective, the Covid-19 pandemic has been catastrophic and killed over one million Americans, but that is not even close to 0.5% of the American population. [255] Some of the reasons for the high death rates in the Revolutionary War and Civil War were:

1. The wars were fought on American soil resulting in more civilian deaths.
2. The Civil War was a conflict between Americans and not a foreign enemy.
3. The stakes for these wars were high since the future existence and survival of the United States were in doubt.
4. The borders of the United States and its sovereignty were directly threatened.

What was more important was that both the Revolutionary War and Civil War were fought over constitutional principles and equal fundamental rights that would define America. That is why the American Revolution and Civil Wars resulted in the establishment of the Constitution and the addition of essential amendments to the Constitution, respectively. No other war led to any legal changes in the Constitution.

The Founding of a Christian Nation [256]

Without the Bible, western society and life in the United States may be completely different since Christianity influenced the Founders and the founding documents (Declaration of Independence and Constitution). The Christian revival in the New World made the Bible the central piece or the cornerstone to the American Revolution, the Declaration of Independence, and Constitution. Without this movement from 1730 to 1770, the United States would be a much different place and may very well not even exist. The names of Founders, the names of their family members, the names of their towns, and their common expressions are more likely than not to have a biblical significance. The Christian revival led to the establishment of colleges to educate the Founders, it united Christian denominations behind common biblical themes, and brought about a desire to replace corruption with the purity of God. The Founders truly believed that America was the new Israel, and it was their responsibility to install a government, which was truly representative of the ethical and moral principles of God and Christianity.

To find God's influence on United States history, look no further than the monuments, museums, and public buildings in Washington DC. The capital is littered with biblical verses and references to God. My favorite is at the Jefferson Memorial "God who gave us life gave us Liberty. Can the Liberties of a Nation be thought secure when we have removed their only firm basis, a conviction in the minds of the people that these Liberties are a gift of God?" In other words, the liberty of citizens protected in the Constitution cannot be secured if the United States is fundamentally transformed into an atheist democracy. Many American and biblical leaders echoed that same sentiment. Pastor Jedidiah Morse warns in a 1799 sermon "Whenever the pillars of Christianity shall be overthrown, our present Republican forms of government, and all the blessings which flow from them, must fall with them." Likewise, Harry Truman warns Americans, "If we don't have the proper fundamental moral background, we will finally wind up with a totalitarian government which does not believe in rights for anybody except the state." Truman's words are representative of the current trajectory of United States governance. Similarly, King Solomon cautioned the people of Israel with these wise words in Proverbs 29:18, "Where there is no [godly] vision, the people are unrestrained, but happy is one who keeps the Law." [257]

Historians widely agree that God had no influence on the Founders drafting of the Constitution. However, Alexander Hamilton, James Madison, George Washington, Benjamin Rush, and Benjamin Franklin would suggest that the Constitution was divinely influenced by the "finger of God" for several reasons. First, the odds of successfully drafting a constitution in such a divisive and polarized political landscape were highly improbable. In fact, the Constitutional Convention was making no progress before Ben Franklin reminded his peers of Psalms 127:1, "Unless the LORD builds a house, they who build it labor in vain." Second, scripture influenced many provisions within the document. [258]

Similarly, the Declaration of Independence can also be linked to the Bible. For example, Genesis 1:28 reads, "God blessed them; and God said to them, 'Be fruitful and multiply, and fill the Earth, and subdue it; and rule over the fish of the sea and over the birds of the sky and over every living thing that moves on the Earth.'" To be fruitful and multiply represents life, to fill the Earth signifies liberty, and to subdue over wildlife denotes happiness or property ownership.

The colonists responded much differently than the Canadians, Irish, Indigenous people, or other nations under oppressive English rule during the 18th century. Why is that? Why were fundamental rights in America so important to fight for but they were not that significant in other countries facing the same oppressive English laws? Historian Bernhard Knollenberg suggests it was because other English colonies were immature politically and did not understand constitutional principles. [259] Case in point, colonial clergymen would regularly give sermons about the natural law theories held by John Locke that planted the seed for revolution in America. John Locke was the primary philosopher mentioned in colonial sermons because his natural law principles of equality and fundamental rights could connect theology, the law, and politics together as one topic. For instance, William Emerson and Jonas Clark were ministers who would regularly reinforce to their congregation that they all had fundamental rights worth fighting for. Emerson and Clark were unlike ministers in other countries under English rule because they would lead the Minute Men at the battles of Lexington and Concord. America was, indeed, unique since John Locke was an unknown quantity in other nations under English rule making natural law unfamiliar to them.

History book theories for the cause of the Revolutionary War do not include God or fundamental rights. To prove the thesis proposed in the Chapter 1, I must demonstrate that the Revolutionary War was fought to protect the fundamental rights of citizens. Since I already gave testimony to illustrate fundamental rights are God-given and if the Revolutionary War was fought to garner those fundamental rights, then history without God is wrong. Furthermore, if my hypothesis is correct, we may conclude that the Revolutionary War may be referred to as the Lockean Revolution.

Revolution Timeline

The American revolution was set in motion in a very slow methodical fashion. Colonial patriots felt they could convince loyalists about their grievances without any conflict: "American writers were profoundly reasonable people. Their pamphlets convey scorn, anger, and indignation; but rarely blind hate, rarely panic and fear. They sought to convince their opponents …." [260] Moreover, "The great social shocks that in the French and Russian Revolutions that sent the foundations of thousands of individual lives crashing into ruins had taken place in America in the course of the previous century, slowly, silently, almost imperceptibly, not as a sudden avalanche but as myriads of individual changes and adjustments, which had gradually transformed the order of society." [261] It is essential to understand that in the years leading up to the Revolutionary War, grievances were generally aired in a non-violent way. What this means is that the purpose and reason for the war were adequately thought out, debated, and the consequences considered. Thus, the American Revolutionary War was one about ideas and constitutional principles instead of a reactionary one regarding any one reason such as economics or imperialism. Many causes of war are unpredictable and impossible to document because they arise from irrational behaviors and emotions. However, since the American Revolution origins were built upon for over a decade, emotions and irrational behaviors are a less likely a cause. Although some historians, such as George Bancroft, believed the American Revolution was a spontaneous event that started with the battles of Lexington and Concord, I do not believe that to be the case. Besides, Bancroft's version of events is said to be a myth or a fabrication of the truth. Consequently, it is hard to give Bancroft's theory any credence concerning his account of the war. [262]

The Events Leading up to the War

Before starting an in-depth look at causation theories, we must first explore the details of the events that preceded the war. The Stamp Act of 1763 and Townshend Duties of 1768, although small, were reasoned to be unlawful by the colonists because they believed parliamentary sovereignty was not absolute, it had limits.

Colonial sovereignty theories evolved over time as to why they opposed the Stamp Act and why parliamentary power was not absolute. Initially, the colonists reasoned that one limit to parliamentary power was that internal excise taxes against the colonies were illegal. The colonists conceded that external taxes such as custom duties to support commerce for the English empire were legitimate taxes. The internal / external tax debate resulted in much confusion. For example, the colonists rejected the Townshend Duties even though parliament held they were an external tax. Consequently, determining the intent of parliament was no easy task. Did parliamentary taxes intend to raise revenue for any purpose, regulate commerce, or both? Nevertheless, the internal / external tax dispute lasted only a short time before colonists were contending all taxes from parliament were illegal citing the home rule theory. The home rule theory reasons that only local governments could decide matters such as taxation and appropriate laws. Later, the dominion theory regarding parliament sovereignty was raised by the colonies. The dominion theory implied the colonies were immune to parliamentary action of any kind since the only link between the colonies and the mother country was the King and not parliament. When the colonies pushed for independence, the dominion theory is precisely the reason parliament was ignored in the Declaration of Independence and all the grievances were directed to the King. The colonists needed help settling on a well-conceived argument to dispute parliamentary sovereignty. [263]

In the early debate over taxes, the colonists erred for several reasons. First, the dominion theory, the home rule theory, and the internal / external argument clearly showed the colonists did not understand that sovereignty could be shared between government entities and the people. And more importantly, they did not realize the people were the most significant sovereign entity in a nation. Second, colonial theories failed to pinpoint that parliamentary power did not allow the passage of any law that would violate the fundamental rights of citizens. The sole purpose of any government is to pass laws to protect the fundamental rights of all citizens equally, not to violate them. It would take a colossal shift in the political philosophies of the colonists before they could unite behind a meaningful theory.

The shift in colonial thinking was initiated when the Virginia legislature passed the Virginia Resolves, consequently printed in many colonial newspapers. The Virginia Resolves detailed precisely why the Stamp Act tax on printed material was illegal. First, it was the first tax paid directly to England and not to the local legislatures in the colonies. Second, it violated the rights of citizens to not only have representation in parliament, but it denied them the right to consent to be governed. The Virginia Resolves would provide the colonists with a meaningful direction that would eventually help them unite behind one theory to protect the fundamental rights of citizens. The primary objection against the Stamp Act was taxation without representation, but it was later recognized that representation was impossible to achieve. Colonial leaders slowly began to realize that even if they had representation in parliament, it would only serve to legitimize parliament to pass taxes. Besides, the difficulty for American representatives to maintain a relationship with their constituents over 3000 miles away was not to be taken lightly in the eighteenth century. Nevertheless, England contended the stamp tax was essential to maintain a standing army in the colonies to protect their imperialistic interests from the French, Spanish, and Indian Tribes. Shortly after the Virginia Resolves made their rounds in neighboring state newspapers, riots originated in many colonial New England states including Massachusetts, Rhode Island, and Connecticut. Stamp distributors in each state resigned because they faced continuous threats against them, their family, and their property. [264] [265]

Within a year of its passage, parliament reluctantly repealed the Stamp Act. The English ruling class harbored much anger and resentment because they believed the colonial response to the Stamp Act in the New England states was uncivil. England's answer to the Stamp Act's failure was the Declaratory Act, which insisted the colonists were virtually represented in parliament. The Declaratory Act of 1766 reads, "the colonies and plantations in America are, and of right ought to be, subordinate unto, and dependent upon the imperial Crown and Parliament of Great Britain". The Declaratory Act may have been the most problematic law levied by England during the pre-revolutionary years. That is because by trying to reinforce parliamentary sovereignty, England encouraged the colonists to pursue the true meaning of sovereignty and develop sound constitutional principles to dispute taxes and other legislation. [266]

The Townshend Duties of 1768 were a tax placed on the importation of lead, glass, paper, tea, and other items. England argued that these taxes were external and were necessary to regulate commerce. The colonists objected because the taxes were not only used to regulate commerce but went into the general treasury to pay for any government expense. Additionally, the Townshend Duties contained both a revenue feature as well as the intrusive Suspension Act that postponed the New York legislature from meeting until they complied with the Quartering Act to house and feed British troops. Thus, the Suspension Act violated a host of fundamental rights including privacy and property rights. [267] Over the next few years colonial merchants responded to the Townshend Duties by refusing to import any taxable items. Eventually, England was again forced to repeal the Townshend Duties except for the duty on tea. [268]

Everything came to a boil with the Tea Act of 1773. The colonist responded with non-violent protests and pamphlet writing, such as the Boston Pamphlets, detailing the "absolute rights" of colonists. When non-violent protests gained no traction, colonial actions turned violent culminating with the Boston Tea Party. The duty on tea from the Tea Act was the same as those found in the Townshend Duties, still the act brought about a more vehement reaction. The reason for the strong response was, in part, to the monopoly on tea provided to the British East India Company. Another reason for the Tea Act outrage may have been from the publication of letters, uncovered around the same time, written by the Loyalist governor of Massachusetts. Governor Thomas Hutchinson's response to the Massachusetts assembly explaining why colonial rights were lesser than English rights poured fuel on the brewing fire. Hutchinson reasoned that colonial proximity to England made it impossible for them to have equal rights. Furthermore, while Hutchinson was maintaining that colonists did not have "all" the rights of Englishmen he said, "I know of no line that can be drawn between the supreme authority of parliament and the total independence of the colonies."[269] Obviously, Hutchinson's remarks sparked much outrage.

England responded to the Boston Tea Party with the so-called Intolerable Acts that included the Boston Port Act, the Impartial Administration of Justice Act (IAJA), the Massachusetts Government Regulatory Act (MGRA), and the Quartering Act. The Boston Port Act closed the Boston Harbor; the IAJA moved trials for royal officials back to England; the MGRA provided that colonial council members and civil officers be appointed by England; and the Quartering Act was much more intrusive than the Quartering Act of 1765 allowing for English troops to be quartered in family residents. At this point, Massachusetts colonists not only believed that their fundamental rights had been violated but they had been rescinded.[270] The colonists' response to the Intolerable Acts was to convene the First Continental Congress in 1774. The First Continental Congress made two crucial decisions. First, they decided to boycott imports and exports with England and second, they agreed that the fundamental rights of the colonists might be defined in a combination of the laws of nature, the English Constitution, and colonial charters.[271] The Founders finally had a clear understanding of the importance of both sovereignty and fundamental rights.

England added insult to injury by passing the American Prohibitory Act in late 1775, which ordered that all trade with the colonies end immediately and any ships trading with the colonies would have their cargo seized. The Prohibitory Act made any reconciliation with England impossible, and the Second Continental Congress responded by opening trade with all countries except England.[272] The lines had been drawn; war was imminent.

Chapter 10: The Revolutionary War Causation Theories and Consequences [273] [274] [275]

There are at least two sides to every historical event, and only one is usually told in history books. History is the study of unique happenings as described by the historian. There are several historical theories for the cause of the Revolutionary War, including imperialism, progressivism, conservativism, the Founders impact, propaganda, and the neo-Whig school of thought. Five of these theories played a part in causing the Revolutionary War. The significance of the Founders impact theory is a result, not a cause, of the war. The theories fail because they do not see what each view has in common: Protecting our God-given fundamental rights.

Imperialism theory suggests that the colonies, as well as other English colonies around the globe, were pawns and that the mother country exploited them for commerce and economic benefits. This theory would suggest that the build up to the Revolutionary War was a long and arduous one, much longer than the 12 years following the passage of the Stamp Act. It focuses on the quartering of troops and navigation laws as the cause for the war. The progressive theory backed the idea that the revolution was an economic dispute about merchant trade and a class struggle between English residents and the American working class. The progressive theory incorrectly suggests that English policy toward the colonies was no different after the French and Indian War. The conservative theory resulting in the Revolutionary War believed that the colonists were wrong to label King George III as a tyrant and to fault him for being the catalyst for the war. To conservative theorists it was not the King, but parliament that grievances resulting in the Revolutionary War should be attributed in the Declaration of Independence. While the conservative theory is correct that the Revolutionary War cause can be attributed to politics, it fails to address the fundamental rights mitigated in the grievances filed in the Declaration of Independence. The Founders' impact theory is a modern theory that historians regard the American Revolution as an internal struggle between the federalist (Washington-Hamilton) and the anti-federalist (Madison-Jefferson). The federalist / anti-federalist battle was won by the federalists and, in the years following the war, it led to the drafting of the Constitution. It is no surprise that historians were on the wrong side of this dispute by incorrectly siding with the federalists. The federalists were correct, but only up to the drafting of the Constitution because the federalists sought more government power and they learned early on how to circumvent the boundaries they placed within the Constitution.

The propaganda theory explains how the colonies became united to fight for fundamental rights and sustain the war effort to fight England even when the outcome looked bleak. Uniting colonists behind a common cause and supporting the war effort was accomplished through the strategic use of propaganda by the colonial leaders. The propaganda theory is correct, but it downplays factual reasons, such as fundamental rights, for the outbreak of the war. In the propaganda theorists' view, it was the propaganda or exaggeration of the truth that caused the war, not the factual reason for the propaganda. The neo-Whig theory focuses on constitutional principles and fundamental natural rights. The neo-Whig theory also explains why the Americans won the Revolutionary War and settled on a constitutional republic. Where neo-Whig theorists fail, they miss the mark to recognize those unenumerated fundamental rights disputed in the other theories were a subset of their theory. Furthermore, the neo-Whig theory does not emphasize the principles and properties that comprise fundamental rights including omitting the idea that these rights are God-given.

Imperialism Theory

The imperialism theory stresses the importance of a standing army. Following the French and Indian War in 1763, France ceded Canada and the western United States to England. Historians, such as Lawrence Gipson, formulated the imperialism theory, which suggests that England had three reasons to have a standing army in the colonies:

1. The colonies had a much larger landmass to defend.
2. They presumed it might be a matter of time before France tried to reclaim its losses.
3. England believed colonial state militias did not have the resources or power to protect the English empire.

Moreover, Gipson suggests that if France had won the French and Indian War, then Americans would have accepted the Sugar, Stamp, and Townshend Acts because they would have needed protection from the French. Imperialism theorists suggest that the French and Indian War turned the British into the enemy of the colonists for not only wanting a standing army to police colonial borders but because colonial merchants were barred from trading with the French West Indies. Gibson and others would argue that once England disposed of the French in North America, the colonist believed they had nothing further to gain by remaining in the English empire. [276]

Gipson needs to understand the larger picture that it was much more than a standing army that upset the colonists. The colonies were at the mercy of the mother country and all her policies because they had no representation in parliament. The colonies had no choice but to support the French and Indian War even though the colonies were never attacked or threatened by the French at any time. If the colonies were at risk and needed a standing army, it was the mother country that put the colonies in danger for its imperialistic lust. Furthermore, Gipson fails to appreciate that the use of a standing army to police colonial territory was a breach of many fundamental rights such as the right to travel or move freely without the threat of constraint as well as privacy and due process violations. Additionally, forcing private citizens to house and feed troops was a direct invasion of their property rights and their right to raise a family without government interference. What's worse, English law provided custom agents the right to perform illegal warrantless searches of colonial residences and ships to uncover smuggled goods. England was denying merchants due process of the law. Some historians would argue that the colonists' fundamental right to security and safety were better enforced with a standing army. Of course, the colonists would argue the infringement of rights from a standing army far outweighs any positives the show of force may provide. [277]

Gipson needs help to grasp the principle of property rights. As we previously learned, Locke had two definitions for property. The first is that property refers to our possessions and the second was property refers to our lives and our personal liberties, including our free will actions or choices to pursue fundamental rights such as free speech and to travel freely. The colonists' right to both tangible and liberty property were violated by requiring them to quarter a standing army. [278] The Founders thought the concept of quartering troops was such an atrocity against civil liberties they expressly prohibit it in both the Declaration of Independence and the Bill of Rights.

Gipson's theory also has its deficiencies when he reasons the taxes imposed on the colonists following the French and Indian War were minor when compared to the taxes that residents in England had to endure for decades to finance both wars and support a vast English empire. True, English citizens may have been paying more in taxes to quench their thirst for empire, but they did not have their daily lives turned upside down with expansive breaches of privacy and property rights. Nor did English residence face martial law type conditions the colonists faced with a standing army.

The imperialism theory also places a significant blame on the outbreak of the Revolutionary War on the restrictive Navigation Acts that were used to regulate commerce. The Navigation Acts were placed on colonial merchants many decades before the outbreak of the French and Indian War and the passage of the Stamp Act. One long standing Navigation Act was called enumeration. Enumeration restricted colonial exports on certain products such as tobacco, rice, and indigo for only English consumption. Gipson rationalizes that enumeration was a massive disadvantage for colonial merchants because it restricted the biggest Southern plantation crops. Historian Oliver Dickerson contradicts Gibson suggesting that most products affected by enumeration were making the colonial merchants wealthy and prosperity in the colonies flourished. Dickerson comes to that conclusion because once the Revolutionary War concluded and the Navigation Acts were removed, crop values declined, and markets were paralyzed for decades when the colonist lost English empire trading partners. Nevertheless, what Gibson and other imperialism theorists fail to recognize is that enumeration was an economic restriction that was the same as a restriction on contract and labor rights. Although the imperialism theory misses badly, it does indirectly highlight many of the fundamental rights violated by English policy. [279] [280] [281]

Progressive Theory [282] [283] [284]

The progressive theory for the outbreak of the Revolutionary War is an economic theory about colonial manufacturing, goods, and services. The progressive theory relies on the premise that English policy toward the colonies was similar in the period of 1763 to 1775 then prior to 1763. If that statement is true, then the war was not a political one, but an economic one. By 1763 England not only relied on the colonies for raw materials but finished goods. Thus, the French and Indian War was seen as a way for England to expand their colonial market in North America for products such as furs, paper, and real estate. The progressive theory concludes, both the colonial and English mercantile systems could not operate jointly and peacefully. Thus, the outbreak of the revolution came about as tensions about expanded markets and products escalated. The progressive theory also suggests that there was a class struggle. Progressive theorists hypothesize that colonists were second-class citizens compared to their English cohorts.

The progressive theory has some serious flaws. First, the colonists may have been regarded less favorably than English citizens, but even English citizens were considered second class citizens compared to English ruling class. For instance, the imperialism theory correctly points out that English citizens were saddled with a much higher tax rate than the colonists. Ironically, the class struggle for equal rights was instead an internal struggle among colonial residents and not between the colonists and English citizens. The colonial class struggle between wealthy merchants and manufacturers with poor farmers is highlighted a bit later in this chapter. Second, England's policies toward the colonies from 1763 to 1775 were much more aggressive than previous years. Prior to 1763, English policy toward the colonies merely influenced commerce and merchants, whereas later policies affected all colonists. For example, new taxes and intrusive quartering laws were directed at all colonists, not just merchants.

Progressive theorist and historian Merrill Jensen suggests that fundamental rights and social reforms were not part of the colonial Revolutionary War movement. Jensen is unequivocally mistaken; the Founders were ingenious and provided Congress and the courts with the tools to overcome social justice barriers and protect the God-given fundamental rights for everyone equally. Unfortunately, referring to the discussion on the Ninth Amendment and Fourteenth Amendment, Congress and the courts both refused to use the tools at their disposal and their ignorance created unnecessary legislative and judicial roadblocks. [285]

We learned that protecting the fundamental rights of women and African Americans was built into the original Constitution. Understanding that the original Constitution protected women is not surprising since Locke goes to great lengths to highlight women's equality and our Founders mirrored Lockean principles in the Constitution. For instance, according to Locke, a man and woman were equals in marriage. Similarly, God views both man and woman as equal (Genesis 1:27). Locke refers to marriage as the first society and the family unit is the second society. Family units make up larger societies such as neighborhoods, organizations, states, and nations. Thus, if men and women are equal in a subset of a state and nation (marriage and family), then by the laws of mathematics, they must be equals in society. [286] Locke and the Founders demonstrated great wisdom because they were centuries ahead of societal norms since God and His laws guided them. Social and equal rights were firmly on the minds of the Founders.

How was Locke's equality principles duplicated in the Constitution? First, equality can be unearthed by viewing what words are excluded in the Constitution's text. The Constitution never mentions race, ethnicity, sexual orientation, or socio-economic status. The Constitution's impartiality was astutely pointed out by the lone dissenter, John Harlan, in *Plessy v. Ferguson* (1896), which upheld segregation. [287] Second, equality is established through the Ninth Amendment and the Bill of Rights because they protect the rights of all American citizens equally regardless of their demographic makeup. The evidence is irrefutable that Jensen was mistaken and the cause for the Revolutionary War must have included those fundamental rights that would foster social reforms. Besides, progressive theorists fail to comprehend that an economic reason for war would encompass economic fundamental rights like the right to work and contract.

The progressive theory is wrong, but again, it does indirectly highlight many economic fundamental rights that were denied to colonists by the English ruling class such as the right to work and contract.

Conservative Theory [288] [289] [290]

The conservative theory insists that the Declaration of Independence was wrong to direct all its grievances toward King George III and not parliament. The King had nothing to do with the Stamp Act, the Declaratory Act, or the Townshend Duties, it was all parliament's doing. Sure, the King okayed these policies, but he was merely a figure head following the lead of parliament. Thus, the conservative theory does not accept the dominion theory, which stated the King was the link between England and the colonies, not parliament.

The conservative theory conflicts with the progressive view because it hypothesizes the war was, indeed, a political one. Thus, the conservative theory suggests that parliament governed the colonies from 1763 to 1775 much differently than before 1763. True, some early navigation acts passed by England were restrictive, but these laws merely affected merchants. The laws passed after 1763 were not only intrusive but the number of invasive laws was amplified. Consequently, the conservative theory is a better explanation of events than the progressive theory.

The conservative theory fails because regardless as to whether parliament or the King should have been blamed in the Declaration of Independence, it ignores or fails to focus on the importance of the grievances filed in that document. Most of the grievances highlight how colonial fundamental rights were being mitigated such as through warrantless searches, the removal of jury trials, free speech restrictions, the quartering of troops, no parliamentary representation, trade limitations, the appointment of judges who were loyal to the cause of England, and the suspension of state legislators. Those grievances encompass a host of fundamental rights violations including due process, free speech, no representation in government, labor and contracts, and privacy.

Propaganda Theory

Locke, like God, understood the power of wisdom and how it could only be obtained via knowledge, truths, proofs, and evidence. Likewise, the colonial clergy were able to back their sermons about natural law with evidence, facts, and truths. Conversely, many elites were able to drive home revolutionary principles and incite violence from angry mobs by building on those moral and natural law principles learned in sermons by presenting them with anecdotal evidence and conspiracy theories. Elites, such as Sam Adams, were able to play on the emotions of the unsuspecting colonists. For example, propagandists circulated conspiracy theories such as King George III was a tyrant when he was only a figure head approving the plans put forth by parliament. Another conspiracy theory put forth was the Stamp Act attempted to enslave the colonists like how colonists enslaved Africans.

Unfortunately, the Intolerable Acts exacerbated the fears of the colonists leading them to believe in many conspiracy theories that were promoted by propagandists. The Boston Massacre was an unfortunate incident between British soldiers and protestors. Propagandists labeled the skirmish a massacre and slaughter when a few British soldiers mistakenly fired on the angry crowd after an agitator shouted "fire." The soldiers' inadvertently thought "fire" was a command coming from their superior officer. The men accused of killing the colonists were defended by John Adams and found not guilty of murder. In fact, the amount of violence between colonists and English troops was surprisingly small. Additionally, although there were very few records of any crimes committed against women and children by the occupied English force, it did not stop the propagandist from printing material claiming otherwise. [291]

Historian James Adams lays out a cleverly crafted hypothesis in support of the propaganda theory. Adams suggests following the passage of the Sugar, Stamp, and Townshend Acts, wealthy merchants were first to question parliamentary power. Consequently, the merchant protests were equally successful to incite lower class members of colonial society to join their cause with the skillful use of propaganda. The message of no taxation without representation and England trying to enslave the colonists resonated among the working class throughout New England. Of course, enslaving colonists was an exaggeration and many of the colonies shrewdly refused parliamentary representation because it would legitimize taxes. Nevertheless, by 1770, after all the English laws had been rescinded, the merchants were again happy and sought no further change or disruption in the English and colonial relationship. [292]

Merchant satisfaction, however, did not stop poor rural farmers, who continued to be influenced by agitators and propaganda, from continuing to pursue equal rights, now against both England and the colonial merchants in a colonial class struggle. Since merchants and wealthier manufacturing workers accounted for less than 10% of the population, the lower-class small farming communities considerably outnumbered them. The class struggle became a social, economic, and political movement about constitutional principles and the laws of nature including equal rights for all men. In fact, it almost turned into an American civil war pitting coastal communities against rural and frontier citizens. For instance, the North Carolina militia thwarted an insurrection led by a group called the Regulators. The Regulators were angry North Carolina citizens located in the western counties seeking equal representation in the state government. It was almost as if England was off the hook for their past indiscretions. It appeared as if England had learned from its past mistakes by repealing all the taxes—until England provided the English owned East India Company a monopoly on the colonial tea market with the passage of the Tea Act. The monopoly on tea reinstated the furor of the colonial merchants who came back into the fold of the revolutionary movement on the side of the lower colonial classes and radical agitators. Moreover, if the Tea Act did not bring merchants back into the revolutionary movement, then they probably would have joined the ranks of the common man once the practice of customs racketeering began. Customs racketeering was a practice used by customs officers to do warrantless searches of merchant ships to seize cargo. The Intolerable Acts, which closed Boston Harbor, would have also enraged merchants enough to rejoin the lower-class colonial ranks to fight against England. The colonists united in a movement that was now about equal rights for all. [293]

It is quite conceivable that the colonial class struggle was exaggerated by some historians, but the Revolutionary War was inevitably the "result of a slow process of social, economic, cultural, and political differentiation." It is entirely possible and probable that the cause of the Revolutionary War was unintentional. Parliamentary actions may have been well intended but their timing and handling of the situation was poor. The British may not have been tyrants trying to enslave the colonists, but their pride and inflexibility were their shortcomings. The English may have been "well-meaning men caught in a situation too complex and demanding for persons with only average talent." [294] Certainly, England was not blameless for the outbreak of the war because they did violate the rights of colonists, but colonial intellectuals were very good at exaggerating circumstances. Whatever the case may be, it is difficult to dispute the role propaganda played to unite citizens into one common cause to fight for constitutional principles including fundamental rights. [295] [296]

The key to a revolution's success, especially the American Revolution, was the ability of intellectuals to exploit all sectors of the population with propaganda. Propaganda targeted any colonials, who may have had a grievance with England, with conspiracy theories to promote constitutional principles and fundamental rights. The propagandist understood what Americans thought, wished, feared, and hated and took advantage of those emotions. After all, all 42 major colonial newspapers were under Whig control and they could, therefore, dictate any narrative they wished. Other than newspapers, Whigs got their messages out in poems, plays, songs, sermons, pictures, pamphlets, and demonstrations. [297]

In fact, without propaganda the vision of independence over the long 7-year war may have fallen flat. For example, when news came of British wanting to talk peace in 1778, the American soldier was undersupplied, under clothed, and in very low spirits. It would have been easy for the Americans to quit and hand the British a victory. However, the propagandist kept the drive for independence alive by lifting the spirits of the soldiers by reminding them that the French may enter the war. They also invented theories that the English troops were more depressed, and thousands were deserting the English army for liberty in America. Some of the propagandist statements were true and some of them were exaggerated, but the intellectuals that ran the governments, newspapers, churches, and wrote pamphlets were able to push the right balance between truth and myth to keep the soldiers motivated. [298]

Most authors who support the propaganda theory for the origins of the Revolutionary War, such as John C. Miller, suggest that propaganda theory did not support fundamental rights as a reason for the war. [299] [300] [301] Miller and other propaganda theorists believed it was the propaganda that triggered the war, not the message behind the propaganda such as to protect fundamental rights. For example, propaganda theorists alleged labelling the Boston Massacre as an intentional act instead of as an unfortunate misunderstanding was much more impactful than discussing the rights violated by the English standing army. In Miller's attempt to downplay fundamental rights, he overlooks that most conservative writings during the pre-Revolutionary War period emphasized the law, natural law, and fundamental rights by making an appeal to ancient law charters (i.e., Magna Carta), natural law philosophers, and the British Constitution and the British rights of man. [302]

While the propaganda theory is a complete and comprehensive hypothesis compared to the other theories, it fails because without recognizing the importance of fundamental rights, there would be no truthful reason or basis for any propaganda to incite a revolution. For the Revolutionary War to be a just war, there had to be a factual reason for the conflict. The American propaganda machine was brilliant because they exaggerated the truth and facts, and the truth and facts should not be underestimated by the propaganda theorists as the cause of the war.

Founders Impact Theory

There was, of course, a federalist and anti-federalist struggle after the passage of the Constitution and it began in the George Washington administration. The Founders impact theory is not a causation theory but an outcome of the Revolutionary War. Some historians are convinced this was the most important struggle of the American Revolution. They may be correct in that assessment because the wrong side won – the federalist school of thought brought forth by George Washington and Alexander Hamilton. Alexander Hamilton was a traitor to the Constitution because he governed much differently than his Federalist Paper writings would suggest.

Treasury Secretary Alexander Hamilton proposed the national bank, and it was adamantly opposed as being unconstitutional by Secretary of State Thomas Jefferson and James Madison. President George Washington would side with Hamilton and a national bank was chartered. Later, the constitutionality of the national bank was taken up by the Supreme Court in *McCulloch v. Maryland* in 1817. The Court incorrectly, in my opinion, held the national bank was indeed constitutional in a landmark majority opinion written by Chief Justice John Marshall. Marshall held the federal government had implied powers beyond those enumerated grants of power in Article I, Section 8 of the Constitution. The national bank dispute was important because there is nothing written in the Constitution about granting the federal government the power to create a bank or any business for that matter. Hamilton argued the Necessary and Proper Clause provided the government with the powers to basically do whatever it deemed necessary to carry out its powers. In this case, the national bank was deemed necessary for the federal government carryout its taxing power. The anti-federalists, James Madison and Thomas Jefferson, reasoned if the federal government could create a bank, then there is no limit to their power. Despite the disagreement between Madison and Hamilton, both they and Marshall agreed that the federal government could use necessary powers if the relationship between the means and ends achieved a constitutional objective, which provided the federal government more power but by no means did they have unlimited power. Although taxing power is a constitutional objective, the government should also be required to use the least evasive method to achieve that constitutional objective. In Chapter 11, the evidence shows that a national bank was by no means the least evasive method to carry out its taxing powers. [303]

Unfortunately, Jefferson and Madison prognosticated what the future had in store for the United States if a national bank was permitted. Fast forward 230 years and federal government powers have become much more intrusive. It is a fact; the United States government overreach of power is much worse today than anything parliament did between 1763 to 1775, which triggered the Revolutionary War. For example, local, state, and federal taxes are much larger per capita than anything proposed by England with the Stamp, Sugar, or Townshend Duties. Colonists paid a tax rate of about 1.5% compared to about 25% today. Furthermore, the value of the dollar is about 35 times lower today as compared with 1776 due to inflation. Between taxes and inflation, a person earning 1,000 dollars in 1776 would need to earn nearly 44,000 dollars today to have equivalent buying power. The above analysis does not include sales taxes, tolls, tips, property taxes, and other hidden fees attached to many present-day purchases and financial transactions. [304] [305] [306]

The Founders impact theory is an important result of the Revolutionary War. In my opinion, the national bank dispute was the unofficial beginning of the progressive movement. Progressivism has been an ongoing non-violent coup d'état that has forever changed the political landscape in America. Progressivism is doing more to mitigate fundamental rights than to protect them. Yes, most progressives seek noble causes, and the movement has accomplished many positive things such as women's suffrage. At the same time, progressivism has led to more government overreach to achieve favorable legislation by any unconstitutional method necessary. For instance, impatience, abuse of power, and lack of tolerance leads political leaders to take advantage of national emergencies to circumvent their expressed grants of power in the Constitution. If the federal government and its political leaders were acting in good faith to help citizens during national emergencies, their expansion of authority would be temporary and not permanent grants of power. When a government reaches beyond its limited constitutional powers, then the fundamental rights of citizens can longer be guaranteed. Group think, identity politics, cancel culture, political correctness, wokeness, and fearmongering have led to the devolving liberty of free speech, parental rights, security rights, and the right to work in modern society. [307]

Neo-Whig Theory [308] [309] [310]

The neo-Whig theory suggests that the war was fought over constitutional principles and fundamental rights is spot on. Other than the neo-Whig theory, every theory describing the reason for the outbreak of war fails to highlight any grievances in the Declaration of Independence and fundamental rights. That said, neo-Whig theorists fail to comprehend that other causation theories are a subset of the neo-Whig theory. Thus, it is fair to propose that a combination of all theories united Americans under one common cause to fight for fundamental rights. Neo-Whig theorists also fail to recognize important principles that define fundamental rights such as being God-given, unanimously accepted, and perfect. Unfortunately, downplaying the impact that God and natural law have on fundamental rights ultimately leads to erroneously rewriting history without God.

Let us evaluate an example of how the progressive theory is a subset of the neo-Whig theory. Louis Hacker, a progressive theorist, wrote that the Revolutionary War was "not over high-sounding political and constitutional concepts .... Natural rights" but "over colonial manufacturing, wild lands and furs, sugar, wine, tea, and currency." Hacker's economic arguments make a great deal of sense since the crackdown on colonial merchant trade, western land speculation, fur trade, and legal currency played a role in colonial outrage. What Hacker and neo-Whig theorists fail to recognize is that limitations and regulations on trade were also restricting the fundamental rights of persons to work a lawful profession. Even Hacker acknowledges this fact when he states colonists were denied "the right to engage in free enterprise" by royal government officials.

Hacker also admits that the right to justice or due process was denied to merchants charged with smuggling goods. Hacker points out how merchants were saddled with the burden of proof to maintain their innocence, trials were moved to England, trial by jury was often denied, and the judges presiding over these cases were biased because they were paid from English taxes and the profits obtained from custom enforcement sieges. Thus, judges were puppets because they served at the pleasure of the crown. In some instances, citizens were sent to England to face trial violating their right to a speedy trial and to have a trial with a jury of their peers. To complicate matters, loyalists arranged to take over or monopolize local government offices, effectively eliminating any avenue to dispute any judicial breaches of power. For example, the passage of the MGRA enabled loyalists to monopolize government offices in Massachusetts. Finally, the passage of the IAJA allowed royal authorities to be tried in England instead of facing their accusers in America.

For a revolution to occur and to be successful, a supermajority of the populous must support the movement. For instance, the imperialism and progressive theories simply do not explain why all colonists, other than merchants, participated in the revolutionary movement. Hacker suggests that poor working-class colonists were brought into the struggle because a recession resulted from the English economic sanctions. Perhaps, but the economic reasons for going to war were vastly dissimilar between merchants and the poor. There had to be a deeper reason that would unite all colonists behind a common cause. Historian Charles Andrews insightfully suggests pinpointing the cause of the complex revolutionary war movement to one reason instead of a multitude of causes acting simultaneously needs to be reconsidered. Andrews recognized that no single reason was common to the entire colonial populous. Andrews observes that only one of twenty-seven grievances in the Declaration of Independence points to an economic cause. Consequently, the only logical explanation is that a combination of all the proposed theories can explain why the colonists were united to fight a Revolutionary War for equal fundamental rights.

Part of the reason historians neglect fundamental rights as a cause for the war is because they fail to recognize unenumerated rights as fundamental rights such as the right to travel, work, family, or marriage. Many rights outlined in Table I are not in the Constitution; they are unenumerated, so they are probably never given much credence by historians. After all, Congress and the courts have yet to formally recognize most of the rights defined in Table I. Most Americans are ignorant of their fundamental rights because they are taken for granted since they are encompassed in our daily routine. For example, no innocent person is concerned that the government will prevent them from travelling to work or eating lunch.

After the war ended, the neo-Whig intellectual philosophy of constitutional principles and natural rights drove the final push for drafting the Republican Constitution and its ratification. Americans came to believe that they were better off than their English counterparts, and what made them better off was better protection of their rights. The two main constitutional principles to arise from the pre-Revolutionary War period were:

1. One region of a country or empire should not dominate another.

2. The government should be inferior to the people.

An important republican principle to emerge from point 1 above was for equal representation in the Senate to prevent heavily populated states from imposing their will on smaller states. Point 2 suggests that sovereignty resided with "We the people" because the Constitution is about curbing government power with checks and balances and other republic principles. Conversely, there is nothing in the Constitution about curbing the rights of the individual or "We the people." [311]

How Did the Americans Overcome the Odds to Win the War?

How did the colonists win the Revolutionary War? The colonists did not win many battles, they were poorly supplied with food, clothing, and ammunition, and many soldiers fled in fear at the start of many battles. State militias performed worse than those in the Continental Army due to their length of enlistment and training. Continental Army enlistment was three years in length while state militia enlistments could be as short as a few months. Most that joined to fight for the colonial cause were poor and non-property owners who were more likely enticed by a bounty payment and the promise of a salary and land after the war. Educated and wealthy persons were less likely to take any chance in the military since they had less to gain personally. [312]

While lower classes had fewer opportunities to pursue rights, such as travelling or owning property, for many, it was worth the risk for them to fight for equal fundamental rights. The Revolutionary War was an opportunity for the less fortunate to pursue rights for themselves and their families. At the same time, the less fortunate were chartered with protecting the liberty and fundamental rights of the privileged and working class. [313] Social classes are not the desire of many Americans who favor socialism and spreading the wealth, but without economic disparities protecting liberty and natural rights is impossible. What makes a country great is competition and the desire of citizens to improve their standing in society. In fact, revolutions are generally about the poor wanting more or furthering their fundamental rights. It was no different in the American Revolution. The lower-class struggle for more rights ultimately led to the Americans' victory. That, along with many English blunders resulted in American independence. While the colonists who fought in the Revolutionary War were willing to die for a cause to better themselves and to secure the future of the United States, the English died to preserve the status quo and the past. The makers of history and those wanting change usually prevail over empires who have no cause and are merely trying to sustain their power. [314]

It may surprise many, but about 20% of the American population were loyalists who did not favor a revolution, but instead wanted to remain loyal to the British crown. Who were the loyalists? The loyalists were rich merchants who obviously knew war would disrupt their business and wealth. Other loyalists were immigrants who did not assimilate to American customs and language. In fact, the New Jersey Dutch population saw a direct correlation between those who did and those who did not assimilate and their support for the war. [315] Thus, assimilation, an internal class struggle, and patriotism were the primary reasons for the American victory and independence.

Consequences of the War

The chief outcome of the war was the Constitution. As already discussed, the Constitution and Bill of Rights primary purpose was to safeguard the sovereignty of the people and the God-given fundamental rights of citizens. These fundamental rights are either enumerated or unenumerated (protected through the Ninth Amendment). Importantly, the structure of the Constitution prevents the federal government from garnering too much power to infringe on the fundamental rights of citizens. These constitutional protections include formulating a republic, separation of powers, federalism, and checks and balances.

The Founders' objective for drafting a constitution was not to bring about huge changes but only minor alterations to society. My theory is that the Founders' chief objective in drafting the United States Constitution was to reinstate a government like how England managed the colonies prior to 1763 with one exception. The Founders placed safeguards in the Declaration of Independence and Constitution to not only protect the fundamental rights of citizens, but to also ensure if for some reason the federal government attempted to go rogue the people had the authority to replace that government. Prior to 1763, parliament basically let the states govern themselves while they only governed trade and commerce, drafted treaties, and provided for national defense. And these are the chief functions of the United States government detailed in the Constitution. All other powers are entrusted with the states through the Tenth Amendment. [316]

Chapter 11: The Civil War Background Information [317]

The major issues leading up to the Civil War are highlighted in this section. What is important to note is how many of the issues are directly related to slavery. The issue of slavery is, of course, synonymous with the fight for equal fundamental rights.

The 1860 Election

Most people regard the 1860 election as one between Abraham Lincoln and Stephen Douglas, but there were two other key players in the election. John Bell was the nominee for the Constitutional Union Party and John Breckinridge was the Southern Democrat Party choice. Although Douglas received nearly 30% of the vote (2nd) he only received 12 electoral votes (4th). Douglas was a Northern Democrat who supported preserving the Union and allowing each state and territory to determine, through popular sovereignty or popular vote, whether the region would be slave or free. No surprise that Breckinridge won a plurality of the Southern states (18% of the vote and 72 electoral votes). Breckinridge was the pro-slavery candidate and President James Buchanan's vice president. Breckinridge believed all states had the right to have slavery and held the position that the only way slavery could be saved was for the South to secede from the Union. The main surprise in the 1860 election may have been the support that Bell received (12% of the vote and 39 electoral votes) winning the second highest vote totals in the South including winning Virginia, Kentucky, and Tennessee. The Constitutional Union Party was the party of choice for many former Whig Party members and their slogan was "The Union as it is, the Constitution as it is." Although Lincoln received fewer than 40% of the vote, he won 18 states and a plurality of the 303 electoral votes (180). The South despised Lincoln so much he was not even on the ballot in ten states. Thus, he probably would have garnered a few more votes than he received.

Southern voters knew they would not win the White House unless two of the three Lincoln opponents withdrew and threw their support behind one candidate. Since that did not come to fruition, the South's hope was Douglas and Lincoln would split electoral votes in the North and no candidate would receive 152 electoral votes to win a plurality of the electoral college. Under such a scenario, the presidency would have been decided by the Democratic controlled House of Representatives that would back Breckinridge. Despite losing the presidency, the 1860 election was not a complete disaster for the Democrats since they still retained a small majority in both the Senate and House. Breckinridge did not muster 45% of the popular vote in the South. Hence, most Southerners, in essence, voted to preserve the Union. [318] So, why did the South start the process to secede from the Union months before Lincoln had a chance to take office and put forth any policies? This is a difficult question to answer and this section on the Civil War tries to determine the root causes for both secession and the war.

The Native American Crisis [319]

The Native American crisis in the South was never really considered a major contributor to the Civil War, but it cannot be completely ignored for escalating tensions between the North and South. Native Americans, who lived in Southern territories, were generally protected by a treaty between the many Indian tribes and the United States. However, Southerners were eager to remove Native Americans so white settlements could expand. The Jackson administration passed the Indian Removal Act of 1830, and it started a mass exodus of Native Americans to territories west of the Mississippi River. Chief Justice John Marshall ruled in *Cherokee Nation v. Georgia* (1831) the Court had no authority to rule on a Georgia law, which allowed them to breach the treaty between the United States and the Cherokee Nation. The Court held the treaty between the United States and the Cherokee Nation was not between two independent nations but instead a nation and a dependent nation, which was outside the scope of Article III of the Constitution. Over the decades prior to the Civil War, tens of thousands of Native Americans would die and countless more would be displaced due to forced migration. Northern views toward Native Americans slowly became more tolerant with the passage of the Northwest Ordinance of 1787. Of course, the North was guilty of irreprehensible actions toward both races in their checkered history, so they were in their infancy of becoming a more tolerant people. In fact, it was Southern brutality that forced Northerners to change their opinions and support the fundamental rights of both Native Americans and African American slaves.

The National Bank Crisis [320]

As alluded to earlier, the national bank dispute arose very early in American politics during the George Washington administration. The national bank became a sectional fight between the North and South, with the North in favor and the South opposed. The South held that the national bank was not only unconstitutional and a corrupt institution, but it favored the more speculative Northern economy. Southerners correctly regarded the national bank as an infringement on states' powers. After all, there is no enumerated power in the Constitution for the federal government to build any company, let alone a national bank monopoly.

In McCulloch, the Court held that the federal government could do what was necessary and proper to conduct its taxing powers and to stabilize United States currency. Nevertheless, was a nationalized bank the best and least evasive method for the federal government to conduct its taxing power? President Andrew Jackson was determined to end the national bank despite its popularity. In fact, when Jackson took matters into his own hands by removing federal funds from the national bank and dispersing them among smaller state banks, his actions were censured. Jackson agreed with Congress' action to censure him because he realized he overstepped his executive powers since dealing with treasury funds was a legislative task. Still, Jackson prevailed when Congress decided not to renew the national bank charter when the Southern coalition was joined with Western support. Thus, Jackson proved a national bank was not a necessary and proper solution to help the government deal with taxing issues or for stabilizing currency since removing the national bank had no ill effect on the economy. The debate over the national bank and how to manage federal treasuries extended into the Van Buren administration and his Treasury Act also had little impact on the economy. The Treasury Act divorced government involvement from all banks with no ill effects on the economy or for the government to collect taxes.

Slavery

Slavery was an embarrassing political issue for the colonists and their fight for independence. The decade leading up to the Revolutionary War, colonists claimed to be slaves of the English empire. Slavery is defined as "anyone who is bound to obey the will of others." [321] I regard slavery as the denial of fundamental rights to any person by another person or institution. Hence, technically, the colonists were right. If their rights were being denied, then they were technically slaves. It is hard to feel sorry for colonists, especially plantation owners, who enslaved millions of Africans. The hypocrisy was alarming. In effect, the slavery colonists felt through English imperialism was nowhere near as harsh as what Africans had to endure in the colonies. For instance, enduring a stamp tax was nothing like the experience of being denied the liberty to travel, religion, free speech, to own and sell property, justice, to enjoy the fruits of their labor, to obtain knowledge, vote, marriage, make family decisions, and so on.

Southern slavery would be a black eye on American politics and constitutional principles for a century and led to the costliest war (death and injury per capita) in American history (Civil War). The Revolutionary War period brought enough attention to the horrors of slavery that the First Continental Congress would ban the importation of slaves. Banning the importation of slaves was a small step in the right direction, but it would fall far short of ending the practice. As James Madison said, "Great as the evil is [slavery], a dismemberment of the Union would be worse." [322] [323]

Slavery had a significant impact on both the constitutions of Virginia and the United States. Virginia's elite witnessed firsthand the horrors of slavery and how it denied men of their fundamental rights. In 1775, George Mason defined the fundamental rights of citizens in the Virginia Declaration of Rights. Many of the rights found in the Bill of Rights or in the Declaration of Independence can be found in the Virginia Declaration of Rights such as all men are created equal and cannot be denied life, liberty, and property. The Virginia Declaration of Rights also mentions due process procedures (justice rights) for warrants, trial juries, and bail requirements as well as term limits for government members and separation of government powers. After the Revolutionary War, Thomas Jefferson also proposed important legislation in Virginia that would find its way into the Bill of Rights. [324] The Virginia Declaration of Rights explains why Virginia was the only Southern slave-holding state to object to the institution of slavery during the drafting of the Constitution.

One significant issue that arose during the Jackson and Van Buren administrations was the Gag Rule of 1836. The Gag Rule of 1836 prohibited petitions relating to slavery from being read or documented within the House of Representatives. Obviously, the Gag Rule of 1836 was an infringement of the First Amendment. More importantly, how could the issue of slavery be addressed if the government wanted to ignore it even existed?

Expansionism[325]

Expansion of United States borders occurred regularly throughout the early formation of the nation. The Louisiana Purchase in 1803 was the first significant expansion of United States borders. The Monroe Doctrine warned European nations that they should cease any effort to form new colonies in the western hemisphere. Therefore, the Monroe Doctrine left the United States as the sole country with the power to expand its borders in the western hemisphere. The sectional rivalry resulting from expansion was primarily over which territories and states would permit slavery and which would prohibit slavery. During the John Tyler administration there were 13 slave states and 13 free states. The anomaly was Missouri. Although Missouri was relatively far North, the Missouri Compromise of 1820 provided it could be admitted as a slave state but any other states above the 36'30" parallel would be free. On Tyler's last day of office, Florida was granted statehood and therefore, slave states maintained a 14 to 13 lead. Obviously, the number of slave or free states was critical in the balance of political power. The North feared that the balance of power was shifting to the South because with the addition of Florida they garnered more House and Senate seats in Congress. Surprisingly, many Southerners were against Texas statehood primarily because of their racial biases. Southerners feared living among Spanish Mexicans who had a darker skin tone, like their supremist attitude toward slaves. And, of course, Northerners objected to Texas statehood because it would be admitted as a slave state expanding the Southern political advantage in Congress.

Thus, there was a notable uproar during the Tyler administration for pursuing Texas statehood. Texas became a republic or nation following its war with Mexico. In 1836, Sam Houston defeated Governor and General Santa Anna's Mexican army. Santa Anna signed a treaty granting Texas its independence. Later, Mexico failed to recognize the treaty because they felt it was coerced. There were several issues at stake for Texas statehood: Slavery, the power of government, and Mexico would fail to recognize its statehood. Additionally, Texas was a large state, and there were Northern concerns it could be divided into more slave states, increasing the Southern congressional advantage. Nevertheless, Texas was finally granted its statehood in 1845. Northerners quit their objection to Texas statehood when President James Polk pursued the Oregon territory, which belonged jointly to American and British interests. Although slave states had a 15 to 13 advantage over the free states, Oregon territory was above the 36'30" parallel allowing for more Northern state expansion in the future. Further complicating matters was a dispute over the Texas border with Mexico that would take a war and years to resolve. When Iowa and Wisconsin entered the Union as free states a few years later, the balance of political power was again equal.

A dispute arose between England and the United States about where to draw the Canadian border to divide the Oregon territory. England favored the 49th parallel while the United States preferred the boundary be placed at 54'40". Polk would attempt to negotiate with both England and Mexico to resolve these border disputes. In Mexico, Polk was willing pay up to 40 million to purchase New Mexico, Utah, California, and to garner a favorable Texas boundary at the Rio Grande River. Mexico rejected any offer put forth by Polk.

Mexican and American hostilities started soon after the failed negotiations when Congress declared war on Mexico. Polk was unwilling to fight both England and Mexico simultaneously, and therefore he agreed to the 49th parallel and a treaty was passed that finally settled the dispute with England over the Oregon territory border. When Mexico surrendered in 1847, a new peace treaty was ratified the following year, and its outcome expanded the continental United States to its current borders. The Polk administration successfully increased the land mass of the United States by 1.2 million square miles. The fight shifted within the United States over whether these territories would be free or permit slavery.

There were several proposals on how to manage the issue of slavery in the newly acquired territories. First, the Wilmot Proviso proposed that the territories acquired from Mexico should prohibit slavery. The Wilmot Proviso was not acceptable to Southerners. Second, the Buchanan proposal suggested that the 36'30" parallel established in the Missouri Compromise should extend to the Pacific. Northerners objected to this because they feared Southern expansion might continue to include parts of Mexico, Latin America, and Cuba. Furthermore, with Northern expansion fixed at the 49th parallel, Northerners knew they had fewer options for expansion. That said, there were two ways to increase political power in Congress: Increase land mass for more states or increase the population. Thus, while the North feared Southern expansion, the South feared Northern population growth since immigrants were flocking to the more industrialize North in great numbers. Third, Lewis Cass was the first to propose popular sovereignty or providing each territory and state with the power to make its own choice. Popular sovereignty would be the compromise suggested by Stephen Douglas in the 1860 election. Generally, congressional votes on expansion policy did not follow party lines, but sectional lines.

The Compromise of 1850 brought California into the Union as a free state, whereas the Utah and New Mexico territories were given the power of popular sovereignty to decide the issue of slavery. It was widely believed that New Mexico and Utah territory would never become a slave state because the people residing in these regions did not have slaves nor did they believe in the institution of slavery. Additionally, it was also reasoned the soil and climate in New Mexico and Utah would not be conducive to the big cash crops that utilize slavery.

The Franklin Pierce administration sought expansion objectives as well. To the Southerners' delight, Pierce pledged to do what Polk could not do, and that was to purchase Cuba from Spain. Although Pierce's efforts failed to obtain Cuba or to expand United States interests in Latin America, many renegades took matters into their own hands. Several Southern men, such as Narciso Lopez and William Walker, attempted sieges to conquer both Cuba and Nicaragua respectively. Eventually, both men failed, and the United States Southern boundaries remained unchanged.

Expansionism also brought about another sectional fight regarding a plan for a national railroad to connect the east coast with the west coast. Of course, Southerners wanted the railroad to originate in the South and follow a Southern course while the opposite was true for Northerners. A railroad fit the expansion narrative because it would allow immigrants and citizens an easier way to migrate west. The railroad question was not resolved until 1862, after the start of the Civil War, when a Northern route was established from eastern cities to Omaha Nebraska and then to the Pacific.

During the railroad debate another controversial expansion and state issue was resolved. Steven Douglas created the Kansas–Nebraska Act that would divide the Nebraska territory into two, making the Northern most Nebraska territory a free-region and the Southernmost Kansas territory a slave region. After a heated debate, the bill passed and although Kansas territory was well above the 36'30" parallel, it was initially a slave region. The bill passed because Northern and Southern Democrats united in support of the bill, whereas Northern Whigs voted against its passage, but Southern Whigs supported the bill. The fracture between Northern and Southern Whigs over slavery led directly to the end of the Whig Party and the formation of the anti-slave Republican Party that would put Abraham Lincoln in the White House.

The Kansas Dispute[326]

The Kansas dispute was about it becoming a free or slave state. The Kansas dispute was the unofficial beginning of the Civil War. While popular sovereignty or majority rule was supposed to be used to decide this problem, the issue was becoming much more complex. The situation was so volatile in Kansas it had 6 governors in 6 years. Initial elections voted for pro-slavery politicians, but those elections were fraudulent. Senator Charles Sumner of Massachusetts gave a speech in support of a free Kansas, and he was nearly beaten to death by Congressman Preston Brooks from South Carolina. Brooks was not expelled but merely censored for his action and was revered in the South as a hero. While a pro-slavery government was initially established in Kansas, a rival free state government was also formed. Neither government was legitimate due to either election fraud or that the free state advocates never won an election to form a recognized government. Pro-slavery factions rode into free areas such as Lawrence, Kansas and would ransack the town. Free state supporters and abolitionists, such as John Brown, would retaliate by dismembering pro-slavery families. John Brown would later become famous for attacking the munitions depot in Harpers Ferry.

The Kansas pro-slavery government drafted a state constitution that was to be ratified by the people. Unfortunately for the pro-slavery movement only one provision of the constitution was voted on: Could slaves be imported from other states and the referendum passed. President James Buchanan and Democrats promised that the entire Kansas constitution would be put to a vote for the people to decide. When that did not happen, the antislavery initiative made it happen because they felt the pro-slavery faction lacked the votes. They were correct; the pro-slavery Kansas constitution was defeated by an overwhelming majority. Buchanan was upset with the result and went behind the backs of the people of Kansas by forwarding the Kansas constitution to Congress seeking their approval. Although the Democrats controlled both houses of Congress, Senator Douglas did not agree with Buchanan's idea to compel the people of Kansas to accept a constitution they overwhelmingly rejected. After all, having Congress approve a state constitution violated their party platform to support popular sovereignty. When Buchanan's stunt failed, and free state forces took control of the Kansas legislature, it was agreed that Kansas statehood would be postponed until its population reached 90,000. Three years later, in 1861, Kansas became the thirty-fourth state and the nineteenth free state. Kansas was a small-scale battle over slavery expansion that foreshadowed the bigger Civil War conflict that was just around the corner. Expansionism benefited many Americans and provided them greater opportunities, but at the same time it brought the issue of slavery to a boil.

The Compromise [327]

The North and South attempted to resolve their differences about slavery with compromises. One such compromise was the passage of the Fugitive Slave Act of 1850, which was an extension of the Fugitive Slave Act of 1793. The objective of the act was to increase fines and prison sentences for those people who failed to abide by the law and return fugitive slaves to their rightful owners. Commissioners, who ruled on Fugitive Slave Act cases, would routinely revert free men to slaves. Commissioners injecting bias was a common practice because commissioners were paid better to return free black men into slavery than to maintain their freedom. For that reason, the Fugitive Slave Act became highly unpopular in the North. The act was neither a deterrent for abolitionists from continuing the practice of freeing slaves nor was it very successful in returning freed slaves.

During the transition between the Buchanan and Lincoln presidencies, the new Congress was seated and worked tirelessly to reach a compromise to resolve the slavery problem, especially after word came that South Carolina seceded. Senator John Crittenden from Kentucky proposed 6 constitutional amendments and 4 resolutions. The amendments were as follows:

1. Slavery would be prohibited in territories north of the 36"30' parallel. South of the 36"30' parallel slavery would be recognized but when territories became states, they could decide whether to adapt slavery or bar slavery in their state constitution.
2. Congress had no power to abolish slavery in any state.
3. Congress had no power to abolish slavery in the District of Columbia.
4. Domestic slave trade should face no government interference.
5. The United States government should reimburse any slaveholder the cost of any unreturned fugitive slaves.
6. No amendment should be made to counteract any of the five previous amendments.

The 4 resolutions were as follows:

1. Slave holding states are entitled to faithful observance of the Fugitive Slave Act.
2. Congress shall recommend states repeal laws that conflict with the Fugitive Slave Act.
3. The commissioner fee should not be a factor when deciding fugitive slave cases. Thus, the fee was to be the same regardless of the outcome of the hearing.
4. Reopen the United States to African-slave trade.

It was speculated had the Crittenden Compromise been put to a popular vote, it would have passed in both the North and South. However, neither the North nor the South was willing to compromise in Congress. Lincoln was a hardliner in that although he felt states should honor the Fugitive Slave Act and Congress should not interfere with slave practices within the states, he would not give an inch to any expansion of the institution in new territories or new states. Although the Crittenden Compromise was most favorable and generous to the Southern position, the South was still not satisfied with some of the proposals. In the end, neither side was really willing to compromise. Representative Thomas Corwin of Ohio said, "I cannot comprehend the madness of the times. Southern men are theoretically crazy. Extreme Northern men are practical fools." Corwin would propose more moderate amendments to resolve the slavery issue.

Had the Crittenden Compromise passed it would have been extremely damaging. Slavery would have been protected in perpetuity and the institution would have been enshrined in our Constitution! Furthermore, the Crittenden Compromise Amendments would have added the word slavery to our Constitution 15 times! The Corwin amendments passed both legislators, but they were never ratified by the states. Although the Corwin amendments do not mention slavery, they too would have protected the institution and allowed it to continue for decades.

Following secession, the South worked quickly to organize their federal government for their newly formed confederacy. The Confederate constitution mimicked the United States Constitution for the most part. Most of the changes to the Confederate constitution, outside of those protecting slavery, were advanced ideas including presidential term limits, presidential line-item veto, legislative bills could only pertain to one subject that was to be clearly stated in the title, and appropriation legislation had to be initiated from the heads of the legislative departments and take two-thirds vote in both branches of the legislature for its passage. These were sound ideas and promote republic principles to prevent against both too much power in one branch of government and majorities imposing their will on minority groups of people. [328] Unfortunately, only presidential term limits would be amended to the United States Constitution after Franklin Delano Roosevelt (FDR) won four terms. It was difficult for biased, opinionated, and angry Northerners to view any changes in the Confederate constitution with any open-mindedness to seek potential benefits that would benefit the entire nation and help the reconstruction process. Thus, the North ignored potential beneficial solutions in the Confederate constitution since the institution of slavery was protected in perpetuity in their constitution.

Secession

Alexander Stephens astutely noted at the Georgia secession conference that Abraham Lincoln's hands were tied since Democrats controlled the legislative branch. Furthermore, he insisted that until Lincoln violated the Constitution the South should not secede. Stephens would inform Lincoln by letter in early December of 1860 "that the people are run mad." By December 20th, 1860, South Carolina voted unanimously, 169-0 to secede. In their secession memorandum they noted that Northern states passed laws nullifying the Fugitive Slave Act of 1850, which violated the Constitution and the compact between the states. Once South Carolina seceded, pressure was on the other states of the deep South to follow South Carolina. [329]

While secession votes in state conferences were overwhelming in favor of the action, only Texas allowed the people to vote on it. About 75% of Texans voted in favor of secession, but the turnout for the special election was small. Thus, it can be surmised that secession was decided by a mere couple hundred of mostly older political leaders in each state. The small sample size may explain the huge turn of events from the 1860 election in November to the start of secession on December 20. Remember, Breckinridge did not even muster 50% of the vote in the South and he ran on the platform of secession. The change of heart may have been influenced by great orators. For example, at the Alabama secession conference, William Yancy was able to change the allegiance of some of his colleagues who wanted to preserve the Union. Whatever the reason, Lincoln (inaugurated until March 4th, 1861) was never provided an opportunity to govern. [330]

Lincoln reasoned states could only secede if they were granted approval from Congress. In no way did he feel a single state could act autonomously and secede without consent. Furthermore, Lincoln felt South Carolina's action to secede was an act of war because they coerced and conspired with other states to influence their secession. Additionally, it was also considered an act of war that the South seized federal property including most forts and ammunition depots located in their newly formed Confederacy. These actions, to Lincoln, were not just an act of war but treasonous. Although border states such as Virginia, Maryland, Kentucky, and Tennessee supported preserving the Union, their legislators decided to "unite their destinies with their sister slave-holding states." Slavery was the one commonality, the one bond that Southern states had in common. According to historian French Chadwick, "it cost more, from every point of view, to be a Union man in the Southern borderland than it did in Massachusetts or Michigan." [331] Virginia would secede shortly after the South fired the first shot in the Civil War and successfully seized Fort Sumter from federal hands. As a result, West Virginia would secede from Virginia and join the Union cause.

The South would gain the initial momentum in the Civil War by being the aggressor, but Southern honor and arrogance would be their downfall. Chadwick suggests that the Southern attack on Fort Sumter was the real reason behind the North's willingness to fight a long bloody war. Slavery, in Chadwick's estimation, was a mere incident or lesser reason. Sure, Sumter was the spark, but decades of slavery disputes that divided the North and South cannot be callously overlooked. After all, slavery was the primary reason that the South seceded and why they felt compelled to protect their institutions and attack Sumter. After Fort Sumter was seized from federal control, Lincoln ordered Union states to organize and recruit for their militias. Lincoln's initial goal was to recruit 75,000 soldiers and retake federal property seized by the South. [332] [333]

Dred Scott v. Sanford [334]

The Supreme Court ruling in *Dred Scott v. Sanford* was one of the biggest factors to precipitate the Civil War. Dred Scott was a slave who resided in Missouri but was taken by his owner to a free state (Illinois) and a free territory (Wisconsin). In a similar case regarding a slave named Rachel (*Rachel v. Walker*), she was also brought to a free state by her owner. The Missouri Supreme Court held that Rachel's liberty was perpetual even after she returned to Missouri. However, the Taney Supreme Court ruled that Dred Scott reverted to a slave once he returned to Missouri.

Taney's decision was flawed for several reasons. First, Taney maintains that Dred Scott was not a citizen of the United States and therefore, he had no standing to argue a case before the Supreme Court. Taney's second error is when he distinguishes between state and national citizenship. The question of citizenship was settled two decades earlier in *Gassies v. Ballon* when Chief Justice Marshall said any citizen of a state is a citizen of the United States. In Taney's opinion (not based on law), slaves were the only people on the face of the Earth who could never earn United States citizenship. Taney's third error is when he refers to the Fifth Amendment Due Process Clause that, "Persons should not be denied life, liberty, and property without due process of the law." Taney suggests that slaves were property and slaveowners could not be denied such property. According to Chief Justice Marshall in *Barron v. Baltimore*, the Bill of Rights and Fifth Amendment did not apply to state laws but only federal laws. Thus, the Fifth Amendment was not applicable to Missouri or Illinois. Therefore, the Fifth Amendment should have had no bearing on the case.

The Dred Scott case may not have made the fracture between Republicans and Democrats any worse, but it did create a serious fracture within the Democratic Party and that was illustrated in the 1860 election were both a Northern and Southern Democrat were on the ticket. The fracture was, in part, caused by Taney's vague opinion over the handling of slavery in the territories. Thus, Northern Democrats had a much different view than Southern Democrats about how slavery in territories should be addressed. Northern Democrats preached popular sovereignty or majority rule in the territories, whereas Southern Democrats expected the federal government to protect slavery in the territories allowing slaveowners to move their slaves into any territory in the country. The fracture in the Democratic Party eliminated the connection that linked Southerners with their Northern cohorts and ensured Abraham Lincoln would win in 1860. [335] Moreover, the division between Democrats made secession much easier for Southern Democrats since they no longer had any political allegiance with Northern Democrats. There is no doubt that the Dred Scott decision brought the nation closer to war. While Republicans feared the decision opened the door to legalizing slavery in free states, the decision forced Southern Democrats to slip further into political isolation.

Chapter 12: The Civil War Causation Theories and Consequences

History book theories for the cause of the Civil War do not include God or fundamental rights. To prove the thesis proposed in Chapter 1, I must show that the Civil War was fought to protect the God-given fundamental rights of citizens.

Just as with the Revolutionary War, the Civil War also has many theories as to what caused the outbreak of war. There is much overlap between Civil War causation theories. The theories include Southern states' powers, the progressive or economic, the cultural, the needless war, and the moral hypothesis. Initial accounts of the war were to vindicate or to rationally explain the actions taken by either side. By end of the 1800s, historians concluded both the North and South had legitimate claims: The South had legitimate state sovereignty reservations and the North was protecting the Union and the moral cause to end slavery. By 1920, the theory accepted by historians was that the Civil War was a struggle for power by two economic factions within the United States. By 1940, historians changed their tune again and this became known as the Revisionist Era. The Revisionists' held the Civil War could have and should have been averted framing it as a needless war. The Revisionists' reasoned that slavery was already an outdated institution, and it was going to end without war. The Revisionist interpretation was the Civil War was fought primarily because agitators, such as the abolitionist, brought about the war with their fanatical views and actions. By the 1950s the causation argument changed again when the moral theory took hold. The moral theory held that the Constitution protected slavery in the states and therefore, the abolitionists were in the right to prevent the expansion of the evil and immoral institution into the new territories and states. [336]

The South was confident that they could defeat the North in a struggle. Although the North had the numbers and industry, Southerners were well adept at hunting and horsemanship skills. Furthermore, Virginia Military Institute and the Citadel trained hundreds of Southern boys to be soldiers and officers. Southerners would almost win the Civil War because as William Yancy of Alabama stated Southern culture was under attack, "Ours is the property invaded; ours are the institutions which are at stake; ours is the peace that will be destroyed; ours is the honor at stake – the honor of our children, the honor of our families, the lives of perhaps of all." Therefore, those fighting for the South had more to lose and usually those with more to lose fare better in any conflict regardless of the odds. Case in point, the colonists had more to lose in the Revolutionary War and were able to overcome the overwhelming odds to defeat the powerful English empire. [337]

Southern States' Powers Theory

South Carolina's "Declaration of the Causes of Secession" refers to states' powers found in the Articles of Confederation, the Constitution, and the Declaration of Independence. Furthermore, the Declaration of Independence provides the people the right to establish a new government. These references are quoted below: [338]

- The Articles of Confederation asserts, "that each state retains its sovereignty, liberty and independence, and every power, jurisdiction, and right which is not, by this Confederation, expressly delegated to the United States in Congress assembled."
- The Constitution's Tenth Amendment pronounces, "powers not delegated to the United States by the Constitution nor prohibited by it to the states, are reserved to the States respectively, or to the people."
- The Declaration of Independence affirms that the colonies "are, and of right out to be, Free and Independent States, that they have the power to levy war, conclude peace, contract alliances, establish commerce, and to do all other acts and things which Independent States may of right do." The South believed if states' powers were breached then they had a duty to secede from the Union because the Declaration of Independence also affirms when any "form of government becomes destructive for which it was established, it is the right of the people to alter or abolish it, and to institute a new government."

States' powers are synonymous with federalism or a dual government system where power is shared between states and the federal government. Those advocating for states' powers usually depends on which political party is in control. History suggests the party in control advocates for federal authority, whereas the minority party promotes states' powers to thwart federal authority. Prior to the Civil War, there were several major disputes between the states and their objection to federal regulations and laws. The national bank discussed earlier is one example. The Kentucky and Virginia Resolutions written by Madison and Jefferson was a states' powers battle over the John Adam's administration passage of the Alien and Seditions Act. Massachusetts and other New England states protested the Jefferson administration's embargo on both the British and French during the Napoleonic Wars. In 1830, South Carolina threatened to nullify protective tariffs that were unfavorable to the local economy. In 1843 Massachusetts, Ohio, and other Northern states protested the annexation of Texas and the expansion of slavery. In 1850, Northern states objected to the passage of the Fugitive Slave Act with their own liberty laws, which nullified the Fugitive Slave Act. Once Lincoln and the Republicans were in power in 1861, it is no surprise the Southern states went back to the states' powers mantra since they were no longer the majority party. [339] Southern states' powers were a sound principle for succession and supported by historical documents. Nevertheless, the Southern reasoning for using states' powers as a cause for succession was misguided at best. [340]

States' powers are often labeled a racist theorem by modern scholars because in their estimation it supported secession and slavery. What scholars and historians fail to remember is that during the first 70 years of United States history from the ratification of the Constitution to the Civil War, it was the federal government that supported slavery and it was the abolitionist movement that was supported by states' powers. In fact,

Northern states threatened to secede from the Union about the issue of slavery before the South acted. The Fugitive Slave Acts of 1793 and 1850 as well as famous Supreme Court cases such as *Prigg v. Pennsylvania, Strader v. Graham,* and *Dred Scott v. Sanford* proved that the federal government, unequivocally, protected slavery prior to the Civil War. Additionally, the South garnered much federal government power from the Three-Fifths Clause in the Constitution. The Three-Fifths Clause enabled the South to gain congressional majorities from slaves who did not have the right to vote for their federal representatives. Once the new anti-slavery Republican Party came to power in 1860, the South knew it was just a matter of time before they outlawed slavery and consequently, they decided to secede from the Union. One can surmise the South was fighting to maintain federal protections for slavery, whereas it was the North that was fighting for states' powers to deny slavery. Thus, the Southern reason for succession was not for states' powers but to maintain the unconstitutional federal protection of slavery and the status quo.

Let us examine an example of why states' powers were just window-dressing. Historian Charles Beard explains that although slave holding citizens and states were a small minority, they controlled the federal government in the years prior to the war. Southern political power was often referred to as slave power. The slave power controlled important House committees and the Supreme Court. Southern Democrats were forced to advocate the policies of slave owners since they were the primary contributors to their campaigns. At the same time, Northern political interests were much more diverse and divided than Southern Democrats. Northern politicians were concerned about many more issues than just appeasing planters and farmers such as manufacturing and industry. Thus, even when non-slave states were a majority in the federal government, they were a minority because their interests were divided. Beard, therefore, gave little credence to Southern states' powers assertions because as he astutely points out that states' powers do not matter much when Southern planters controlled many aspects of the federal government. [341]

States' powers and nationalism were at the core of the Civil War dispute. Both reasons may be related to patriotism, maintaining law and order, power, and preservation of local, state, and federal governments. The North strongly held the institution of slavery threatened the existence of the United States because it diminished national power. Power is both the perception of strength held by nations as well as the pride and patriotism, which is felt by its citizens. A powerful country, such as the United States, harbors a large and well-equipped military. Powerful nations are also generally supported by large populations and a large land mass with diverse industries. The North sensed that not only were government and other institutions seriously threatened by secession and slavery, but secession threatened the strength, economy, and patriotism of the entire nation. Thus, secession threatened the survival of the United States because it would weaken the Union and may make it more susceptible to enemy attacks. Consequently, nationalism was a better reason for war than states' powers and sectionalism. [342]

Economic Theory

Economic roots for the outbreak of war make sense since slavery was the primary component of the Southern economic system. Slavery was considered both capital and labor. Instead of investing in machinery and innovation the South invested in slaves. Although the South's economy grew, it failed to develop. Slavery was linked to cotton and the demand for cotton and slavery boomed in the years prior to the Civil War. Thus, it would come as no surprise that the South wanted to reopen African slave trade to keep up with growing cotton demands. Even South Carolina voted to expand slave trade despite a crumbling cotton economy and a dwindling need for slaves in their state. [343]

The South regarded any danger to slavery as an economic threat to destroy their monopoly on cotton and other agriculture crops. As the North modernized education, industry, farming, communication, and transportation, the South remained stagnant with high rates of illiteracy and an archaic feudal economic structure with no middle class. Although the South's economy boomed, their methods and institutions remained unchanged. The Northern capitalist and free labor system were the opposite of the Southern institution of slavery. [344]

Other than slavery, the biggest economic issue facing the South was taxes. The South did not want to pay taxes that exploited their citizens while at the same time strengthened and benefited the North. The South understood all too well that most taxes and federal policies favored the North. Protective tariffs, a homestead act, a liberal immigration policy, government subsidies for internal improvements, and a transcontinental railway all favored Northern states. Furthermore, policies such as better communication and transportation would unite the West and North to oppose the South. To unite the Southern coalition behind secession, the South pardoned the debts owned by Southern traders to Northern businesses. The pardoning of debts united non-slave owning Southern traders with the Southern slavocracy. [345]

The South sensed it was an economic dominion of the North paying taxes to build their cities, canals, and railroads. Specifically, the South objected that their taxes went into a general national treasury, which functioned as a "suctioned-pump to drain away our substance." Of course, the North realized if Southern secession succeeded then that would hamper the Northern economy not only through reduced tax revenues but an independent South would be forced to bolster their manufacturing and trade and would most likely return the favor and place higher tariffs on Northern exports to the South. [346]

Most citizens throughout United States history would not object to taxes if they had a choice where their tax money was being spent instead of it going into the general treasury fund. Moreover, all citizens object to excessive government spending and waste. Wasteful spending and tax rates are considerably worse now than back in the 1850s leading up to the Civil War. Today, the government oversees dozens of unconstitutional departments such as education, agriculture, energy, housing and urban development, and so forth. All these agencies drain the tax base and waste money, but the fact remains no one is complaining about it or sees it as a reason to start a revolution or civil war. Thus, there must be more to the economic reason for the Civil War besides taxes and protecting Southern economic markets.

Whenever the South fell on hard times, they always blamed Northern exploitation for their incompetence, problems, and ignorance to keep up with the changing times. Industrialization, innovation, and common sense were not going to stand in the way of a plantation owners' pride. The South was not going to terminate slavery and appease the North even if they would benefit economically. In 1862, case in point, even when Lincoln proposed to provide plantation owners with compensation for each emancipated slave, the South refused both the proposal and any idea that would include ending slavery. One writer suggested, "The more economically debilitating their way of life, the more they clung to it." Another historian wrote, "one plain and obvious effect of the slaveholding system is to deaden every class of society and the spirit of industry essential to the increase of public wealth." In other words, the South would go into financial ruin before giving up slavery. [347] [348]

Cultural Theory

The cultural theory suggests that the Civil War was fought by two very different regions. There is no question there were stark differences between the North and South in terms of climate, dialects, clothing, fashion, and customs. While the South remained static and resistant to change, the North flourished with new cities and advancements in transportation and communication. In fact, some historians suggest that the South was a nation within a nation because it was vastly different culturally. [349]

There were educational opportunities in the South, but only for the wealthy. Education was much different in the North than in the South and that can be best illustrated through their dramatic literacy differences. Books, publishers, magazines, and bookstores were uncommon in the South. Hence, it should come as no surprise that most Southerners were illiterate. Yet, Southerners thought they belonged to a superior race of people. In fact, despite many shortcomings, Southerners believed it was the North that maintained an inferior civilization. [350]

New Englanders mimicked English shopkeepers, border states mimicked English farmers, but the deep South had evolved into a new race of people. Powerful Southern political families remained static, and their social intercourse was limited to their immediate family and local community. Conversely, the Northerner was mobile and constantly on the move looking for opportunities to meet the American dream and strike it rich whether speculating in western lands, minerals and resources, or in manufacturing with new ideas and innovation. Southern nationalism was about localism to protect their institutions such as slavery, whereas Northern nationalism was global with a vast number of interests and objectives.

Southern nationalism of the nineteenth century stressed national pastimes and traditions, whereas their eighteenth-century nationalism stressed rationalism and natural rights. Hence, Southern culture devolved over time, and it was the North that was superior in most aspects of cultural life. For the South to submit to the North was difficult because it would mean an end to not only slavery but the entire way of Southern life and more importantly, the power of the plantation owner both politically, economically, and socially. Additionally, the fear factor cannot be taken lightly in the cultural theory. The South feared living side by side with free slaves for many reasons including retribution. However, the thought of a black man free to court and marry a white Southern belle brought about the fear of God and further fueled the growth of white supremacy in the South. [351]

The South was a feudal system with a few slaveowners imposing their tyrannical power on not only poorer white citizens, but a population of millions of slaves. Slavery fueled feudalism and feudalism fueled slavery. In a true feudal system, there was a mutual friendship between a lord who provides protection and the vassal who provides services. In such a feudal system, vassals had many rights because they controlled most aspects of their lives, but this was not the case with the Southern feudal system during the nineteenth century. Slaves had no liberty because they had no control over any aspect of their lives. Furthermore, the lower socioeconomic class of white Southern citizens were also denied many rights such as voting and free speech rights. [352]

The Southern feudal system had a few rich families but was dominated by the poor. There was no middle class. There were wealthy planters and very poor planters and slaves. The poor planters were too ignorant to be disgruntled with their situation. The poor were controlled by the wealthy politicians and were easily brainwashed into not only believing in Southern nationalism, but fighting for it. Southern nationalism was very strong and although many in the South supported the Union because their forefathers had taken part in creating the United States, they wanted a nation that preserved their way of life and their institutions. [353]

Some historians place the blame for exacerbated cultural differences, between the two sections, directly on a lack of tolerance and self-respect for different customs between the North and South. During the founding era and through the 1820s both the North and South found a way to work out their differences and were able to compromise. Tolerance and compromise started to decline once the Missouri slave question arose and it devolved into nitpicking criticisms such as over the different foods they ate. Nitpicking criticisms were coined egocentric centralism and eventually led to "war psychosis." The Civil War generation of Americans was not as intellectually inclined as the Founders to find middle ground. The decades leading up to the war were the start of partisanship when the objective of the majority party was to punish those in the minority. [354]

Southern political leaders became the cheerleaders or the central force behind the propaganda initiative that included mudslinging and stereotypes to incite Northerners and to unite the citizens of the South. Conversely, Northern attacks to destroy Southern reputations or to humiliate their way of life was seen as a real threat to their honor. In the South honor was earned through the community. Thus, any attack on a Southerner was not just an attack on their honor, but the honor of the entire community or the entire South. [355]

Cultural theorists, such as Allan Nevins, fail to blame the cause of the war on the primary reason there were stark cultural differences between the North and South. The divergence between the two sections of the United States was directly related to slavery. Slavery explains why the culture of the South evolved much differently than those citizens of the North. Thus, the marginalization of slavery by cultural theorists is a gross oversight that fails to comprehend that without slavery the cultural differences would be far less exacerbated.

Needless War Theory

The needless war theory encompasses an emotional factor for the cause of the Civil War. Both the North and South had what were labelled as instigators and agitators who influenced the emotions of the populous. The agitators in the North were the abolitionists and the agitators in the South were "fire-eaters" or the pro-slavery faction. Supporters of needless war theory suggest the intense passion of the abolitionists and fire-eaters drowned out the reasonable voices of people, such as Senator Stephen Douglas, who wanted to pursue popular sovereignty to decide the issue of slavery. What needless war theorists suggest is that the Civil War should have never happened because it was provoked by agitators and strong negative emotions. [356]

The abolitionist movement expanded following the passing of the 1793 Fugitive Slave Act. Although the movement freed an estimated 100,000 slaves, it had its shortcomings. Northerners could not decide what to do with freed slaves and feared that the uneducated and out of work slaves would drain or burden the economy. Some thought that the best solution was to colonize slaves by moving them back to Africa or segregating them in a territory like what was done to Native Americans. However, these ideas never gained traction both because they were costly, and racist. Women, who were part of the abolitionist movement, started their own equal rights movement by the mid-1850s. The women's rights movement caused a fracture in the abolitionist movement. Combining both the women and slave rights movements into one group would have been powerful, unfortunately, it never materialized. [357]

Abolitionist propaganda flooded the South especially following slave uprisings such as those led by Nat Turner. Southerners, of course, became paranoid and fearful. The South tried to use the federal government to silence the First Amendment rights of abolitionists, but that failed. Abolitionists' aggressive behavior also upset Northerners who wanted to preserve the Union. Many Northerners thought abolitionists were needlessly stirring the pot and growing animosity. That may have been the biggest error of the abolitionist movement, they wanted to end slavery at any cost, even at the expense of the Union. Although abolitionists succeeded in bringing the debate of slavery to forefront, their extremism scared away many potential sympathizers both in the North and South. [358]

If fanatical abolitionists were the primary reason for causing the war, then needless war theorists are wrong about mitigating the role that slavery played in the war's origins. After all, without slavery there are no abolitionists. Like the relationship between culture and slavery, the two subjects of slavery and abolitionism are closely related. Confederate President, Jefferson Davis, points to the relationship between slavery and abolitionists for the outbreak of war when he suggests that the Northern way of life was not under attack, but it was the South that was under constant attack by abolitionists including the death of citizens for protecting their slave property. Southerners point to abolitionist, John Brown, and his raid on an arsenal at Harpers Ferry as conclusive evidence that abolitionist were a threat to slavery. Brown's objective was to arm slaves and create a rebellion. That said, Brown's raid failed, and he and those involved were hanged. Brown was seen as a martyr by some Northerners, one Northern newspaper would opine, "that John Brown has twice as much right to hang Governor Wise than Governor Wise has to hang him." While the South's fear and paranoia about abolitionists was real, Brown's ambitious plan to lead a Southern slave insurrection from the Appalachian Mountains had absolutely zero chance of succeeding. [359]

Strong emotions were certainly part of the reason for the Revolutionary and Civil Wars. Still, the two wars had something else in common: It took decades of ill feelings before hostilities erupted. Decades of ill feelings suggests that people had ample time to work out differences and to formulate constitutional arguments for their disagreements. These wars were by no means spontaneous and led solely by propagandists, agitators, or politicians trying to sway public interest by invoking fear and emotions. Historian James Randall rationalizes the only plausible cause for any war is that psychopaths, agitators, misguided politicians, and propagandists pushed for it to happen. Nevertheless, as long as there is a factual substance and a moral reason for catalyzing the instigation of war, strong emotions are not disqualifying to justify a war. After all, slavery is a justifiable moral reason for instigating strong emotions in the most rational human beings. As discussed earlier, natural law and God justify wars that meet certain criteria, and they are unquestionably fulfilled by the North's cause to end the evil institution of slavery. [360]

While needless war historian James Randall agrees that slavery was immoral, but he also believed that if the nation pursued peace, the institution of slavery would have eventually ceased to exist because industrial innovations would have made the institution obsolete. In fact, Randall suggests the issue of slavery was "highly artificial, almost fabricated." The needless war theory is interesting, but it is not history. Unlike other Civil War causation theories, we will never know the true outcome of slavery had war been averted. Randall's theory is worth discussing, but it is pure speculation. [361]

Randall reasons had both the North and South agreed with Stephen Douglas' compromise of popular sovereignty, slavery would have never expanded westward because the land and climate were not conducive for popular Southern crops such as cotton. In fact, Randall would suggest that slavery reached its zenith by 1860 and would have completely disappeared in a generation because profit and land limits were already maximized. Randall may have been correct, but who knows if slavery would go extinct in a decade or thrive for another century or longer. For those who harbor any thoughts industrialization would eventually end slavery must keep in mind that the practice of slavery still exists in portions of the world today including in the United States (human trafficking). Thus, the argument that Southern slavery was "ready to break under its own weight" because it was inefficient, overcapitalized, and stood in the way of industrialization probably holds little credibility. [362]

Randall also believes there was a leadership failure leading up to the Civil War, which he called "weak." Not surprisingly, he labels the decade proceeding the Civil War as the "blundering generation." Political tensions were high in Congress in the late 1850s. Not only did members fail to compromise to resolve the issue of slavery, but its members were also attending work armed with revolvers and knives. Even challenges to duels were quite common. [363] Randall's leadership theories are flawed because he poses no policy examples that may have prevented war.

French Chadwick, however, proposes one potential failure in leadership during the lame duck period between the Buchanan and Lincoln administrations. Chadwick suggests had Buchanan been bold and reinforced the federal forts in the deep South with more men and munitions then the South may have thought twice about seceding from the Union or seizing federal property. In Chadwick's opinion, Buchanan not only had the resources to achieve this task, but he could have easily replaced troops when the time arose. Chadwick, like other Revisionists, emphasize that Buchanan was weak or tended to "always seek to work the lines of least resistance." Chadwick concludes, in part, that blame for the war may have been the long transition between the election and the new administration. During the transition Buchanan wanted to maintain the status quo by recognizing the South's right to slavery, protecting the right to slavery in all territories, and enforcement of the fugitive slave law. [364] In short, both Chadwick and Randall insist weak leadership and fanaticism led to a political misunderstanding culminating in a needless war.

The best theory of a failed or weak political system leading up to the Civil War was written by David Donald in *An Excess of Democracy*. In this paper, Donald details how a decline in the performance of government, at all levels, failed to manage issues such as slavery in territories, issues with Oregon and California territories, Texas annexation, the Mexican War, and the Supreme Court decision in Dred Scott explains why the Civil War became imminent. Donald explains how suffrage expanded to include all white males and political candidates had a problem connecting with all the voter groups. Thus, not to alienate any voters, politicians avoided controversial subjects that "inevitably produced leaders without policies and parties without principles." Consequently, an excess of democracy left the people leaderless. And each subtle and delicate issue, such as Dred Scott, was a "shock" to the political system that broke down the political order and culminated in war. [365] Donald is correct and his theory is like the needless war theory that poor leadership was responsible for the war. Donald distinguishes himself, however, from Randall and Chadwick because he emphasizes the importance of failed policies surrounding slavery. The Civil War was inevitable because slavery was more than a shock to the political landscape, it was an earthquake that rocked the nation. One can certainly extrapolate Donald's leadership and democracy theory to modern politics to explain why the United States is so polarized and divided. Donald's theory also explains how the Founders fear of democracy materialized in American politics.

Randall's suggestion that slavery issues such as emancipation, returning fugitive slaves to their owners, and the territorial question of slavery had no bearing on the war is hard to fathom. These were hotly contested issues that remained unsolved for decades. To dismiss the evils of slavery and the fight for equal fundamental rights is wrong. Randall's assertion that most of the blame of the Civil War falls with Northern abolitionists agitators, not only excludes the entire moral and humanitarian issue of slavery but it overlooks the entire paradox of Southern liberty for its white citizens and slavery for its black population. The Southern principle that slavery was a "positive good" explains why war was a necessity. [366] [367]

Opinions persist that the cost to save the Union was not worth the cost in life and the destruction of the economy that would lead to a generation of poverty following the war. After all, many nations in world history separated without dire consequences such as Norway and Sweden. In fact, there were no consequences when the American English Empire split from the Canadian English Empire. Nevertheless, the needless war theorists fail to consider the humanitarian crisis of slavery. Would it be acceptable for the North to allow the South to secede and to wipe its hands clean from any association with slavery? That was not possible since that would make the North equally as guilty as the South by allowing that barbaric practice to continue. When the humanitarian crisis is taking place within the United States borders, it would be criminal to ignore it and not use any means necessary to put an end to the institution and practice of slavery. [368]

Needless war historian Avery Craven notices the lives of 75% of lower-class non-slave holding Southern whites and the lives of the slave did not change much after the Civil War. It was not until the cotton industry was updated in the 1930s that ex-slaves' lives changed for the better. [369] That the lives of former slaves did not improve immediately following the war is irrelevant. Craven and Randall for some inexplicable reason fail to grasp that the tools to provide former slaves and poor Southerners equal rights was amended to the Constitution (Thirteenth, Fourteenth, and Fifteenth Amendments). The process to provide African Americans and poor whites an unfettered chance to achieve a better life had started. Unfortunately, stereotypes, biases, and bigotry are never eliminated from society, but the process to reform the South's way of living and thinking had begun. It takes time to change customs and perceptions no matter how immoral they may be. A war to protect the rights of 25% of the nation's population from an evil custom and culture was not needless, it was necessary.

Moral Theory [370]

The moral issue of slavery was a common topic in the North during the 1850s. Specifically, the difference between slavery and liberty (freedom) was often discussed. Senator William Seward claimed, "slavery is a temporary, accidental, partial, and incongruous one [institution]; liberty, on the contrary, is a perpetual, organic, universal one [institution], in harmony with the Constitution of the United States." In another speech, Seward suggests, "Our country is a theatre which exhibits in full operation two radically different political systems; one resting on the basis of servile labor, the other on the voluntary labor of free men." William Herndon, who was Lincoln's law partner, stated, "Liberty and slavery – civilization and barbarianism are absolute antagonists." James Lowell proclaimed that "liberty is also an institution deserving some attention in a Model Republic." President Lincoln made an astute observation when he said the world looks at the American experiment with not only skepticism but views it entirely hypocritically when Americans preach liberty in the face of Southern slavery. Another paper noted that the North was just as guilty as the South about the issue of slavery because they "encouraged it." I do not know that they encouraged it, but looking the other way when the liberty of others is at stake is wrong.

The South countered Northern arguments of morality and liberty with cries that slaves were not equal to whites or the institution of slavery was humane. For example, Alexander Stephens declaration that race equality was an "error" and "that the negro is not equal to the white man" were common Southern statements. Southerners provided examples of their bigotry, for instance, in a New Orleans Bee editorial that read, "as long as false and pernicious theories are cherished respecting the inherent equality and right of every human being, there can be no satisfactory political Union between the two sections." Ironically, future Confederate President, Jefferson Davis, argues the objective of the North was not to eliminate Southern inhumanity but to stifle slave numbers because they count toward their federal representation in Congress (one slave was 3/5 of person in the census count). The hypocrisy of the South was overwhelming, they felt slaves had no human value other than labor and to help the South garner more political power in Congress that was used to keep the institution of slavery perpetually protected.

In Davis' estimation slavery was humane because it "elevated brutal savages into docile, intelligent, and civilized laborers." Southerners argued that slaves had a better life when compared with the lower class of the North, "The difference between us is, that our slaves are hired for life and well compensated (food, clothing, shelter), your [lower class] are hired by the day, not cared for, and scantly compensated." What the above quotes neglect to mention is that slaves are denied family, work, travel, property, contract, voting, marriage, and other rights. Moreover, the above quotes also dismiss the point that slavery eliminates any motivation for self-improvement, which is needed for economic growth. [371]

The Southern case to support slavery put forth by Senator John Calhoun (1850) was quite different than those theories offered by the North. Senator Calhoun was not only the most influential person in South Carolina politics in the pre-Civil War era, he was the face of Southern politics. His constitutional doctrines would serve as a meaningful model to not only protect the institution of slavery, but to be the basis of secession arguments in 1861 (ten years after his death). Calhoun insists it was Northern power over the federal government and other institutions that not only threatened the institution of slavery but was attempting to destroy Southern ways of life, dismantling the equilibrium between the North and South, and subject every Southerner to poverty. Calhoun asks for a constitutional amendment to restore Southern power and protect its institutions. [372]

To downplay the moral reason for the war, historians had to mitigate the role of slavery for causing the war. Those historians who supported the moral theory erred because they believed the Constitution supported slavery. Even modern moral theorists argue that slavery was protected by the Constitution. If slavery is immoral and the Constitution is divinely influenced by God, then it cannot protect slavery or any criminal behavior. That said, history up to the Civil War demonstrated the federal government protected slavery time and time again. For example, the Fugitive Slave Acts and cases such as *Prigg v. Pennsylvania, Dred Scott v. Sanford,* and *Strader v. Graham* all defend slavery using constitutional reasoning. The government's tendency to favor slavery led to a fracture in the abolitionist movement with those in favor of the Constitution and those who wanted to discard the document because they thought it supported slavery. [373]

The fracture in the abolitionist movement led many historians, such as Paul Calore, to erroneously argue slavery was protected by the Constitution. There are several reasons why the Constitution does not support slavery:

1. Why did Calhoun, Crittenden, and others want to amend the Constitution to protect slavery if it was already protected? That is because the Constitution and its principles were the antithesis of slavery.

2. Slavery or any class of persons or a tiered level of citizenship are never mentioned or defined in the Constitution. The preamble states the Constitution protects "We the people" not "We the white people." Henceforth, even slaves were citizens and protected by the Constitution. In 1863 attorney general Edward Bates provided a solid argument for citizenship that refuted *Dred Scott v. Sanford.* Dred Scott held that blacks, free or slave, were the only category of persons who could never be citizens of the United States. Bates explained that not only was the Constitution "silent" about color, but the Constitution did not grant citizenship. Bates elaborated that the Constitution only protects citizenship or those persons who were natural born citizens or foreigners who were naturalized citizens. There is nothing in the Constitution to deny citizenship to free or slave blacks who were born in the United States. [374]

3. The Importation Clause allowed the practice of slavery importation to continue, but only to 1807 when it was banned by the Jefferson administration.

4. The Three-Fifths Clause infers that slaves were more than property; they were citizens because they counted toward the census. The Three-Fifths Clause would suggest slaves had fewer rights but that did not preclude them from being considered citizens. During this era women also had mitigated rights, but they were citizens. [375]

5. The Fugitive Clause guaranteeing the return of escaped slaves was the only provision that protected slavery, but the federal government had no way to enforce the provision. It was not until the unconstitutional passage of the Fugitive Slave Act of 1793 did the federal government step in and provide a law to enforce the Fugitive Clause. Future Supreme Court Chief Justice, Salmon Chase, would argue before the courts that the federal government had no power to enforce the Fugitive Clause because it was located in Article IV of the Constitution. The location of the Fugitive Clause in the Constitution was significant because Article IV outlines a few powers and principles of state governments, but the federal government is not provided any expressed grant of power to enforce Article IV. Article IV is a

compact or agreement between the states and therefore, can only be enforced by the states. For instance, the Privileges and Immunities Clause, located in Article IV, Section 2, never provides the federal government with the power to prohibit states from infringing on the privileges and immunities of citizens. If the federal government had such powers, then the Privileges and Immunities Clause of the Fourteenth Amendment would never have been a necessary upgrade to the Constitution. What Article IV, Section 2 accomplishes was to ensure all privileges and immunities permitted to citizens of a certain state were also provided to citizens of another state who are visiting the jurisdiction. Although Chase's arguments in *Prigg v. Pennsylvania* (1842) would fall on deaf ears, he was 100% correct, the Constitution did not yield the federal government power to defend slavery or the Fugitive Clause. [376]

The conundrum posed by the meaning of Article IV, Section 2 is that, although states had to treat citizens from other states visiting their jurisdiction the same as residents of the state, it did not preclude them from violating the privileges and immunities of residents and visitors. The conundrum posed in the preceding sentence was true for several reasons. First, *Barron v. Baltimore* failed to apply the Bill of Rights to the states and second, Article IV, Section 2 did not pertain to protecting privileges and immunities. Article IV, Section 2 only pertained to treating nonresidents the same as residents. Thus, one might reasonably assume states could enslave residents or non-residents visiting the state. The discrepancy in understanding Article IV, Section 2 was not a failure of the Constitution; it was a failure of the Supreme Court in *Barron v. Baltimore*. The ruling in Baron prevented the federal government from protecting citizens from rogue state laws because it held the Bill of Rights did not apply to the states. The Republican Party platform of 1860 tried resolve the glaring mistake made in Barron by changing its definition of Article IV, Section 2 to resolve this conundrum, implying that Article IV, Section 2 did, in fact, allow the federal government to protect the privileges and immunities of citizens. Although the new Republican point of view for Article IV, Section 2 tried to correct the error that the Bill of Rights did not apply to the states in Barron, it incorrectly refuted the argument held by fellow Republican Salmon Chase in Prigg. Thus, Republicans finally agreed that the Fourteenth Amendment was necessary, in part, to repudiate Barron. Had it not been for Barron it would be obvious the Constitution did not protect slavery. [377]

6. At the same time the Constitution was being ratified, the Northwest Ordinance abolished slavery in the territories of Ohio, Michigan, Indiana, Illinois, and Wisconsin. Although passed under the Articles of Confederation Congress, the Supreme Court upheld its constitutionality in *Strader v. Graham (1851)*. While Strader upheld the constitutionality of territories to be free, it failed to protect free states. In Strader, the Court held that the status (free or slave) of three slaves who travelled to Ohio from Kentucky was dependent on Kentucky law. Thus, Strader held the three slaves reverted to slaves once they

returned to Kentucky. Although the Court recognized the authority of the Northwest Ordinance when Ohio was a territory, it did not extend the Northwest Ordinance to Ohio when it became a state. The Northwest Ordinance made it clear that Ohio would never be a slave region whether a territory or state. In fact, no free territory ever became a slaveholding state in United States history! If the Supreme Court can uphold a ban of slavery in the territories it begs to reason they could have upheld a of ban slavery in free states for instance, using Ohio state law instead of Kentucky state law in Strader. Strader is an example of a case that was decided 50% correctly and 50% atrociously. [378]

7. It seems preposterous that language such as "All men are created equal" or "We the people" are ignored when slavery is defended. The Bill of Rights and the Declaration of Independence protect the rights of all citizens equally regardless of race, gender, or socioeconomic standing. Without the egregious mistake made by the Barron decision, the Constitution would be an obvious prohibition on slavery. Former slave, Frederick Douglass, would defend both the Declaration of Independence and Constitution as a prohibition against slavery.

Historian French Chadwick downplayed the role of slavery for the outbreak of the war. Chadwick reasoned that a majority of the slaveowners treated slaves humanely, slaves were content with their lives, and slaves showed no signs of assimilation. Even if Chadwick's anecdotal evidence is true, what he fails to comprehend is that anyone who is not given opportunities to experience the benefits of liberty may not know any better. Today, this is known as Narcissistic Abuse Syndrome when people accept a horrific situation such as domestic abuse. Furthermore, it is the role of the government and free people to protect the rights of those who cannot speak for themselves such as those persons with disabilities, the unborn, children, the dead, and especially anyone held in servitude. Protecting those who cannot speak for themselves is precisely why the protection of fundamental rights is a necessity. [379]

Chadwick argues if slavery was the cause for the war, then the Southern military would not have been primarily comprised of poor white non-slaveholding Southerners. The question that Chadwick should raise is why would poor Southerners fight a war to protect an institution that left them serfs to the Southern feudal system? While slaves who were unaware of the benefits of liberty may have been content with their situation, similarly, the ignorance of the poor white Southerner may explain why they would protect a system that did not benefit them – they knew no better. [380]

Historian Charles Beard's also diminishes the impact of slavery as a primary reason for the war. Beard argues that abolishment of slavery was not even a Republican platform issue for the 1860 election and he, therefore, erroneously concludes that ending slavery was not a popular political point of view in the North. The Republican Party initially did not intend to end slavery, they did intend, however, to stop it from spreading in new territories and states. [381]

It is often advised that historians should remain neutral when writing about past conflicts. As moral theory historian Arthur Schlesinger advises, sometimes it is so obvious that the position taken by one side is so evil and immoral, for history to be accurate, sides must be taken. The Revisionists contend the Civil War was a neutral war or a needless war fought because of agitators or cultural, economic, and political differences. Schlesinger astutely points out that slavery is one commonality in the states' powers, cultural, economic, political, and needless war theories. Schlesinger argues for historians to remain neutral; they were tasked with marginalizing the significance that slavery played in the outbreak of the Civil War. [382]

Schlesinger's morality theory has one major flaw. Sure, he acknowledges the obvious: Slavery is evil and wrong. However, he fails to detail why slavery is evil and wrong. Why is slavery intuitively immoral? Because it violates God's law of moral principles which, in turn, violate the laws of human nature or the laws of right and wrong. Schlesinger fails to identify those properties that comprise fundamental rights including downplaying the significance of natural law and God since fundamental rights are God-given.

Consequences of the War [383]

In effect, the Civil War was a continuation of the American Revolutionary War to resolve the issue of slavery that remained unsolved at the Constitutional Convention in 1787. Our Founders put the Union first and kicked the issue of slavery down the road to be settled later. Historian Charles Beard regards the Civil War as the second American revolution. Beard argues the Civil War could be viewed as a revolution because it ends in a new government (power shifted from Democrats to Republicans), it saw vast changes in socio economic classes that saw more wealth distribution, it resulted in a revised Constitution (at least amended), and it brought about the industrial revolution. [384]

The Thirteenth, Fourteenth, and Fifteenth Amendments were passed following the Civil War and are important because they not only protected the fundamental rights of all citizens, but they made it impossible for states to violate the rights of anyone ever again (not just slaves). There is nothing in these amendments about resolving cultural difference or economic inequalities between the North and South. Each amendment infers slavery was the reason for the Civil War. For historians to suggest that slavery was merely a smoke screen for the outbreak of Civil War is negligent.

By 1865 the executive and legislative branches were dominated by Republicans who believed the purpose of the Civil War was to eradicate slavery. To build on the emancipation proclamation and the Military Act of 1862, Congress proposed the Thirteenth Amendment. The Thirteenth Amendment used very similar language to the Northwest Ordinance to abolished slavery, but Southern states responded to this amendment with black codes or a set of laws whose purpose was to keep free black people oppressed. To secure passage, both Republicans and Democrats erroneously agreed that the Thirteenth Amendment did not protect political rights, but only the natural and civil rights of freed slaves. [385]

Congress responded to the black codes with the Civil Rights Act of 1866. It was debated if Congress had the authority to pass such an act and if so, what constitutional provision provided the federal government authority to enforce civil rights legislation. The Ninth Amendment should have been the tool used by the federal government to enforce civil rights legislation, but it was ignored. In fact, it was precisely the purpose of the amendment! Instead, proponents of the Civil Rights Act of 1866 theorized the Thirteenth Amendment or Article IV, Section 2 (the Privileges and Immunities Clause) provided them authority to pass civil rights legislation. Opponents argued the Thirteenth Amendment and Article IV, Section 2 gave them no authority to regulate work contracts or civil rights. Again, to increase the chances of its passage the purpose of the Civil Rights Act of 1866 was confined to the protection of natural or civil rights, not political rights such as the right to vote, hold public office, or sit on juries. [386]

When Congress ignored the Ninth Amendment to pass civil rights legislation many senators, such as John Bingham, felt Republicans had no recourse except to pass a new amendment to enforce the Civil Rights Act of 1866. Bingham and many Republicans felt the Civil Rights Act may not be able to survive legal challenges without an amendment to defend its passage. After all, the legislation was originally vetoed by President Andrew Johnson before Congress got the votes to override the veto. In 1868, the Fourteenth Amendment was ratified. Again, to enhance the chance of its passage, the purpose of the Fourteenth Amendment was confined to protect natural and civil rights, but not political rights. [387]

Nine years later the Civil Rights Act of 1875 was passed and it became known as the Accommodations Act. The Civil Rights Act of 1875 held that it was unlawful for places of business to discriminate. In the *Civil Rights Cases of 1883*, the Civil Rights Act of 1875 was found unconstitutional. In that case Justice Bradley would define slavery "as a restraint on travel, the inability to buy and sell property, the inability to make contracts, the inability to have standing in court, the inability to be a witness against a white person, and severer punishment for crimes." Nevertheless, Bradley correctly pointed out that the Civil Rights Act of 1875 violated the implied First Amendment right to associate. The Civil Rights Act of 1964 and the cases such as *Atlanta Motel v. United States* and *Katzenbach v. McClung* would reinstate controversial accommodation laws. [388]

Finally, the Fifteenth Amendment provided that all male citizens should garner the political right to vote including former slaves. The Fifteenth Amendment has been superseded by the Nineteenth Amendment that provides all non-felon citizens over 18 with voting privileges. Some scholars argue that the passage of the Fifteenth Amendment was proof that the meaning of the Thirteenth Amendment, the Civil Rights Act of 1866, and the Fourteenth Amendment did not protect political rights (such as the right to vote) as privileges and immunities. I disagree and rationalize the Republicans excluding political rights was merely a strategic political move to ensure the passage of the amendments and legislation. We will never know for sure what was discussed in private to pass the civil rights bill and amendments, but compromise is a significant part of congressional political strategy. I find the exclusion of political rights by Congress following the Civil War very odd. It was almost as if it was a bargaining chip to pass legislation and not because political rights are not fundamental rights. Notwithstanding, I enshrine political rights as fundamental rights for many reasons:

1. The Constitution does not support two classes of citizenship.
2. Sir William Blackstone agreed that political rights were fundamental rights.
3. *Strauder v. West Virginia, ex Parte Virginia,* and *Virginia v. Rivas* all protected the political right to sit on juries in 1880.
4. Political rights are a subset of natural rights.
5. Political rights are encompassed within the Ninth Amendment.
6. Political rights are God-given because they are discerned in the Bible.
7. Voting privileges were expanded only a year and a half after the passage of the Fourteenth Amendment by the same men who said fundamental rights did not include political rights.

Despite the dispute about the constitutionality of the accommodation laws and the definition of a fundamental right, the outcome of the Civil War was clear: Improved protections of fundamental rights for all citizens. [389]

Chapter 13: Conclusion

Key Points

Below are the main takeaways from this book:

- Science cannot disprove God. In fact, the hypothesis that a God exists is more logical than any scientific theory to explain the creation of the universe and life.
- Through heavy contemplation and prayer, one can rationalize the many stories and miracles that happen in the Bible.
- Fundamental rights are God-given and can be decerned in the Bible, the Constitution, and historical legislation.
- The process for identifying and protecting fundamental rights has become convoluted and has done a disservice to the Constitution and protecting rights.
- The federal government has invented many techniques and methods to infringe upon, mitigate, and violate our God-given fundamental rights.
- Few God-given fundamental rights have escaped detrimental laws or regulations at the hands of the federal government.
- Historical causation theories for the Revolutionary and Civil Wars are incorrect because they neglect the importance of fundamental rights and God.
- There has been an ongoing trend to rewrite the history of the United States as a secular nation. The information supplied in treatise demonstrates the United States is, without question, a Christian nation.
- The United States is drifting away from the vision conveyed by the Founders, which has been detrimental to both the constitutional principles and the fundamental right protections enshrined in the Constitution.
- Since God is the most logical solution for the creation of the universe and the Bible is His word, then fundamental rights discerned in the Bible must be God-given. The government and historians have been trying to rewrite United States history without God by mitigating fundamental rights and fabricating secular causation theories for the Revolutionary and Civil Wars. The evidence supplied by this book proves unequivocally that United States history without God is wrong. God strongly influenced the Founders and the Declaration of Independence and Constitution, and God-given Fundamental rights were the basis for fighting both the Revolutionary and Civil Wars.

Fundamental Rights, Natural Law, and God Never Stood a Chance

Historian Charles Beard agrees with remarks made by Civil War Era Senator William Seward that economic rebellions primarily fought to attain property reform have never had much historical success. Beard and Seward are both right and wrong. They were right the Civil War was about more than economic reasons. They were wrong because they only view property as something tangible. They never realized that property is more than an economic right but according to the Bible and natural law it also includes ownership of oneself and our personal liberty. [390] Romans 14:12 teaches us that people are accountable for their liberty or their actions. If people are accountable for their actions, then they own their actions. Romans 14:12 reads, "So then each one of us will give an account of himself to God." To be sure, the cause for both the Revolutionary and Civil Wars was much more involved than a dispute about tangible property rights. Instead, the wars were a dispute about those property rights which encompass the personal liberty of people to pursue fundamental rights. In fact, successful and justifiable conflicts are primarily fought to protect the personal liberty of citizens to pursue their God-given fundamental rights.

The preceding paragraph reveals an ugly truth. A leading Civil War historian (Beard) and the Civil War's most famous anti-slavery Senator (Seward) both fail to understand a vital natural law principle regarding property rights and, therefore, fail to comprehend what caused the Civil War. There is absolutely no way fundamental rights, natural law, and God stood a chance to survive the test of time if the so-called experts, such as Beard and Seward, did not understand that property rights were, indeed, the real reason for fighting the Civil War.

Next Steps

At the moment I do not have any future research planned on the subject of fundamental rights. If I were to delve deeper into the subject of God-given fundamental rights, I might focus my attention on the Ninth Amendment. Making the Ninth Amendment relevant would go a long way to protecting our God-given fundamental rights. I am also contemplating turning this book into a short version for young adults since it is easier to shape the minds and perceptions of younger people than older people. I am also considering running for Congress as a libertarian, but that is contingent on my health and the health of my family. Libertarians are lucky if they garner 1% of the vote but running for Congress is a great way to introduce new ideas. I wish there was a comprehensive list of books on fundamental rights I could recommend for the reader. There is little research available on subject of privileges and immunities or fundamental rights outside the work of a few law scholars. Unfortunately, the work of law scholars is not intended for the layperson to understand.

The next steps for people wanting to change minds and perceptions about our God-given fundamental rights is twofold. First, people should support a state amendment constitutional convention to suggest amendments proposed in Chapter 1 to bring back the Founders' vision for the Constitution and to protect our fundamental rights. [391] Second, political independents should continue to grow support for a viable third-party. There is no better way to bring about meaningful change in the political process if the parties in power receive a vote of no confidence. At the very least Americans should support an initiative to add "None of the above" on election ballots as a mechanism to emphasize a vote of no confidence in our political leaders.

Appendix

Table A1: Timeline of Events

Year	Event
2000–500 BC	Old Testament is written
0	Christ is Born
30	Jesus Dies
41–70	New Testament is written
1607	Jamestown Settlement in New World is Established
1687	Isaac Newton Discovers Gravity
1754–1763	French and Indian War
1765	Stamp Act Passed
1766	Declaratory Act Passed
1768	Townshend Duties Passed
1770	Boston Massacre
1773	Tea Act Passes / Boston Tea Party
1774	Intolerable Acts Passed
1775–1783	American Revolutionary War
1776	Declaration of Independence
1781–1789	Articles of Confederation is the Law of the America
1787	Northwest Ordinance
1789	The Constitution is Ratified
1793	Chisholm v. Georgia / Fugitive Slave Act of 1793 Passed
1798	Calder v. Bull
1803	Marbury v. Madison / Louisiana Purchase
1807	Importation of Slaved Banned
1817	McCulloch v. Maryland
1820	Missouri Compromise
1823	Corfield v. Coryell / Monroe Doctrine
1824	Second Law of Thermodynamics Discovered
1830	Indian Removal Act
1831	Cherokee Nation v. Georgia
1833	Second National Bank Dissolved

1836	**Gag Rule**
1842	**Prigg v. Pennsylvania**
1846	**Oregon Territory Treaty**
1848	**Spanish American Treaty Ratified**
1850	**Fugitive Slave Act of 1850**
1851	**Strader v. Graham**
1854	**Kansas–Nebraska Act Passed**
1857	**Dred Scott v. Sanford**
1859	**John Brown's Raid on Harpers Ferry / Charles Darwin's Theory of Evolution**
1860	**Abraham Lincoln Elected President / Crittenden Compromise Proposed**
1861–1865	**The American Civil War**
1864	**James Maxwell Discovers the Electromagnetic Force**
1865	**Thirteenth Amendment Ratified**
1866	**Civil Rights Act of 1866**
1868	**Fourteenth Amendment is Ratified**
1870	**Fifteenth Amendment is Ratified**
1873	**Slaughter-House Cases / Bradwell v. Illinois**
1875	**Civil Rights Act of 1875 (Accommodations Act)**
1880	**Strauder v. West Virginia, Ex Parte Virginia**
1883	**Civil Rights Cases**
1893	**Prout v. Starr**
1895	**Pollock v. Farmers Loan and Trust**
1896	**Plessy v. Ferguson**
1905	**Albert Einstein Discovers the Special Theory of Relativity**
1913	**Sixteenth and Seventeenth Amendments Ratified**
1915	**Einstein Discovers General Relativity**
1917	**Espionage Act**
1918	**Max Planck Discovers Quantized Energy Levels**
1919	**Schenck v. United States / Debs v. United States / Abrams v. United States**
1920	**The Beginning of Quantum Mechanics**

1923	**Meyer v. Nebraska**
1925	**Pierce v. Society of Sisters**
1927	**Heisenberg Uncertainty Principle / Buck v. Bell**
1931	**Georges Lemaitre Proposes the Big Bang Theory**
1934	**Nebbia v. New York**
1935	**Strong Nuclear Force is Discovered**
1938	**United States v. Carolene Products**
1942	**Wickard v. Filburn**
1944	**Korematsu v. United States**
1947	**Everson v. Board of Education**
1954	**Brown v. School Board / Berman v. Parker**
1957	**Civil Rights Act of 1957**
1962	**Baker v. Carr**
1963	**Sherbert v. Verner**
1964	**Civil Rights Act of 1964 / Katzenbach v. McClung / Atlanta Motel v. US / Reynolds v. Simms**
1965	**Griswold v. Connecticut**
1969	**Brandenburg v. Ohio**
1970	**String Theory Begins**
1973	**Roe v. Wade**
1978	**Penn Central v. New York City**
1983	**Weak Nuclear Force is Discovered**
1986	**Loop Theory Begins**
1989	**Deshaney v. Winnebago**
1992	**Lee v. Weisman**
2002	**Zelman v. Simmons-Harris / Tahoe-Sierra v. Tahoe Regional Planning**
2003	**Lawrence v. Texas / Grutter v. Bollinger**
2004	**Locke v. Davey**
2005	**Kelo v. New London / Castle Rock v. Gonzales**
2007	**Gonzales v. Raich**
2008	**D.C. v. Heller**
2010	**McDonald v. Chicago**

2014	**McCullen v. Coakley**
2015	**Obergefell v. Hodges**
2018	**Masterpiece Cakeshop v. Colorado**

List A1: Moral Principles and Corresponding Biblical Verses

- **Treat others as you expect to be treated** Matthew 7:12, Luke 6:31
- **Do no harm. Evil cannot be done even if it may result in good** Romans 3:9, (Proverbs 11:13, 17:13), Matthew 5:29, Galatians 6:1
- **Do not cheat** Leviticus 19:11; **lie**, Matthew 26:59–61, John 15:26, Exodus 23:1–2, Philippians 1:18, Isaac 60:1, Ephesians 4:25; **steal** (Matthew 15:15–20, 19:18), Ephesians 4:28, (Exodus 23:4–5 and 23:8), (Proverbs 6:16–19, 6:30–31), (Ezekiel 18:7, 22:12); **be deceitful** Matthew 5:15–23, (Proverbs 24:28–29, 26:19, 26:24, 26:26), Ezekiel 22:29; **commit adultery** Matthew 5:27–28, Ezekiel 18:6, Leviticus 18:1–30, (Proverbs 5 and 7); **fall to temptation** Luke 8:5–15; or **commit murder** Matthew 5:21
- **Forgive those whom do you harm** (Matthew 5:11, 22–24, 38–42, 6:12, 18:21–35), Mark 11:25–26, (Psalms 25, 32, 94:1), Proverbs 25:21–22, Romans 12:17–21, 1 Thessalonians 5:12–15, 1 Peter 3:8–14, (Luke 6:28–29, 15:11–32), Colossians 3:13, John 8:11, Galatians 6:1
- **Profess love** (Matthew 5:44-46, 19:19), (Luke 6:27, 6:32), (John 3:16, 13:35, 15:9, 15:12), 1 John 4:7–21, 1 Corinthians 13:1–13, Colossian 3:14, Proverbs 10:12; **joy** (Matthew 5:12, 7:1–5), 1 Peter 1:8–9, John 17:13; **peace** Luke 6:35, John 14:27, Philippians 4:6–7; **tolerance** Matthew 7:1–5, (Romans 12:9–21,14:3–15:7), 2 Corinthians 5:11–21, Proverbs 21:15; **kindness** Genesis 4:1–12, Psalms 4:4, (Matthew 5:21–22, 18:21–25), (Ephesians 2:6–7,4:25–5:2), James 1:19–21, Colossians 3:12, 1 Peter 4:9, 5:5, 2 Peter 1:7, (Proverbs 11:16–17,14:22, 25:11), (Isaac 58:6–7); **goodness** Luke 6:33, Numbers 12:3, Galatians 6:9–10, Titus 2:5–6; **faithfulness and hope** Mathew 23:23, Ephesians 6:13, Romans 5:10, 1 John 3:3, Proverbs 3:3, Revelation 2:10, Hebrews 3:6; **gratitude** Matthew 6:25–34; **self-control or patience** Psalms 39:1, (Proverbs 10:18–20, 14:17, 14:29, 25:28, 29:11, 29:22), Matthew 15:1–20, (James 1:4, 3:1–12, 5:8–9), 1 Peter 2:23, 2 Peter 1:6, Isaac 40:31, Romans 15:1, Titus 2:11–12, 1 Timothy 1:16
- **Be modest and humble** Mark 10:35–45, Romans 12:3, Philippians 2:1–11, 1 Peter 3:15, (Matthew 11:29, 25:34–40), (Luke 12:13–21, 14:8–11), 1 Timothy 6:3–19, Hebrews 13:5, (James 2:1–17, 4:6), 1 Corinthians 8:1, 2 Corinthians 10:1–18, Galatians 6:1–18, (Proverbs 8:12–14, 15:11, 15:27, 22:4, 25:27, 27:1–2, 29:23), John 13:14–15
- **Have empathy** Matthew 19:23, (Proverbs 14:21, 14:31)
- **Follow the laws of society** (Matthew 23:23, 26:39–61), Luke 11:42, (Romans 4:19, 13:1–7), 1 Peter 2:13–15, 2 Peter 2:10, Jude 1:8, (Proverbs 28:4–5, 28:9, 29:4, 29:18), Ecclesiastes 8:2–5

- **Mind your own business and do not judge or envy others** Matthew 7:1–2, Luke 6:37, 1 Thessalonians 4:11–12, 2 Thessalonians 3:11, 1 Timothy 5:13, (Proverbs 6:24, 23:17, 24:1, 25:17, 27:4), 1 Corinthians 3:3, Exodus 20:17, Philippians 4:11–12
- **Honor contracts** Matthew 21:33–46, (Leviticus 19:35 and 25:16–34), Numbers 30:1–16, (Proverbs 20:10, 20:23, 22:26–27), (Ezekiel 18:6, throughout the Bible, there are dozens of references to a covenant [contract] between God and the people to honor God's law
- **Honor your parents and elders** (Matthew 15:1–9, 19:19), Ephesians 6:1–4, Colossians 3:20, (Leviticus 19:3 and 19:32), (Proverbs 13:1, 19:13, 19:26, 20:20, 23:22, 30:11, 30:17)
- **Never seek revenge** Romans 12:17–21, 1 Peter 3:9, Leviticus 19:18, (Proverbs 24:17–18, 25:21)
- **Do not be greedy** Numbers 11:31–34, (Proverbs 13:25, 19:17), the Book of Ecclesiastes, 1 Corinthians 10:24, Acts 20:35, John 15:13
- **Develop friendships** Proverbs 27:9–10
- **Do not complain or argue** Philippians 2:14, Numbers 11:1–3, Proverbs 23:29–35
- **Do not use vulgar language** Ephesians 5:4, Ephesians 4:29–30, James 5:12, Leviticus 19:12
- **Trials for Crimes** Numbers 35:24–25
- **Creation of the institution of marriage** Genesis 2:18–25

List A2: Biblical Virtues and Corresponding Biblical Verses

- **Have grit, dedication, determination, perseverance, bravery, and courage in the face of adversity** Luke 16:19–31, (Romans 8:31, 15:1), James 5:16, 1 Peter 4:8
- **Be Energetic** (Proverbs 6:6–11, 10:4–5, 24:10, 28:1), Ephesians 5:15–15, Philippians 2:12–13, (1 Thessalonians 4:11–12, 3:6–15), 1 Corinthians 3:8
- **Trust** Isaac 14:24, Philippians 4:6, Romans 8:28
- **Have Integrity and Compassion** (Matthew 9:13, 12:7), Luke 10:30–37, (Proverbs 15:1, 28:13)
- **Serve others in need, be Generous, and be Charitable** 2 Chronicles 6:13–42, Ecclesiastes 9:10, Luke 12:13–21, 1 Corinthians 9:6–15, Ephesians 5:3–7, John 3:16–18, (Matthew 6:1–8. 20:1–16, 25:34–40), Mark 10:35–45, Romans 12:3, (Philippians 2:1–11, 3:1–8), (Luke 6:30, 6:35, 14:12–14), (2 Corinthians 8:13–14, 9:6–7), 1 Thessalians 5:14, (Leviticus 19:10, 25:35–42), (Proverbs 4:14–15, 8:12–14, 21:13, 22:9, 28:27, 30:15), Ezekiel 18:7, (Psalms 34:2, 49:6–7), James 1:27, 1 Peter 3:15
- **Be Loyal to others and God** (Matthew 26:14–16, 27:1–5, 26:69–75) (Proverbs 20:6, 20:28, 21:21), Luke 16:1–18, the entire Book of Ecclesiastes
- **Hard Work and Dedication** 1 Thessalonians 4:11–12, 2 Thessalonians 3:9–12, 1 Peter 4:9, (Proverbs 10:4–5, 12:24, 13:4–5, 13:11, 20:4, 21:25, 22:29, 26:14–16, 28:19), Ecclesiastes 5:19
- **Develop Wisdom or Prudence** The entire Book of Proverbs, Matthew 7:24–27, Numbers 25:10–13, Ecclesiastes 9:10, Mathew 25:1–13, Luke 12:35–48, 1 Thessalonians 5:1–11, (Revelations 3:1–6, 14–22), Romans 12:2, Colossians 4:5–6, 2 Peter 1:5, Samuel 15:23
- **Responsibility or Justice** Luke 7:1–10, Mark 10:35–45, 1 Corinthians 16:13–14, Galatians 6:9–10, (Proverbs 3:21–27, 19:20), 2 Kings 11:5–7, The Bible is littered with stories about the wrath of God demonstrated in wars and cataclysmic climate events. While these stories are often viewed by naysayers as evil actions, they are merely God seeking justice and retribution from sinners for failing to follow His Law or moral principles. The purpose of justice and retribution is for people to fear God so they will live righteous life. The Book of Hosea is short, but it does an excellent job detailing all the sins committed by Israel and Judah, which brought about God's wrath. Murder, stealing, deceit, disloyalty, lack of compassion, greed, pride, lack of faith, adultery, lack of wisdom, and lying are a few of the sins mentioned. The bottom line is what we should learn from God's wrath is that we are responsible and accountable for our actions.
- **Women's Traits, Characteristics, and Rights** Proverbs 31:10–31
- **Respect and accept everyone equally, or treat everyone with Dignity** (Numbers 12:1–15, 16:1–35), (Galatians 5:13–15, 19–21), James 3:13–18, Leviticus 19:14, (Proverbs 17:5, 22:2, 28:3) Matthew

21:33–46, James 2:9, (Exodus 23:3, 23:6, and 23:9), (Leviticus 19:15 and 19:33–34), Samuel 16:7, (Proverbs 24:23, 28:21, 29:7, 29:13, 31:8), (Ezekiel 18:8)

- **Do not be materialistic or Temperance** Matthew 6:19–20, Luke 19:11–27, the entire Book of Ecclesiastes

Table A2: Fundamental Rights and Corresponding Virtues and Moral Principles

Fundamental Right	Acquired Virtue	Moral Principles to Follow
To Free Speech	Compassion, Trust, Integrity, Dignity, Responsibility, Prudence	Compassion, kindness, modest, humility, treat others how you wish to be treated, do no harm, be charitable and tolerant, do not judge others, use no foul language; practice forgiveness, gratitude, do not seek revenge, and do not be greedy
To Enter into Contracts	Justice, Trust, Responsibility, Integrity, Dignity	Honor contracts, follow the laws of society, show gratitude, do not be greedy, and do not seek revenge
To Justice	Justice, Trust, Responsibility, Women's Rights, Dignity, Integrity, Prudence, Temperance	Trials, no murder, no lying, no deceit, no cheating, follow the laws of society, treat everyone as you wish to be treated, forgiveness, do not seek revenge, and do no harm
To Life	Justice, Trust, Responsibility, Dignity, Integrity, Prudence, Temperance, Loyalty	Do not murder, treat everyone as you wish to be treated, do no harm, follow the laws of society, practice gratitude, goodness, tolerance, love, and kindness
To Work in a Lawful Profession	All Virtues Apply	Do not complain, do not envy others, be humble, be modest, treat others how you wish to be treated, be grateful, tolerance, and do no harm
To Obtain Knowledge and Wisdom	Determination, Discipline, Integrity, Perseverance, Prudence, Fortitude, Service	Practice gratitude, humility, modesty, patience, self-control, and tolerance
To Own and Sell Property	Responsibility, Dedication, Perseverance, Prudence, Integrity, Temperance, Dignity	Honor contracts, do not envy others, follow the laws of society, and show gratitude

To Pursue Health and Happiness	Responsibility, Perseverance, Dedication, Prudence, Integrity, Dignity	Do not envy others, practice gratitude, humility, modesty, patience, tolerance, and self-control, and do not judge
To Recreation	Temperance, Dignity, Integrity, Perseverance, Dedication, Fortitude, Service, Dignity, Responsibility, Charitable, Energetic	Be humble, modest, and honest, have self-control, tolerance, and patience, do not lie, do not cheat, do not steal, do not be deceitful, treat everyone as you expect to be treated, do not argue, show gratitude, and do not judge
To Marriage and Family Rights	Compassion, Trust, Dedication, Loyalty, Integrity, Responsibility, Dignity, Women's Rights	Marriage, love, kindness, loyalty, do no harm, forgiveness, patience, gratitude, no adultery, tolerance, empathy, do not judge, honor contracts, be humble, modest, and show goodness
To Raise a Family	Compassion, Trust, Dedication, Loyalty, Integrity, Dignity, Responsibility, Women's Rights	Marriage, love, kindness, loyalty, do no harm, forgiveness, patience, gratitude, tolerance, honor your parents, empathy, do not judge, be humble, modest, and show goodness
To Friendships	Compassion, Trust, Dedication, Loyalty, Integrity, Dignity, Responsibility, Women's Rights	Friendships, love, kindness, loyalty, treating others how you wish to be treated, doing no harm, being charitable; practicing forgiveness, patience, gratitude, tolerance, empathy, do not judge; be humble, modest, and show goodness
To Vote	Service, Responsibility, Trust, Prudence. Loyalty, Integrity, Dignity	Practice honesty, gratitude, tolerance, humility, and modesty
To Privacy	Responsibility, Trust, Loyalty, Integrity	Do no harm, treat others as you wish to be treated, do not judge, and tolerance

To Choose	Responsibility, Prudence, Compassion, Temperance, Service, Charity	Do no harm, show forgiveness, patience, gratitude, and tolerance, do not judge others, do not envy others, treat others as you wish to be treated, practice empathy, forgiveness, and goodness, do not seek revenge, do not be greedy, show humility, modesty, love, and kindness
To Travel	Responsibility, Trust, Integrity, Prudence	Follow the laws of society, gratitude, tolerance, patience, and self-control
To Consent	Service, Loyalty, Responsibility, Trust, Prudence	Honor contracts and follow the laws of society
To Self-defense	Justice, Courage, Responsibility, Perseverance, Fortitude, Temperance, Prudence, Integrity, Dignity	Do not murder, empathy, tolerance, self-control, and patience
To Religious Liberty	All Virtues Apply	All moral principles apply

Index

Bibliography

The Book of Mormon

Randy Barnett and Evan Bernick, *The Original Meaning of the 14th Amendment: The Letter and Spirit, Harvard University Press*, Cambridge, MA, 2021

Stephen C. Meyer, *Return of the God Hypothesis*, Harper One, New York NY, 2021

Henry M Morris III, *The Book of the Beginnings: A Practical Guide to Understand and Teach Genesis*, Institute for Creation Research, Dallas TX, 2012

David Barton, *The Founders Bible*, Shiloh Road Publishing, Newberry Park CA, 2012

Robert Morgan, *100 Bible Verses that Made America*, W Publishing, Nashville TN, 2020

Carl Richard, *The Founders, and the Bible*, Lanham MD, Rowman and Littlefield, 2016

Harvey Silverglate, *Three Felonies a Day: How the Feds Target the Innocent*, Encounter Books, New York NY, 2009

Roger Alliman, *Broken*, 2022

The American Standard Bible

Carlo Rovelli, *Reality is not what it Seems: The Journey to Quantum Gravity*, Riverhead Books, New York, NY, 2017

John Gribbin, *13.8: The Quest to Find the True Age of the Universe and the Theory of Everything*, Yale University Press, New Haven CT, 2016

Michio Kaku, *The God Equation: The Quest for a Theory of Everything*, Doubleday, New York, NY, 2021

Corey S. Powell, *God in the Equation: How Einstein Became the Prophet for the New Religious Era,* Free Press, New York, NY, 2002

Amir D. Aczel, *God's Equation: Einstein, Relativity, and the Expanding Universe*, Four Walls Eight Windows Publishing, New York, NY, 1999

Bernard Bailyn, *The Ideological Origins of the American Revolution*, Harvard University Press, Cambridge MA, 1967

Robert Middlekauff, *The Glorious Cause: The American Revolution 1763–1789*, Oxford University Press, Oxford UK, 1982

Esmond Wright, *Causes and Consequences of the American Revolution*, Quadrangle Books, Chicago IL, 1966

Patrick Bohan, *Defending Freedom of Contract: Constitutional Solutions to Resolve Our Political Divide*, Inside Edge Publishing, Houston TX, 2020

Patrick Bohan, *How a Neurological Disorder Changed My Life for the Better: The Science Behind Nerve, Muscular, and Neuromuscular Disorders and their Effects on Cycling*, Inside Edge Publishing, Houston TX, 2021

John W. Yolton, *The Locke Reader: A Selection from the Works of John Locke*, Cambridge University Press, Cambridge UK, 1977

John Locke, *The Second Treaties of Government*, The Liberal Arts Press, New York NY, 1952

Kenyon C. Cramer, *The Causes of War: The American Revolution, Civil War, and World War* I, Scott, Foresman, and Co., Northbrook IL, 1965

John C. Wahlke, *The Causes of the Revolutionary War*, DC Heath and Company, Boston MA, 1974

Kenneth Stampp, *The Causes of the Civil War*, Prentice Hall, Englewood Cliffs NJ, 1965

French Ensor Chadwick, *The Causes of the Civil War, 1859–1861*, Harper Brothers, New York NY, 1906

Paul Calore, *The Causes of the Civil War: The Political, Cultural, Economic, and Territorial Disputes between the North and South*, McFarland and Company, Jefferson NC, 2008

J. Budziszewski, *Written on the Heart: The Case for Natural Law*, Intervarsity Press, Downers Grove IL, 1997

Francis S. Collins, *The Language of God: A Scientist Presents Evidence for Belief*, First Press, New York NY, 2006

C.S. Lewis, *Mere Christianity*, Harper Collins, New York NY, 2001

C.S. Lewis, *Christian Reflections*, William B Eerdmans Publishing Company, Grand Rapids Michigan, 1971

C.S. Lewis, *Miracles: A Preliminary Study*, New York NY, Simon and Schuster, 1996

Richard Rohr, *The Devine Dance*, The Whitaker House, Kensington PA, 2016

Rose Book of Bible Charts, Maps, and Timelines, Rose Publishing, 2005

Dr. Chuck Missler, *Cosmic Codes: Hidden Messages from the Edge of Eternity*, Koinonia House Publishing, Coeur d'Alene Idaho, 2004

Thomas Dages, *The Lancing of My Soul*, NEWW Publishing, Centennial Colorado, 2019

Roger Alliman, *Pressing on to Maturity*, CreateSpace Publishing, Scotts Valley CA, 2017

Pat Williams, *Character Carved in Stone*, Revel Publishing, Grand Rapids, MI, 2019

Kitty Ferguson, *Fire in the Equation: Science, Religion, and the Search for God*, W.B. Eerdmans Publishing Company, Grand Rapids, MI, 1995

Shannon Bream, *The Women of the Bible Speak*, Harper Collins, New York, NY, 2021

[1] The Fifth Amendment's "Takings" Clause - FindLaw

[2] How to judge Judge Gorsuch (chicagotribune.com)

[3] Randy Barnett and Evan Bernick, *The Original Meaning of the 14th Amendment: The Letter and Spirit, Harvard University Press*, Cambridge, MA, 2021, 375 – 381

[4] Randy Barnett and Evan Bernick, *The Original Meaning of the 14th Amendment: The Letter and Spirit, Harvard University Press*, Cambridge, MA, 2021, 375 – 381

[5] Randy Barnett and Evan Bernick, *The Original Meaning of the 14th Amendment: The Letter and Spirit, Harvard University Press*, Cambridge, MA, 2021, 375 – 381

[6] Kenyon C. Cramer, *The Causes of War: The American Revolution, Civil War, and World War* I, Scott, Foresman, and Co., Northbrook IL, 1965, 72 – 75

[7] Patrick Bohan, *Defending Freedom of Contract: Constitutional Solutions to Resolve Our Political Divide*, Inside Edge Publishing, Houston TX, 2020

[8] Patrick Bohan, *Defending Freedom of Contract: Constitutional Solutions to Resolve Our Political Divide*, Inside Edge Publishing, Houston TX, 2020

[9] Harvey Silverglate, *Three Felonies a Day: How the Feds Target the Innocent*, Encounter Books, New York NY, 2009

[10] Randy Barnett and Evan Bernick, *The Original Meaning of the 14th Amendment: The Letter and Spirit, Harvard University Press*, Cambridge, MA, 2021, 305 – 316

[11] Harvey Silverglate, *Three Felonies a Day: How the Feds Target the Innocent*, Encounter Books, New York NY, 2009

[12] God Created the Universe Painting by Lois Viguier - Fine Art America

[13] Michio Kaku, *The God Equation: The Quest for a Theory of Everything*, Doubleday, New York NY, 2021, 117 – 122, 178, 186, 195 – 196

[14] Carlo Rovelli, *Reality is not what it Seems: The Journey to Quantum Gravity*, Riverhead Books, New York, NY, 2017, 123

[15] Michio Kaku, *The God Equation: The Quest for a Theory of Everything*, Doubleday, New York NY, 2021, 3, 5, 56 – 68, 94 – 100, 146 – 148

[16] Patrick Bohan, *How a Neurological Disorder Changed My Life for the Better: The Science Behind Nerve, Muscular, and Neuromuscular Disorders and their Effects on Cycling*, Inside Edge Publishing, Houston TX, 2021

[17] Corey S. Powell, *God in the Equation: How Einstein Became the Prophet for the New Religious Era,* Free Press, New York, NY, 2002, 54

[18] Michio Kaku, *The God Equation: The Quest for a Theory of Everything*, Doubleday, New York NY, 2021, 27

[19] David Barton, *The Founders Bible*, Shiloh Road Publishing, Newberry Park CA, 2012, 391 – 392

[20] Roger Alliman, *Broken*, 2022, 5 – 11

[21] Dr. Chuck Missler, *Cosmic Codes: Hidden Messages from the Edge of Eternity*, Koinonia House Publishing, Coeur d'Alene Idaho, 2004

[22] David Barton, *The Founders Bible*, Shiloh Road Publishing, Newberry Park CA, 2012, 442 – 447, 1298, 1889

[23] David Barton, *The Founders Bible*, Shiloh Road Publishing, Newberry Park CA, 2012, 1879, 1952

[24] C.S. Lewis, *Miracles: A Preliminary Study*, New York NY, Simon and Schuster, 1996, 187 – 217

[25] Dr. Chuck Missler, *Cosmic Codes: Hidden Messages from the Edge of Eternity*, Koinonia House Publishing, Coeur d'Alene Idaho, 2004

[26] Corey S. Powell, *God in the Equation: How Einstein Became the Prophet for the New Religious Era,* Free Press, New York, NY, 2002, 241 – 258

[27] Stephen C. Meyer, *Return of the God Hypothesis*, Harper One, New York NY, 2021, 443 – 450

[28] Dr. Chuck Missler, *Cosmic Codes: Hidden Messages from the Edge of Eternity*, Koinonia House Publishing, Coeur d'Alene Idaho, 2004

[29] Stephen C. Meyer, *Return of the God Hypothesis*, Harper One, New York NY, 2021, 175

[30] Stephen C. Meyer, *Return of the God Hypothesis*, Harper One, New York NY, 2021, 150, 275

[31] Michio Kaku, *The God Equation: The Quest for a Theory of Everything*, Doubleday, New York NY, 2021, 174 – 175

[32] Kitty Ferguson, *Fire in the Equation: Science, Religion, and the Search for God*, W.B. Eerdmans Publishing Company, Grand Rapids MI, 1995, 164 – 171

[33] Stephen C. Meyer, *Return of the God Hypothesis*, Harper One, New York NY, 2021, 146 – 163

[34] Carlo Rovelli, *Reality is not what it Seems: The Journey to Quantum Gravity*, Riverhead Books, New York, NY, 2017, 237 – 247

[35] John Gribbin, *13.8: The Quest to Find the True Age of the Universe and the Theory of Everything*, Yale University Press, New Haven CT, 2016, 44

[36] Kitty Ferguson, *Fire in the Equation: Science, Religion, and the Search for God*, W.B. Eerdmans Publishing Company, Grand Rapids MI, 1995, 200 – 210

[37] Michio Kaku, *The God Equation: The Quest for a Theory of Everything*, Doubleday, New York NY, 2021, 14 – 16, 24, 42 – 47, 94, 126 – 128, 149 – 155

[38] Carlo Rovelli, *Reality is not what it Seems: The Journey to Quantum Gravity*, Riverhead Books, New York, NY, 2017, 69 – 84

[39] Corey S. Powell, *God in the Equation: How Einstein Became the Prophet for the New Religious Era,* Free Press, New York, NY, 2002, 20

[40] *Rose Book of Bible Charts, Maps, and Timelines, Rose Publishing*, 2005, 48 – 59

[41] Stephen C. Meyer, *Return of the God Hypothesis*, Harper One, New York NY, 2021, 307 – 315, 346 – 353

[42] Stephen C. Meyer, *Return of the God Hypothesis*, Harper One, New York NY, 2021, 164 – 188, 263 – 267, 301 – 325

[43] Stephen C. Meyer, *Return of the God Hypothesis*, Harper One, New York NY, 2021, 189 – 211, 307 – 315

[44] Stephen C. Meyer, *Return of the God Hypothesis*, Harper One, New York NY, 2021, 189 – 211, 307 – 315

[45] Carlo Rovelli, *Reality is not what it Seems: The Journey to Quantum Gravity*, Riverhead Books, New York, NY, 2017, 69 – 84, 89, 116 – 129, 165 – 180, 220 – 230

[46] Michio Kaku, *The God Equation: The Quest for a Theory of Everything*, Doubleday, New York NY, 2021, 3, 5, 56 – 68, 94 – 100, 146 – 148

[47] Michio Kaku, *The God Equation: The Quest for a Theory of Everything*, Doubleday, New York NY, 2021, 3, 5, 141 – 145, 158, 163 – 164

[48] Michio Kaku, *The God Equation: The Quest for a Theory of Everything*, Doubleday, New York NY, 2021, 3, 5, 141 – 145, 158, 163 – 164

[49] Carlo Rovelli, *Reality is not what it Seems: The Journey to Quantum Gravity*, Riverhead Books, New York, NY, 2017, 69 – 84, 89, 116 – 129, 165 – 180, 220 – 230

[50] Stephen C. Meyer, *Return of the God Hypothesis*, Harper One, New York NY, 2021, 326 – 347

[51] Corey S. Powell, *God in the Equation: How Einstein Became the Prophet for the New Religious Era,* Free Press, New York, NY, 2002, 6 – 14, 198 – 209

[52] Amir D. Aczel, *God's Equation: Einstein, Relativity, and the Expanding Universe*, Four Walls Eight Windows Publishing, New York, NY, 1999, 171 – 175, 207 – 220

[53] Stephen C. Meyer, *Return of the God Hypothesis*, Harper One, New York NY, 2021, 104 – 105

[54] Stephen C. Meyer, *Return of the God Hypothesis*, Harper One, New York NY, 2021, 388 – 406

[55] Stephen C. Meyer, *Return of the God Hypothesis*, Harper One, New York NY, 2021, 346, 368 – 387

[56] Kitty Ferguson, *Fire in the Equation: Science, Religion, and the Search for God*, W.B. Eerdmans Publishing Company, Grand Rapids MI, 1995, 84

[57] Kitty Ferguson, *Fire in the Equation: Science, Religion, and the Search for God*, W.B. Eerdmans Publishing Company, Grand Rapids MI, 1995, 84

[58] David Barton, *The Founders Bible*, Shiloh Road Publishing, Newberry Park CA, 2012, 1642

[59] United Methodist Church split: New denomination announces May launch (usatoday.com)

[60] Henry M Morris III, *The Book of the Beginnings: A Practical Guide to Understand and Teach Genesis*, Institute for Creation Research, Dallas TX, 2012, 45 – 50, 53, 60 – 61, 63, 66 – 76, 78, 79 87, 94, 215 – 216, 232

[61] Henry M Morris III, *The Book of the Beginnings: A Practical Guide to Understand and Teach Genesis*, Institute for Creation Research, Dallas TX, 2012, 98

[62] Henry M Morris III, *The Book of the Beginnings: A Practical Guide to Understand and Teach Genesis*, Institute for Creation Research, Dallas TX, 2012, 45 – 50, 53, 60 – 61, 63, 66 – 76, 78, 79 87, 94, 215 – 216, 232

[63] Amir D. Aczel, *God's Equation: Einstein, Relativity, and the Expanding Universe*, Four Walls Eight Windows Publishing, New York, NY, 1999, 167 – 171

[64] Carlo Rovelli, *Reality is not what it Seems: The Journey to Quantum Gravity*, Riverhead Books, New York, NY, 2017, 165 – 180

[65] Henry M Morris III, *The Book of the Beginnings: A Practical Guide to Understand and Teach Genesis*, Institute for Creation Research, Dallas TX, 2012, 45 – 50, 53, 60 – 61, 63, 66 – 76, 78, 79 87, 94

[66] Astronomers witness the explosive death of a giant star for first time (nbcnews.com)

[67] Black Holes - Definition, How are Black Holes Formed, Types, Properties and FAQs (byjus.com)

[68] Henry M Morris III, *The Book of the Beginnings: A Practical Guide to Understand and Teach Genesis*, Institute for Creation Research, Dallas TX, 2012, 45 – 50, 53, 60 – 61, 63, 66 – 76, 78, 79 87, 94, 215 – 216, 232

[69] Henry M Morris III, *The Book of the Beginnings: A Practical Guide to Understand and Teach Genesis*, Institute for Creation Research, Dallas TX, 2012, 128, 131, 137, 146, 149

[70] Henry M Morris III, *The Book of the Beginnings: A Practical Guide to Understand and Teach Genesis*, Institute for Creation Research, Dallas TX, 2012, 171 – 172

[71] Henry M Morris III, *The Book of the Beginnings: A Practical Guide to Understand and Teach Genesis*, Institute for Creation Research, Dallas TX, 2012, 158 – 165

[72] Water, Wind and Fire: The Holy Spirit in Scripture – Notes from Class 1 – Christ Church NYC

[73] The Mystical Nature of the Universe: Everything is Connected - The Creation Frequency

[74] Henry M Morris III, *The Book of the Beginnings: A Practical Guide to Understand and Teach Genesis*, Institute for Creation Research, Dallas TX, 2012, 54, 101,105, 111 – 121, 136, 139

[75] Francis S. Collins, *The Language of God: A Scientist Presents Evidence for Belief*, First Press, New York NY, 2006

[76] Ask not what your country can do for you (Kennedy's inaugural address) (ushistory.org)

[77] Corey S. Powell, *God in the Equation: How Einstein Became the Prophet for the New Religious Era,* Free Press, New York, NY, 2002, 50 – 51, 251 – 253

[78] Corey S. Powell, *God in the Equation: How Einstein Became the Prophet for the New Religious Era,* Free Press, New York, NY, 2002, 255 – 258

[79] Amir D. Aczel, *God's Equation: Einstein, Relativity, and the Expanding Universe*, Four Walls Eight Windows Publishing, New York, NY, 1999, 13, 17, 20, 123, 218

[80] Why Thousands of New Animal Species Are Still Discovered Each Year - Atlas Obscura

[81] C.S. Lewis, *Miracles: A Preliminary Study*, New York NY, Simon and Schuster, 1996, 132 – 140

[82] C.S. Lewis, *Miracles: A Preliminary Study*, New York NY, Simon and Schuster, 1996, 132 – 140

[83] C.S. Lewis, *Miracles: A Preliminary Study*, New York NY, Simon and Schuster, 1996, 185 – 200

[84] Can Positive Thinking Help You Heal? | Psychology Today

[85] Kitty Ferguson, *Fire in the Equation: Science, Religion, and the Search for God,* W.B. Eerdmans Publishing Company, Grand Rapids MI, 1995, 160 – 165, 190 – 195

[86] Kitty Ferguson, *Fire in the Equation: Science, Religion, and the Search for God*, W.B. Eerdmans Publishing Company, Grand Rapids MI, 1995, 260 – 264, 270 – 274

[87] C.S. Lewis, *Miracles: A Preliminary Study*, New York NY, Simon and Schuster, 1996, 185 – 200

[88] C.S. Lewis, *Miracles: A Preliminary Study*, New York NY, Simon and Schuster, 1996, 187 – 217

[89] Henry M Morris III, *The Book of the Beginnings: A Practical Guide to Understand and Teach Genesis*, Institute for Creation Research, Dallas TX, 2012, 222

[90] David Barton, *The Founders Bible*, Shiloh Road Publishing, Newberry Park CA, 2012, 323 – 325

[91] Henry M Morris III, *The Book of the Beginnings: A Practical Guide to Understand and Teach Genesis*, Institute for Creation Research, Dallas TX, 2012, 207 – 209

[92] Shannon Bream, *The Women of the Bible Speak*, Harper Collins, New York NY, 2021

[93] Henry M Morris III, *The Book of the Beginnings: A Practical Guide to Understand and Teach Genesis*, Institute for Creation Research, Dallas TX, 2012, 192 – 195

[94] J. Budziszewski, *Written on the Heart: The Case for Natural Law*, Intervarsity Press, Downers Grove IL, 1997, 120, 133

[95] David Barton, *The Founders Bible*, Shiloh Road Publishing, Newberry Park CA, 2012, 611 – 616, 1042

[96] Robert Morgan, *100 Bible Verses that Made America*, W Publishing, Nashville TN, 2020, 47 – 50

[97] David Barton, *The Founders Bible*, Shiloh Road Publishing, Newberry Park CA, 2012, 1040 – 1041, 1763 – 1770

[98] Kitty Ferguson, *Fire in the Equation: Science, Religion, and the Search for God*, W.B. Eerdmans Publishing Company, Grand Rapids MI, 1995, 128 – 147

[99] Kitty Ferguson, *Fire in the Equation: Science, Religion, and the Search for God*, W.B. Eerdmans Publishing Company, Grand Rapids MI, 1995, 242 – 264, 276

[100] Kitty Ferguson, *Fire in the Equation: Science, Religion, and the Search for God*, W.B. Eerdmans Publishing Company, Grand Rapids MI, 1995, 242 – 264, 276

[101] Corey S. Powell, *God in the Equation: How Einstein Became the Prophet for the New Religious Era,* Free Press, New York, NY, 2002, 134 – 135

[102] What book did Founding Fathers most often quote? (wnd.com)

[103] Shannon Bream, *The Women of the Bible Speak*, Harper Collins, New York NY, 2021, 151

[104] C.S. Lewis, *Mere Christianity*, Harper Collins, New York NY, 2001

[105] Pat Williams, *Character Carved in Stone*, Revel Publishing, Grand Rapids MI, 2019, 18

[106] Patrick Bohan, Defending Freedom of Contract, Inside Edge Publishing, Houston TX, 2020

[107] Randy Barnett and Evan Bernick, *The Original Meaning of the 14th Amendment: The Letter and Spirit, Harvard University Press*, Cambridge, MA, 2021, 141 – 145

[108] Randy Barnett and Evan Bernick, *The Original Meaning of the 14th Amendment: The Letter and Spirit, Harvard University Press*, Cambridge, MA, 2021, 235 – 250

[109] Randy Barnett and Evan Bernick, *The Original Meaning of the 14th Amendment: The Letter and Spirit, Harvard University Press*, Cambridge, MA, 2021, 235 – 250

[110] John Locke, *The Second Treaties of Government*, The Liberal Arts Press, New York NY, 1952

[111] J. Budziszewski, *Written on the Heart: The Case for Natural Law*, Intervarsity Press, Downers Grove IL, 1997, 21 – 33

[112] Richard Rohr, *The Devine Dance*, The Whitaker House, Kensington PA, 2016, 96 – 98

[113] David Barton, *The Founders Bible*, Shiloh Road Publishing, Newberry Park CA

[114] J. Budziszewski, *Written on the Heart: The Case for Natural Law*, Intervarsity Press, Downers Grove IL, 1997, 123 – 133

[115] Bernard Bailyn, *The Ideological Origins of the American Revolution*, Harvard University Press, Cambridge MA, 1967, 76 – 78, 188 – 194

[116] The Debate Over a Bill of Rights – Center for the Study of the American Constitution – UW–Madison (wisc.edu)

[117] Randy Barnett and Evan Bernick, *The Original Meaning of the 14th Amendment: The Letter and Spirit, Harvard University Press*, Cambridge, MA, 2021, Preface

[118] Randy Barnett and Evan Bernick, *The Original Meaning of the 14th Amendment: The Letter and Spirit, Harvard University Press*, Cambridge, MA, 2021, 40 – 45

[119] Randy Barnett and Evan Bernick, *The Original Meaning of the 14th Amendment: The Letter and Spirit, Harvard University Press*, Cambridge, MA, 2021, Preface, 24, 175 – 185

[120] John C. Wahlke, *The Causes of the Revolutionary War*, DC Heath and Company, Boston MA, 1974, 70 – 85

[121] Patrick Bohan, Defending Freedom of Contract, Inside Edge Publishing, Houston TX, 2020

[122] Randy Barnett and Evan Bernick, *The Original Meaning of the 14th Amendment: The Letter and Spirit, Harvard University Press*, Cambridge, MA, 2021, Preface, 24

[123] Randy Barnett and Evan Bernick, *The Original Meaning of the 14th Amendment: The Letter and Spirit, Harvard University Press*, Cambridge, MA, 2021, 229 – 233

[124] Randy Barnett and Evan Bernick, *The Original Meaning of the 14th Amendment: The Letter and Spirit, Harvard University Press*, Cambridge, MA, 2021, 229 – 233

[125] Randy Barnett and Evan Bernick, *The Original Meaning of the 14th Amendment: The Letter and Spirit, Harvard University Press*, Cambridge, MA, 2021, Preface, 24, 185 – 192

[126] Randy Barnett and Evan Bernick, *The Original Meaning of the 14th Amendment: The Letter and Spirit, Harvard University Press*, Cambridge, MA, 2021, 171 – 176

[127] Randy Barnett and Evan Bernick, *The Original Meaning of the 14th Amendment: The Letter and Spirit, Harvard University Press*, Cambridge, MA, 2021, 171 – 176, 348, 361

[128] Randy Barnett and Evan Bernick, *The Original Meaning of the 14th Amendment: The Letter and Spirit, Harvard University Press*, Cambridge, MA, 2021, 351 – 361

[129] Randy Barnett and Evan Bernick, *The Original Meaning of the 14th Amendment: The Letter and Spirit, Harvard University Press*, Cambridge, MA, 2021, 205 – 226, 279

[130] Randy Barnett and Evan Bernick, *The Original Meaning of the 14th Amendment: The Letter and Spirit, Harvard University Press*, Cambridge, MA, 2021, 123, 188, 196, 210

[131] Randy Barnett and Evan Bernick, *The Original Meaning of the 14th Amendment: The Letter and Spirit, Harvard University Press*, Cambridge, MA, 2021, 27 – 28

[132] John W. Yolton, *The Locke Reader: A Selection from the Works of John Locke*, Cambridge University Press, Cambridge UK, 1977, 302, 308, 309

[133] Patrick Bohan, *How a Neurological Disorder Changed My Life for the Better: The Science Behind Nerve, Muscular, and Neuromuscular Disorders and their Effects on Cycling*, Inside Edge Publishing, Houston TX, 2021

[134] John W. Yolton, *The Locke Reader: A Selection from the Works of John Locke*, Cambridge University Press, Cambridge UK, 1977, 325 – 329

[135] John Locke, *The Second Treaties of Government*, The Liberal Arts Press, New York NY, 1952, xiii

[136] John W. Yolton, *The Locke Reader: A Selection from the Works of John Locke*, Cambridge University Press, Cambridge UK, 1977, 308

[137] Randy Barnett and Evan Bernick, *The Original Meaning of the 14th Amendment: The Letter and Spirit, Harvard University Press*, Cambridge, MA, 2021, 6 – 10, 15, 24

[138] John W. Yolton, *The Locke Reader: A Selection from the Works of John Locke*, Cambridge University Press, Cambridge UK, 1977, 319 – 322

[139] Declaration of Independence, 1776

[140] John W. Yolton, *The Locke Reader: A Selection from the Works of John Locke*, Cambridge University Press, Cambridge UK, 1977, 307 – 309

[141] John Locke, *The Second Treaties of Government*, The Liberal Arts Press, New York NY, 1952, xv

[142] David Barton, *The Founders Bible*, Shiloh Road Publishing, Newberry Park CA, 2012, 122 – 123, 273 – 277

[143] David Barton, *The Founders Bible*, Shiloh Road Publishing, Newberry Park CA, 2012, 812, 965 – 971, 1215

[144] John Locke, *The Second Treaties of Government*, The Liberal Arts Press, New York NY, 1952, xv

[145] John W. Yolton, *The Locke Reader: A Selection from the Works of John Locke*, Cambridge University Press, Cambridge UK, 1977, 258, 267

[146] Pat Williams, *Character Carved in Stone*, Revel Publishing, Grand Rapids MI, 2019, 109

[147] Statue Of Liberty A Symbol Of Freedom - Gets Ready

[148] Patrick Bohan, *Defending Freedom of Contract: Constitutional Solutions to Resolve Our Political Divide*, Inside Edge Publishing, Houston TX, 2020, Prerequisite or Concurrent reading.

[149] The Progressive Era (Progressive movement) (article) | Khan Academy

[150] David Barton, *The Founders Bible*, Shiloh Road Publishing, Newberry Park CA, 2012, 147 – 148

[151] Robert Middlekauff, *The Glorious Cause: The American Revolution 1763 – 1789*, Oxford University Press, Oxford UK, 652 – 658

[152] J. Budziszewski, *Written on the Heart: The Case for Natural Law*, Intervarsity Press, Downers Grove IL, 1997, 33 – 37

[153] Esmond Wright, *Causes and Consequences of the American Revolution*, Quadrangle Books, Chicago IL, 1966, 279 – 283

[154] David Barton, *The Founders Bible*, Shiloh Road Publishing, Newberry Park CA, 2012, 147 – 148

[155] Harvey Silverglate, *Three Felonies a Day: How the Feds Target the Innocent*, Encounter Books, New York NY, 2009, 92 – 94

[156] Bernard Bailyn, *The Ideological Origins of the American Revolution*, Harvard University Press, Cambridge MA, 1967, 289, 293, 304

[157] John C. Wahlke, *The Causes of the Revolutionary War*, DC Heath and Company, Boston MA, 1974, 74

[158] David Barton, *The Founders Bible*, Shiloh Road Publishing, Newberry Park CA, 2012, 1860 – 1861

[159] Robert Morgan, *100 Bible Verses that Made America*, W Publishing, Nashville TN, 2020, 22 – 24

[160] Bernard Bailyn, *The Ideological Origins of the American Revolution*, Harvard University Press, Cambridge MA, 1967, 68 – 70

[161] Robert Morgan, *100 Bible Verses that Made America*, W Publishing, Nashville TN, 2020, 50 – 52, 104, 108

[162] Robert Morgan, *100 Bible Verses that Made America*, W Publishing, Nashville TN, 2020, 50 – 52, 104, 108

[163] Robert Morgan, *100 Bible Verses that Made America*, W Publishing, Nashville TN, 2020, 60, 61, 65 – 68, 71, 85

[164] John Locke, *The Second Treaties of Government*, The Liberal Arts Press, New York NY, 1952, xiv

[165] John W. Yolton, *The Locke Reader: A Selection from the Works of John Locke*, Cambridge University Press, Cambridge UK, 1977, 287 – 296, 298

[166] John Locke, *The Second Treaties of Government*, The Liberal Arts Press, New York NY, 1952, xvii – xviii

[167] David Barton, *The Founders Bible*, Shiloh Road Publishing, Newberry Park CA, 2012, 332, 1723

[168] David Barton, *The Founders Bible*, Shiloh Road Publishing, Newberry Park CA, 2012, 1067

[169] Here's what the 20 Republicans voting against Kevin McCarthy say they want (mercurynews.com)

[170] Freedom Caucus earns major concessions from Kevin McCarthy (nypost.com)

[171] Bernard Bailyn, *The Ideological Origins of the American Revolution*, Harvard University Press, Cambridge MA, 1967, 198 – 203

[172] Esmond Wright, *Causes and Consequences of the American Revolution*, Quadrangle Books, Chicago IL, 1966, 69, 76

[173] David Barton, *The Founders Bible*, Shiloh Road Publishing, Newberry Park CA, 2012, 914 – 915

[174] About The 1619 Project | Pulitzer Center: 1619 Project (1619education.org)

[175] David Barton, *The Founders Bible*, Shiloh Road Publishing, Newberry Park CA, 2012, 162 – 169, 1975

[176] David Barton, *The Founders Bible*, Shiloh Road Publishing, Newberry Park CA, 2012, 162 – 169, 1975

[177] David Barton, *The Founders Bible*, Shiloh Road Publishing, Newberry Park CA, 2012, 1020 – 1028

[178] Bernard Bailyn, *The Ideological Origins of the American Revolution*, Harvard University Press, Cambridge MA, 1967, 54 – 63

[179] John C. Wahlke, *The Causes of the Revolutionary War*, DC Heath and Company, Boston MA, 1974, 52

[180] C.S. Lewis, *Mere Christianity*, Harper Collins, New York NY, 2001, 3 – 18, 37, 62, 102 – 110, 161 – 179

[181] C.S. Lewis, *Christian Reflections*, William B Eerdmans Publishing Company, Grand Rapids Michigan, 1971, 70 – 85

[182] Patrick Bohan, *Defending Freedom of Contract: Constitutional Solutions to Resolve Our Political Divide*, Inside Edge Publishing, Houston TX, 2020, 141 – 166

[183] Patrick Bohan, *Defending Freedom of Contract: Constitutional Solutions to Resolve Our Political Divide*, Inside Edge Publishing, Houston TX, 2020

[184] William Anderson, *The Book of Revelation*, Liguori Publications, Liguori MO, 2014, 114

[185] Francis S. Collins, *The Language of God: A Scientist Presents Evidence for Belief*, First Press, New York NY, 2006, 28, 40 – 54, 65 – 75, 148 – 158

[186] Patrick Bohan, *Defending Freedom of Contract: Constitutional Solutions to Resolve Our Political Divide*, Inside Edge Publishing, Houston TX, 2020

[187] J. Budziszewski, *Written on the Heart: The Case for Natural Law*, Intervarsity Press, Downers Grove IL, 1997, 65 – 75, 92, 101 – 122, 167, 174, 189, 213 – 228

[188] Francis S. Collins, *The Language of God: A Scientist Presents Evidence for Belief*, First Press, New York NY, 2006, 28, 40 – 54, 65 – 75, 148 – 158

[189] What Democrats Learned from LeBron James - POLITICO

[190] These 10 states still have COVID emergency orders in place | The Hill

[191] What 100 Years of History Tells Us About Racism in Policing | News & Commentary | American Civil Liberties Union (aclu.org)

[192] Are White Men Really the Problem? | Psychology Today

[193] There's A Growing Educational Gap Between Rural and Urban Areas, Connectivity Could Help Solve It (hundred.org)

[194] Yes, Trump and Biden Both Broke the Rules. Here's Why It's Not the Same. – DNyuz

[195] Flashback: Biden suggested Trump's coronavirus travel ban was 'xenophobic' | Fox News

[196] Bernard Bailyn, *The Ideological Origins of the American Revolution*, Harvard University Press, Cambridge MA, 1967, 76 – 78, 188 – 194

[197] Randy Barnett and Evan Bernick, *The Original Meaning of the 14th Amendment: The Letter and Spirit, Harvard University Press*, Cambridge, MA, 2021, 293 – 298

[198] Patrick Bohan, *Defending Freedom of Contract: Constitutional Solutions to Resolve Our Political Divide*, Inside Edge Publishing, Houston TX, 2020

[199] David Barton, *The Founders Bible*, Shiloh Road Publishing, Newberry Park CA, 2012, 681 – 688, F1 – F8, 1667 – 1676

[200] David Barton, *The Founders Bible*, Shiloh Road Publishing, Newberry Park CA, 2012, 681 – 688, F1 – F8, 1667 – 1676

[201] Patrick Bohan, *Defending Freedom of Contract: Constitutional Solutions to Resolve Our Political Divide*, Inside Edge Publishing, Houston TX, 2020

[202] Patrick Bohan, *How a Neurological Disorder Changed My Life for the Better: The Science Behind Nerve, Muscular, and Neuromuscular Disorders and their Effects on Cycling*, Inside Edge Publishing, Houston TX, 2021

[203] Disability Impacts All of Us Infographic | CDC

[204] C.S. Lewis, *Mere Christianity*, Harper Collins, New York NY, 2001, 3 – 18, 37, 62, 102 – 110, 161 – 179

[205] Patrick Bohan, *Defending Freedom of Contract: Constitutional Solutions to Resolve Our Political Divide*, Inside Edge Publishing, Houston TX, 2020

[206] Math education: US scores stink because of how schools teach lessons (usatoday.com)

[207] U.S. government - budget, by agency 2022 | Statista

[208] USDA ERS - Rural Poverty & Well-Being

[209] Harvey Silverglate, *Three Felonies a Day: How the Feds Target the Innocent*, Encounter Books, New York NY, 2009

[210] 19 Ridiculous Federal Criminal Laws and Regulations | LibertyWorks

[211] Patrick Bohan, *Defending Freedom of Contract: Constitutional Solutions to Resolve Our Political Divide*, Inside Edge Publishing, Houston TX, 2020 (advised prerequisite reading for this section)

[212] Patrick Bohan, *how a Neurological Disorder Changed My Life for the Better: The Science Behind Nerve, Muscular, and Neuromuscular Disorders and their Effects on Cycling*, Inside Edge Publishing, Houston TX, 2021

[213] USDA ERS - Rural Poverty & Well-Being

[214] Patrick Bohan, *Defending Freedom of Contract: Constitutional Solutions to Resolve Our Political Divide*, Inside Edge Publishing, Houston TX, 2020

[215] Patrick Bohan, *Defending Freedom of Contract: Constitutional Solutions to Resolve Our Political Divide*, Inside Edge Publishing, Houston TX, 2020

[216] New York Times (nytimes.com)

[217] What is critical race theory? | Fox News

[218] Patrick Bohan, *Defending Freedom of Contract: Constitutional Solutions to Resolve Our Political Divide*, Inside Edge Publishing, Houston TX, 2020

[219] J. Budziszewski, *Written on the Heart: The Case for Natural Law*, Intervarsity Press, Downers Grove IL, 1997, 44

[220] Gun laws in the United States by state - Wikipedia

[221] Smart guns: How smart are they? - BBC News

[222] Why the NRA hates smart guns | TechCrunch

[223] TRACKER: Pro-abortion attacks in the U.S. continue (updated) | Catholic News Agency

[224] Patrick Bohan, *Defending Freedom of Contract: Constitutional Solutions to Resolve Our Political Divide*, Inside Edge Publishing, Houston TX, 2020

[225] DHS tries to right controversial rollout of its 'disinformation governance board' - The Washington Post

[226] Patrick Bohan, *Defending Freedom of Contract: Constitutional Solutions to Resolve Our Political Divide*, Inside Edge Publishing, Houston TX, 2020

[227] Patrick Bohan, *Defending Freedom of Contract: Constitutional Solutions to Resolve Our Political Divide*, Inside Edge Publishing, Houston TX, 2020

[228] Patrick Bohan, *Defending Freedom of Contract: Constitutional Solutions to Resolve Our Political Divide*, Inside Edge Publishing, Houston TX, 2020

[229] Accommodation laws has caused a great deal of cognitive dissonance. Therefore, I have reached out to 14th Amendment scholars seeking clarity on this subject. Unfortunately, I have not heard back.

[230] David Barton, *The Founders Bible*, Shiloh Road Publishing, Newberry Park CA, 2012, 1742 – 1743, 1778 – 1790, 1803 – 1812

[231] David Barton, *The Founders Bible*, Shiloh Road Publishing, Newberry Park CA, 2012, 1742 – 1743, 1778 – 1790, 1803 – 1812

[232] David Barton, *The Founders Bible*, Shiloh Road Publishing, Newberry Park CA, 2012, 307 – 309, 1599 – 1602, 1721

[233] David Barton, *The Founders Bible*, Shiloh Road Publishing, Newberry Park CA, 2012, 708

[234] Violent Crime Increases in 2021 | Crime in America.Net

[235] David Barton, *The Founders Bible*, Shiloh Road Publishing, Newberry Park CA, 2012, 311 – 315

[236] David Barton, *The Founders Bible*, Shiloh Road Publishing, Newberry Park CA, 2012, 337 – 340

[237] Randy Barnett and Evan Bernick, *The Original Meaning of the 14th Amendment: The Letter and Spirit, Harvard University Press*, Cambridge, MA, 2021, 275 – 280, 286

[238] Historical Poverty Tables: People and Families - 1959 to 2020 (census.gov)

[239] If The US Spends $550 Billion On Poverty How Can There Still Be Poverty in The US? (forbes.com)

[240] The World's Most Generous Countries (usnews.com)

[241] Joe Biden Wants 2 Million More Immigrants a Year | ImmigrationReform.com

[242] Job Growth by Year Statistics - WhatToBecome

[243] Fact check: How much does illegal immigration cost America? Not nearly as much as Trump claims. (nbcnews.com)

[244] Cost of Illegal Immigration by State 2022 (worldpopulationreview.com)

[245] The Cost of Illegal Immigration to US Taxpayers | FAIR (fairus.org)

[246] US Immigration and Border Security Statistics and Data | USAFacts

[247] Patrick Bohan, *Defending Freedom of Contract: Constitutional Solutions to Resolve Our Political Divide*, Inside Edge Publishing, Houston TX, 2020

[248] David Barton, *The Founders Bible*, Shiloh Road Publishing, Newberry Park CA, 2012, 905 – 906

[249] Facts About Abortion: U.S. Abortion Statistics (abort73.com)

[250] Patrick Bohan, *Defending Freedom of Contract: Constitutional Solutions to Resolve Our Political Divide*, Inside Edge Publishing, Houston TX, 2020, Prerequisite or Concurrent reading.

[251] American Revolutionary War - Timeline Express (wp-timelineexpress.com)

[252] Esmond Wright, *Causes and Consequences of the American Revolution*, Quadrangle Books, Chicago IL, 1966, 12 – 14

[253] Kenyon C. Cramer, *The Causes of War: The American Revolution, Civil War, and World War* I, Scott, Foresman, and Co., Northbrook IL, 1965, 18

[254] United States military casualties of war - Wikipedia

[255] Coronavirus in the U.S.: Latest Map and Case Count - The New York Times (nytimes.com)

[256] John W. Yolton, *The Locke Reader: A Selection from the Works of John Locke*, Cambridge University Press, Cambridge UK, 1977, 31 – 34, 174, 190, 192, 195, 198, 210, 220

[257] Robert Morgan, *100 Bible Verses that Made America*, W Publishing, Nashville TN, 2020, 130 – 132, 229 – 231

[258] Robert Morgan, *100 Bible Verses that Made America*, W Publishing, Nashville TN, 2020, 113 – 155

[259] John C. Wahlke, *The Causes of the Revolutionary War*, DC Heath and Company, Boston MA, 1974, 53

[260] Bernard Bailyn, *The Ideological Origins of the American Revolution*, Harvard University Press, Cambridge MA, 1967, 18

[261] Bernard Bailyn, *The Ideological Origins of the American Revolution*, Harvard University Press, Cambridge MA, 1967, 19

[262] Kenyon C. Cramer, *The Causes of War: The American Revolution, Civil War, and World War* I, Scott, Foresman, and Co., Northbrook IL, 1965, 13, 23

[263] Robert Middlekauff, *The Glorious Cause: The American Revolution 1763 – 1789*, Oxford University Press, Oxford UK, 1982, 132 – 135

[264] Robert Middlekauff, *The Glorious Cause: The American Revolution 1763 – 1789*, Oxford University Press, Oxford UK, 1982, 77 – 83, 99 – 107

[265] John C. Wahlke, *The Causes of the Revolutionary War*, DC Heath and Company, Boston MA, 1974, 60 – 62

[266] Robert Middlekauff, *The Glorious Cause: The American Revolution 1763 – 1789*, Oxford University Press, Oxford UK, 1982, 150, 156

[267] Robert Middlekauff, *The Glorious Cause: The American Revolution 1763 – 1789*, Oxford University Press, Oxford UK, 1982, 150, 156

[268] Robert Middlekauff, *The Glorious Cause: The American Revolution 1763 – 1789*, Oxford University Press, Oxford UK, 1982, 208

[269] Robert Middlekauff, *The Glorious Cause: The American Revolution 1763 – 1789*, Oxford University Press, Oxford UK, 1982, 218, 225 – 231

[270] Robert Middlekauff, *The Glorious Cause: The American Revolution 1763 – 1789*, Oxford University Press, Oxford UK, 1982, 218, 225 – 231

[271] Robert Middlekauff, *The Glorious Cause: The American Revolution 1763 – 1789*, Oxford University Press, Oxford UK,1982, 248

[272] Robert Middlekauff, *The Glorious Cause: The American Revolution 1763 – 1789*, Oxford University Press, Oxford UK, 1982, 315, 322

[273] Bernard Bailyn, *The Ideological Origins of the American Revolution*, Harvard University Press, Cambridge MA, 1967, 94 – 120, 172 – 175

[274] John W. Yolton, *The Locke Reader: A Selection from the Works of John Locke*, Cambridge University Press, Cambridge UK, 1977, 31 – 34, 174, 190, 192, 195, 198, 210, 220

[275] Esmond Wright, *Causes and Consequences of the American Revolution*, Quadrangle Books, Chicago IL, 1966, 137 – 142, 150 – 155, 174 – 176, 188 – 192, 215 – 217

[276] John C. Wahlke, *The Causes of the Revolutionary War*, DC Heath and Company, Boston MA, 1974, 55

[277] John C. Wahlke, *The Causes of the Revolutionary War*, DC Heath and Company, Boston MA, 1974, 55

[278] Robert Middlekauff, *The Glorious Cause: The American Revolution 1763 – 1789*, Oxford University Press, Oxford UK, 1982, 118 – 119

[279] Esmond Wright, *Causes and Consequences of the American Revolution*, Quadrangle Books, Chicago IL, 1966, 74 – 75, 87 – 94, 99 – 102, 143, 167

[280] Kenyon C. Cramer, *The Causes of War: The American Revolution, Civil War, and World War* I, Scott, Foresman, and Co., Northbrook IL, 1965, 38 – 42, 58

[281] John C. Wahlke, *The Causes of the Revolutionary War*, DC Heath and Company, Boston MA, 1974, 22 – 49

[282] Esmond Wright, *Causes and Consequences of the American Revolution*, Quadrangle Books, Chicago IL, 1966, 74 – 75, 87 – 94, 99 – 102, 143, 167

[283] Kenyon C. Cramer, *The Causes of War: The American Revolution, Civil War, and World War* I, Scott, Foresman, and Co., Northbrook IL, 1965, 38 – 42, 58

[284] John C. Wahlke, *The Causes of the Revolutionary War*, DC Heath and Company, Boston MA, 1974, 22 – 49

[285] John C. Wahlke, *The Causes of the Revolutionary War*, DC Heath and Company, Boston MA, 1974, 70 – 85

[286] John W. Yolton, *The Locke Reader: A Selection from the Works of John Locke*, Cambridge University Press, Cambridge UK, 1977, 238, 243, 273 – 277, 286

[287] Patrick Bohan, *How a Neurological Disorder Changed My Life for the Better: The Science Behind Nerve, Muscular, and Neuromuscular Disorders and their Effects on Cycling*, Inside Edge Publishing, Houston TX, 2021, 50 – 58

[288] Esmond Wright, *Causes and Consequences of the American Revolution*, Quadrangle Books, Chicago IL, 1966, 74 – 75, 87 – 94, 99 – 102, 143, 167

[289] Kenyon C. Cramer, *The Causes of War: The American Revolution, Civil War, and World War* I, Scott, Foresman, and Co., Northbrook IL, 1965, 38 – 42, 58

[290] John C. Wahlke, *The Causes of the Revolutionary War*, DC Heath and Company, Boston MA, 1974, 22 – 49

[291] Robert Middlekauff, *The Glorious Cause: The American Revolution 1763 – 1789*, Oxford University Press, Oxford UK, 1982, 126

[292] John C. Wahlke, *The Causes of the Revolutionary War*, DC Heath and Company, Boston MA, 1974, 104 – 112, 115, 116, 126

[293] John C. Wahlke, *The Causes of the Revolutionary War*, DC Heath and Company, Boston MA, 1974, 104 – 112, 115, 116, 126

[294] John C. Wahlke, *The Causes of the Revolutionary War*, DC Heath and Company, Boston MA, 1974, 104 – 112, 115, 116, 126

[295] Robert Middlekauff, *The Glorious Cause: The American Revolution 1763 – 1789*, Oxford University Press, Oxford UK, 1982, 126

[296] John C. Wahlke, *The Causes of the Revolutionary War*, DC Heath and Company, Boston MA, 1974, 104 – 112

[297] Kenyon C. Cramer, *The Causes of War: The American Revolution, Civil War, and World War* I, Scott, Foresman, and Co., Northbrook IL, 1965, 44 – 46

[298] Kenyon C. Cramer, *The Causes of War: The American Revolution, Civil War, and World War* I, Scott, Foresman, and Co., Northbrook IL, 1965, 60 – 63

[299] Kenyon C. Cramer, *The Causes of War: The American Revolution, Civil War, and World War* I, Scott, Foresman, and Co., Northbrook IL, 1965, 48

[300] John C. Wahlke, *The Causes of the Revolutionary War*, DC Heath and Company, Boston MA, 1974, 66 – 70

[301] John C. Wahlke, *The Causes of the Revolutionary War*, DC Heath and Company, Boston MA, 1974, 66 – 70

[302] Kenyon C. Cramer, *The Causes of War: The American Revolution, Civil War, and World War* I, Scott, Foresman, and Co., Northbrook IL, 1965, 44 – 46

[303] Randy Barnett and Evan Bernick, *The Original Meaning of the 14th Amendment: The Letter and Spirit, Harvard University Press*, Cambridge, MA, 299 – 303

[304] The tax rates that led American colonists to rebel – Philip Greenspun's Weblog

[305] How Much Does the Average American Pay in Taxes? (thebalancemoney.com)

[306] $1 in 1776 → 2022 | Inflation Calculator (officialdata.org)

[307] Free Speech and Its Present Crisis: In today's America, the right to express one's opinion is threatened by activists and authorities alike. | City Journal (city-journal.org)

[308] Kenyon C. Cramer, *The Causes of War: The American Revolution, Civil War, and World War* I, Scott, Foresman, and Co., Northbrook IL, 1965, 25 – 27, 33

[309] John C. Wahlke, *The Causes of the Revolutionary War*, DC Heath and Company, Boston MA, 1974, 1 – 21

[310] John C. Wahlke, *The Causes of the Revolutionary War*, DC Heath and Company, Boston MA, 1974, 57

[311] Kenyon C. Cramer, *The Causes of War: The American Revolution, Civil War, and World War* I, Scott, Foresman, and Co., Northbrook IL, 1965, 60, 61, 62, 63

[312] Robert Middlekauff, *The Glorious Cause: The American Revolution 1763 – 1789*, Oxford University Press, Oxford UK, 1982, 496 – 511

[313] Robert Middlekauff, *The Glorious Cause: The American Revolution 1763 – 1789*, Oxford University Press, Oxford UK, 1982, 496 – 511

[314] Esmond Wright, *Causes and Consequences of the American Revolution*, Quadrangle Books, Chicago IL, 1966, 86

[315] Robert Middlekauff, *The Glorious Cause: The American Revolution 1763 – 1789*, Oxford University Press, Oxford UK, 1982, 547 – 550

[316] Esmond Wright, *Causes and Consequences of the American Revolution*, Quadrangle Books, Chicago IL, 1966, 265 – 267

[317] Patrick Bohan, *Defending Freedom of Contract: Constitutional Solutions to Resolve Our Political Divide*, Inside Edge Publishing, Houston TX, 2020, Prerequisite Reading

[318] French Ensor Chadwick, *The Causes of the Civil War, 1859 – 1861*, Harper Brothers, New York NY, 1906, 123 – 135

[319] Paul Calore, *The Causes of the Civil War: The Political, Cultural, Economic, and Territorial Disputes between the North and South*, McFarland and Company, Jefferson NC, 2008, 69 – 75

[320] Paul Calore, *The Causes of the Civil War: The Political, Cultural, Economic, and Territorial Disputes between the North and South*, McFarland and Company, Jefferson NC, 2008, 88 – 92, 111, 115

[321] Bernard Bailyn, *The Ideological Origins of the American Revolution*, Harvard University Press, Cambridge MA, 1967, 233, 244

[322] Bernard Bailyn, *The Ideological Origins of the American Revolution*, Harvard University Press, Cambridge MA, 1967, 265

[323] Robert Middlekauff, *The Glorious Cause: The American Revolution 1763 – 1789*, Oxford University Press, Oxford UK, 1982, 646

[324] Robert Middlekauff, *The Glorious Cause: The American Revolution 1763 – 1789*, Oxford University Press, Oxford UK, 1982, 603 – 608, 615 – 619

[325] Paul Calore, *The Causes of the Civil War: The Political, Cultural, Economic, and Territorial Disputes between the North and South*, McFarland and Company, Jefferson NC, 2008, 130 – 150, 155 – 219

[326] Paul Calore, *The Causes of the Civil War: The Political, Cultural, Economic, and Territorial Disputes between the North and South*, McFarland and Company, Jefferson NC, 2008, 231 – 247

[327] French Ensor Chadwick, *The Causes of the Civil War, 1859 – 1861*, Harper Brothers, New York NY, 1906, 166 – 186

[328] French Ensor Chadwick, *The Causes of the Civil War, 1859 – 1861*, Harper Brothers, New York NY, 1906, 252 – 260

[329] French Ensor Chadwick, *The Causes of the Civil War, 1859 – 1861*, Harper Brothers, New York NY, 1906, 135 – 150

[330] French Ensor Chadwick, *The Causes of the Civil War, 1859 – 1861*, Harper Brothers, New York NY, 1906, 135 – 150

[331] French Ensor Chadwick, *The Causes of the Civil War, 1859 – 1861*, Harper Brothers, New York NY, 1906, 267, 279 – 284

[332] French Ensor Chadwick, *The Causes of the Civil War, 1859 – 1861*, Harper Brothers, New York NY, 1906, 267, 338 – 342

[333] Paul Calore, *The Causes of the Civil War: The Political, Cultural, Economic, and Territorial Disputes between the North and South*, McFarland and Company, Jefferson NC, 2008, 290

[334] Patrick Bohan, *Defending Freedom of Contract: Constitutional Solutions to Resolve Our Political Divide*, Inside Edge Publishing, Houston TX, 2020, Chapter 11

[335] Paul Calore, *The Causes of the Civil War: The Political, Cultural, Economic, and Territorial Disputes between the North and South*, McFarland and Company, Jefferson NC, 2008, 252 – 255

[336] Kenyon C. Cramer, *The Causes of War: The American Revolution, Civil War, and World War* I, Scott, Foresman, and Co., Northbrook IL, 1965, 108

[337] French Ensor Chadwick, *The Causes of the Civil War, 1859 – 1861*, Harper Brothers, New York NY, 1906, 17 – 36, 112

[338] Paul Calore, *The Causes of the Civil War: The Political, Cultural, Economic, and Territorial Disputes between the North and South*, McFarland and Company, Jefferson NC, 2008, 267 – 268

[339] Kenneth Stampp, *The Causes of the Civil War*, Prentice Hall, Englewood Cliffs NJ, 1965, 66 – 70

[340] Kenneth Stampp, *The Causes of the Civil War*, Prentice Hall, Englewood Cliffs NJ, 1965, 60 – 62

[341] Kenyon C. Cramer, *The Causes of War: The American Revolution, Civil War, and World War* I, Scott, Foresman, and Co., Northbrook IL, 1965, 72 – 75

[342] Kenneth Stampp, *The Causes of the Civil War*, Prentice Hall, Englewood Cliffs NJ, 1965, 72 – 82

[343] French Ensor Chadwick, *The Causes of the Civil War, 1859 – 1861*, Harper Brothers, New York NY, 1906, 60 – 66

[344] Kenneth Stampp, *The Causes of the Civil War*, Prentice Hall, Englewood Cliffs NJ, 1965, 94 – 106

[345] Kenneth Stampp, *The Causes of the Civil War*, Prentice Hall, Englewood Cliffs NJ, 1965, 94 – 106

[346] Kenneth Stampp, *The Causes of the Civil War*, Prentice Hall, Englewood Cliffs NJ, 1965, 86 – 91

[347] Kenyon C. Cramer, *The Causes of War: The American Revolution, Civil War, and World War* I, Scott, Foresman, and Co., Northbrook IL, 1965, 97, 100 – 102, 113

[348] Kenneth Stampp, *The Causes of the Civil War*, Prentice Hall, Englewood Cliffs NJ, 1965, 21 – 31, 50

[349] Kenyon C. Cramer, *The Causes of War: The American Revolution, Civil War, and World War* I, Scott, Foresman, and Co., Northbrook IL, 1965, 78

[350] Kenneth Stampp, *The Causes of the Civil War*, Prentice Hall, Englewood Cliffs NJ, 1965, 205 – 244

[351] Kenneth Stampp, *The Causes of the Civil War*, Prentice Hall, Englewood Cliffs NJ, 1965, 205 – 244

[352] J. Budziszewski, *Written on the Heart: The Case for Natural Law*, Intervarsity Press, Downers Grove IL, 1997, 45

[353] Kenyon C. Cramer, *The Causes of War: The American Revolution, Civil War, and World War* I, Scott, Foresman, and Co., Northbrook IL, 1965, 78

[354] Kenneth Stampp, *The Causes of the Civil War*, Prentice Hall, Englewood Cliffs NJ, 1965, 36 – 40, 55 – 57

[355] Kenneth Stampp, *The Causes of the Civil War*, Prentice Hall, Englewood Cliffs NJ, 1965, 205 – 244

[356] Kenneth Stampp, *The Causes of the Civil War*, Prentice Hall, Englewood Cliffs NJ, 1965, 108 – 112, 125

[357] Paul Calore, *The Causes of the Civil War: The Political, Cultural, Economic, and Territorial Disputes between the North and South*, McFarland and Company, Jefferson NC, 2008, 13, 18, 20 – 30

[358] Paul Calore, *The Causes of the Civil War: The Political, Cultural, Economic, and Territorial Disputes between the North and South*, McFarland and Company, Jefferson NC, 2008, 13, 18, 20 – 30

[359] French Ensor Chadwick, *The Causes of the Civil War, 1859 – 1861*, Harper Brothers, New York NY, 1906, 66 – 89

[360] Kenyon C. Cramer, *The Causes of War: The American Revolution, Civil War, and World War* I, Scott, Foresman, and Co., Northbrook IL, 1965, 88, 92 – 93, 100, 111

[361] Kenyon C. Cramer, *The Causes of War: The American Revolution, Civil War, and World War* I, Scott, Foresman, and Co., Northbrook IL, 1965, 97, 100 – 102, 113

[362] Slavery Still Exists In These 6 Countries And More | Very Real (oxygen.com)

[363] French Ensor Chadwick, *The Causes of the Civil War, 1859 – 1861*, Harper Brothers, New York NY, 1906, 93 – 94, 105

[364] French Ensor Chadwick, *The Causes of the Civil War, 1859 – 1861*, Harper Brothers, New York NY, 1906, 150 – 165, 184 – 208, 247

[365] Kenneth Stampp, *The Causes of the Civil War*, Prentice Hall, Englewood Cliffs NJ, 1965, 128 – 132

[366] Kenyon C. Cramer, *The Causes of War: The American Revolution, Civil War, and World War* I, Scott, Foresman, and Co., Northbrook IL, 1965, 88, 92 – 93, 100, 111

[367] Kenneth Stampp, *The Causes of the Civil War*, Prentice Hall, Englewood Cliffs NJ, 1965, 115 – 121, 162 – 172

[368] Kenneth Stampp, *The Causes of the Civil War*, Prentice Hall, Englewood Cliffs NJ, 1965, 72 – 82

[369] Kenyon C. Cramer, *The Causes of War: The American Revolution, Civil War, and World War* I, Scott, Foresman, and Co., Northbrook IL, 1965, 110, 112

[370] Kenneth Stampp, *The Causes of the Civil War*, Prentice Hall, Englewood Cliffs NJ, 1965, 137 – 185

[371] Paul Calore, *The Causes of the Civil War: The Political, Cultural, Economic, and Territorial Disputes between the North and South*, McFarland and Company, Jefferson NC, 2008, 13, 18, 20 – 30

[372] French Ensor Chadwick, *The Causes of the Civil War, 1859 – 1861*, Harper Brothers, New York NY, 1906, 66 – 89

[373] Randy Barnett and Evan Bernick, *The Original Meaning of the 14th Amendment: The Letter and Spirit, Harvard University Press*, Cambridge, MA, 2021, 90 – 100

[374] Randy Barnett and Evan Bernick, *The Original Meaning of the 14th Amendment: The Letter and Spirit, Harvard University Press*, Cambridge, MA, 2021, 90 – 100

[375] Paul Calore, *The Causes of the Civil War: The Political, Cultural, Economic, and Territorial Disputes between the North and South*, McFarland and Company, Jefferson NC, 2008, 8 – 15

[376] Randy Barnett and Evan Bernick, *The Original Meaning of the 14th Amendment: The Letter and Spirit, Harvard University Press*, Cambridge, MA, 2021, 83 – 85, 104, 113, 122 – 123, 129

[377] Randy Barnett and Evan Bernick, *The Original Meaning of the 14th Amendment: The Letter and Spirit, Harvard University Press*, Cambridge, MA, 2021, 83 – 85, 104, 113, 122 – 123, 129

[378] Paul Calore, *The Causes of the Civil War: The Political, Cultural, Economic, and Territorial Disputes between the North and South*, McFarland and Company, Jefferson NC, 2008, 8 – 15

[379] French Ensor Chadwick, *The Causes of the Civil War, 1859 – 1861*, Harper Brothers, New York NY, 1906, 17 – 36, 112

[380] French Ensor Chadwick, *The Causes of the Civil War, 1859 – 1861*, Harper Brothers, New York NY, 1906, 17 – 36, 112

[381] French Ensor Chadwick, *The Causes of the Civil War, 1859 – 1861*, Harper Brothers, New York NY, 1906, 17 – 36, 112

[382] Kenyon C. Cramer, *The Causes of War: The American Revolution, Civil War, and World War* I, Scott, Foresman, and Co., Northbrook IL, 1965, 102 – 105, 113 – 114

[383] Patrick Bohan, *Defending Freedom of Contract: Constitutional Solutions to Resolve Our Political Divide*, Inside Edge Publishing, Houston TX, 2020, Chapter 11

[384] Kenyon C. Cramer, *The Causes of War: The American Revolution, Civil War, and World War* I, Scott, Foresman, and Co., Northbrook IL, 1965, 154 – 156

[385] Randy Barnett and Evan Bernick, *The Original Meaning of the 14th Amendment: The Letter and Spirit, Harvard University Press*, Cambridge, MA, 2021, 109 – 127

[386] Randy Barnett and Evan Bernick, *The Original Meaning of the 14th Amendment: The Letter and Spirit, Harvard University Press*, Cambridge, MA, 2021, 109 – 127

[387] Randy Barnett and Evan Bernick, *The Original Meaning of the 14th Amendment: The Letter and Spirit, Harvard University Press*, Cambridge, MA, 2021, 109 – 127

[388] Patrick Bohan, *Defending Freedom of Contract: Constitutional Solutions to Resolve Our Political Divide*, Inside Edge Publishing, Houston TX, 2020

[389] Randy Barnett and Evan Bernick, *The Original Meaning of the 14th Amendment: The Letter and Spirit, Harvard University Press*, Cambridge, MA, 2021, 347

[390] Kenyon C. Cramer, *The Causes of War: The American Revolution, Civil War, and World War* I, Scott, Foresman, and Co., Northbrook IL, 1965, 72 – 75

[391] COSAction (conventionofstates.com)

For more information contact:

Patrick Bohan
info@advbooks.com

To purchase additional copies of this book or other books published by Advantage Books, visit our online bookstore at: www.advbookstore.com

Orlando, Florida, USA
"we bring dreams to life"™
www.advbookstore.com

www.ingramcontent.com/pod-product-compliance
Lightning Source LLC
Chambersburg PA
CBHW080236270326
41926CB00020B/4260

* 9 7 8 1 5 9 7 5 5 7 4 7 4 *